Erik S. Lunde and Douglas A. Noverr, Film Studies

D1520064

Selected Course Outlines and
Reading Lists from American
Colleges and Universities

Film
Studies

edited by Erik S. Lunde and Douglas A. Noverr
Michigan State University

 Markus Wiener Publishing, Inc.
New York

For information write to
Markus Wiener Publishing,
225 Lafayette Street, New York, NY 10012

Library of Congress Cataloging-in-Publication Data

Film studies.

    (Selected reading lists and course outlines from American colleges and
universities)
    Bibliography: p.
    Contents: v. 1. Introductory courses, interdisciplinary courses, courses
about directors, and about film and literature -- v. 2. Film history, film
genres, and foreign films.
    1. Motion pictures -- Study and teaching. 2. Motion pictures--Bibliogra-
phy. I. Lunde, Erik S. (Eric Sheldon) II. Noverr, Douglas A. III. Series.
PN1993.7.F5 1988   791.43'01'5   88-17395
ISBN 1-55876-001-6 (v. 1)

Printed in America

FILM STUDIES:
SELECTED COURSE OUTLINES AND READING LISTS

ERIK S. LUNDE
DOUGLAS A. NOVERR

TABLE OF CONTENTS

IV. Film And Literature

V. Women In Film

VI. Interdisciplinary And Cultural Approaches To Film

I. THE EVOLUTION OF FILM STUDIES

INTRODUCTION AND OVERVIEW

In his influential "The Study of Motion Pictures in Colleges and Universities" (The Educational Record Winter 1965: 33-67) David C. Stewart made a series of ten recommendations to promote and improve the study of film in institutions of higher education. His second recommendation stated: "There is immediate need for the publication and wide distribution of a book which will describe, in detail, a variety of courses in motion picture history, criticism, and appreciation, and also reflect the broad range of current film courses of high quality. Such a book should contain the titles of texts and films used in the courses, listings of principal film distributors, and other information that would make it a valuable and useful reference source." Stewart's study provided information on course titles and descriptions at a number of institutions, listings of films, and sample reading lists.

Stewart's call for such a book was answered by the publication of The American Film Institute Guide to College Courses in Film and Television, which has been published in seven editions since its inception. The American Film Institute also created a syllabus bank as part of its Education Services Resources, making its repository of syllabi available on request. In 1974 The American Historical Association sponsored the publication of Teaching History with Film, written by John E. O'Connor and Martin Jackson. The pamphlet, part of the AHA's Discussions on Teaching series, provided valuable information on how to integrate film into the history curriculum as well as numerous examples of specific integrations. The August 1977 publication of Film and the Humanities, edited by John E. O'Connor, as the outgrowth of the October 1976 Rockefeller Foundation Humanities program on "Film and the Humanities" included reprinted articles that documented materials for courses on film and history, the American Dream, literature and film, philosophy and film, and anthropology and film. Both of these reports resulted from film-study conferences that involved a wide spectrum of academics, professionals, government agency officials, and educators. In 1979 the American Studies Association published a special issue (Winter 1979) of the American Quarterly on Film and American Studies with excellent survey essays by John E. O'Connor ("Teaching Film and American Culture: A Survey of Texts") and Peter C. Rollins ("Film, Television, and American Studies: Questions, Activities, Guides").

This present volume of course materials on film studies continues this practice of making significant materials available with the goals of wider distribution, representative and inclusive sampling of courses, ready availability, and highest utility to teachers of film studies. In our letter of solicitation to prospective contributors, we stated our purposes in developing the volume.

> Our purposes in compiling and editing this text are fourfold. First, we would like this volume to serve as a valuable and instructive aid to teachers who are developing, revising, or expanding film courses. Second, such a resource work documents the current rich diversity of approaches and formats for film studies courses and thus enables practitioners to learn what others are doing in similar courses and curriculums. Third, we hope that this volume will encourage further research in matters of teaching strategies and methodologies as well as the general field of film studies. Fourth, the book will serve as historical documentation of the evolving state of film studies in the United States and indicate current trends and emphases.

Our hopes for developing this volume have more than been fulfilled by the wide ranging and substantial course materials our highly cooperative contributors have so generously made available. Originally, we planned one volume, but the extent of our contributions dictated that we publish two volumes, this volume on film studies and another volume on film history. Our publisher and editor, Dr. Markus Wiener, readily agreed to publish two volumes, thus enabling us to give full presentation of the materials contributed to our project as well as to present the contributions in a more organized and interrelated format.

It is not the purpose of this introductory essay to provide a history of the development of film studies or to survey the field in detail. That important task is admirably undertaken and fulfilled by Professor Barry K. Grant's richly detailed essay "Film Study in the Undergraduate Curriculum: An Overview", which follows this introduction. His essay is a revision of his introduction to Film Study in the Undergraduate Curriculum. Others who have contributed to surveying and documenting this development include David C. Stewart, John E. O'Connor, Jack C. Ellis, Richard Dyer McCann, Anthony Schillaci and John M. Culkin (in Films Deliver: Teaching Creatively with Films, 1970) and T.J. Ross, (Film and the Liberal Arts, 1970), among many others. The purpose of this introduction is to comment upon and highlight certain salient features of film studies courses and their common characteristics.

First, it should be stressed that these film studies courses are rooted in the experience of the film text. The study of film, of course, has as its primary purpose an active involvement of the viewer's mind, viewing skills, imagination, and sensibility in a close "reading" of the film text. Out of this close viewing and focused attention to the complex details and patterns of the film text comes an understanding of the film's themes, purpose, implications and extensions beyond the film, along with many other perceptions. Parallel to these is an appreciation of the filmic elements of the film as the vision of a director and the product of a creative collaboration between those involved in the film's creation and execution. The "seeing" of the film is crucial to its understanding and to the fruitful perception of complex meanings. Thus, an introductory course to film studies is an essential beginning point to learning about the medium's ways of presenting versions of drama and narratives.

Section II of this volume illustrates a rich variety of approaches and methodologies by nine teachers of film with an emphasis on the dialogic process of viewing, responding, and formulating responses in an informed and intelligent manner. This process of directing and guiding student responses to film is common to all film courses but particularly critical and challenging in introductory courses where students need viewing skills as well as the benefit of technical and conceptual knowledge. The teacher of film needs to make the exploration of film a collaborative enterprise where students' perceptions are valued, supported, challenged, and reformulated to higher levels of understanding. This mutual thrill of discovery -- and often rediscovery for the teacher -- is at the heart of film study, as film has the remarkable ability to evoke emotions, passions, and opinions.

The teacher brings enthusiasm and insight to the shared experience of film as well as provides instruction in the technical elements of filmmaking, especially those that significantly affect what we see and how we see it. One way of focusing a film study course is to use the work of a noted director as a means of analyzing that director's vision, style, use of the technical production staff, work with actor and actresses, and particular directorial trademarks. Section III of this volume features course materials on a number of famous directors and their work.

The course materials presented in Sections IV, V, and VI illustrate the solidly interdisciplinary and cross-disciplinary nature of film studies and the invaluable quality of film as a cultural document. Film studies has been enriched and vitalized by its connections with other fields and with new areas of knowledge and theory: feminist studies, aesthetics, concepts of visualization and the spectatorship, art, sociology, anthropology, recent developments in literary criticism like deconstruction and narrativity, popular culture, political science, law, and economics, to highlight some of the areas. Some may see this proliferation of connections between film and other related areas as a diffusion of attention away from the proper study of film as film. However, as David Shepard has pointed out in his "Film Study and Filmmakers" (Cinema Journal, Summer 1985), film study should aim at providing students with perspective on their culture and world community, encourage wide and interdisciplinary learning, and make them aware of the great minds of the past and present. Quite rightly, Professor Shepard, one of the contributors to this volume, argues that film study "sits squarely within the tradition of the academy to preserve and encourage wide learning" and that film study is a means of making a liberal arts education more meaningful and vital. Of course, Professor William Arrowsmith eloquently made this same case for film study earlier in his important essay titled "Film as Educator," published in the Journal of Aesthetic Education in 1969. While many administrators and rigidly oriented disciplinarians have even yet to be persuaded, teachers and students of film enthusiastically know how the medium has served as a significant catalyst for cultural reexamination and reassessment. Indeed, film study is, and has been, moving in a number of directions, but the diffusion has been exciting and promising.

The course materials in this volume illustrate the diversity of approaches and the varied uses of film to explore areas that hold meaning and significance about our lives and culture. Film study serves as a focus of spirited intellectual discourse and exchange in the university community as well as a focus for shared cultural experience. Film has developed as an international language and as a means of providing students with a global perspective on the world community. As these course syllabi document, film study serves to bridge the print generation and the visual generation by demonstrating to students that reading in history, cultural studies, and other disciplines not only informs and enriches their response to film but also enhances their ability to learn in an interdisciplinary mode. The process of making connections and integrations is essential to the learning process; it is the central activity of the university.

Viewing films and reading significant material are corollary activities, and this combination puts film solidly in the context of society, culture, and history, where it originates and where it finds its stimulus for development. Film study courses illustrate a great degree of innovation and creativity in their development as teachers synthesize information, apply new areas of knowledge to the study of film, appropriate established knowledge, and break new theoretical ground. These courses illustrate the enthusiasm of film studies teachers for their subject and the sense of being involved in an enterprise that is evolving and actively keeping up with the new developments in film while exploring the past.

The excitement involved in this activity has many causes. First, a newer generation of film study textbooks has provided more sophisticated, updated, and visually documented instruction. Certain texts have become standard reading in film study courses, and all focus on the complex process of viewing films and understanding what one sees, and the how and why. These newer texts include the following (which is not an inclusive or exclusive list but a representative one): Joseph M. Boggs, The Art of Watching Films (2nd ed. 1988); David Bordwell and Kristin Thompson, Film Art: An Introduction (2nd ed. 1986); Leo Braudy, The World in a Frame: What We See in Films (1984); Louis Giannetti, Understanding Movies (Fourth ed. 1987); Bruce F. Kawin, How Movies Work (1987); James Monaco, How to Read a Film (1977); William H. Phillips, Analyzing Films (1983); Thomas Sobchack and Vivian C. Sobchack, An Introduction to Film (2nd ed. 1987); George Weed and George Lellis, Film: Form and Function (1981). Many of these texts originated from courses and were developed to meet the needs of students. They have been revised, expanded, updated, and improved to include the latest developments and directions in the field.

Another exciting development in film study courses has been the technological revolution in videotape equipment, laserdiscs, and equipment for the intensive and systematic study of film. Professor Robert Carringer's material on the Criterion Collection Edition of The Magnificent Ambersons in Section VIII of this volume illustrates one of the most effective uses of the new technology to provide a complete context for the study of a particular film masterpiece. This important Criterion Collection now includes ten laserdisc editions of classic American films. With the development of videotape and the ready accessibility of hundreds of films, past and present, students have opportunities to view films not previously available. While videotapes certainly cannot replace projected film, they are invaluable to the intensive study of film and make film more widely and easily available to the classroom or film laboratory for review and for study of particular sequences or scenes.

Another important development in film study courses is the beginning availability of specific books that help students to write cogently and purposefully about films and to learn methodologies of film criticism. Books that deserve special mention in this respect include Harris J. Elder, Writing about Film and Timothy Corrigan, A Short Guide to Writing about Film (1988). Solid sections on writing about film can also be found in Bruce F. Kawin, How Movies Work (1987); Thomas Sobchack and Vivian C. Sobchack, An Introduction to Film (Second ed. 1987); William H. Phillips, Analyzing Films (1983), a selection of which is included in Section VIII. of this volume; and Elizabeth McMahan, Susan Day, and Robert Funk, Elements of Writing about Literature and Film (1988). This is an area of instruction that has been notably lacking, but it appears that the need for texts and materials on writing about film has been recognized.

Overall, film study courses illustrate the diversity, innovation, and currency of information and knowledge that should, and does, characterize the best of American higher education. Film study clearly can serve as a focal point of interdisciplinary, integrative, and global education. It has earned its place in the university curriculum and established its vitality as an area of scholarship and learning.

To the contributors to this volume, we express our deepest thanks and appreciation for their willingness to make these rich materials available to a wide audience. Our contributors have offered much appreciated words of encouragement and support, and we have enjoyed corresponding with them and learning more about their teaching and research. The "About the Contributors" section documents their contributions to film scholarship and the growth of film studies. Other individuals who could not contribute to the book, for various reasons, also offered their encouragement and stated the need for such a resource and reference work.

To our publisher, Dr. Markus Wiener, we extend our appreciation for his enthusiasm and support of this project and for the personal contacts that he made with a number of our contributors in New York City. He has made possible the publication of two volumes on film course materials, this book and <u>Film History: Selected Course Outlines and Reading Lists</u>, which will be published simultaneously.

Erik S. Lunde
Douglas A. Noverr

Michigan State University
East Lansing, Michigan

"FILM STUDY IN THE UNDERGRADUATE CURRICULUM: AN OVERVIEW"

by Barry Keith Grant

Less than a century old, film history begins in 1895 with
the first public showing of the Lumiere brothers' films in Le
Grand Cafe in Paris.   Thus the academic study of film, in comparison to, say, that of literature or painting, has not had adequate time to acquire a firm sense of tradition.   From the 1920s
through the 1950s, the occasional college course in film was offered -- Dudley Andrew points out that the University of Iowa
offered film courses during World War 1[1] -- but these scattered
few were of necessity tentative in approach.   By the 1940s five
universities had established film departments (USC, UCLA, CCNY,
NYU, and Boston University), and by the 50s a number of other
universities were offering individual courses in film.   Yet it
has been estimated that at this time there were still less than
100 persons in the United States engaged in film teaching, and for
most of them it was regarded as a secondary field of interest.[2]

In the history of film theory, it was not until Andre Bazin's
writings in the late 1940s that the narrow formative aesthetics
of Sergei Eisenstein, Rudolf Arnheim, Bela Belazs, and others was
challenged to any significant extent.   In the 1950s, the enthusiasm of Cahiers du Cinema and other journals for American
auteurs, followed by Andrew Sarris's pioneering articles in
English beginning in 1963 (and his long-running weekly column in

8

The Village Voice) generated a new intellectual curiosity among Americans seriously interested in film. The so-called "Hitch-cocko-Hawksians" of la nouvelle vague praised the work of many Hollywood directors in wildly enthusiastic terms, and if some of the more excessive writing verged on the mystical, it presaged a new way of talking about the cinema that demanded informed response. British critics, writing in such newer journals as Movie, rebelled against the conservative, content-oriented criticism of the established periodicals and adopted approaches similar to what Richard Roud in Sight and Sound called "The French Line."[3] And then Robin Wood, a frequent contributor to Movie, in his influential work Hitchcock's Films (1965) asserted -- a claim that for many amounted to nothing less than heresy -- that the films of the Master of Suspense were as complex as the plays of the Bard of Avon and that they required an equally elaborate exegesis.

By this time auteurism was enshrined as the privileged critical methodology in film studies, since it claimed to base its approach on both the economic (acknowledgement of the studio system) and aesthetic (mise-en-scene) properties of the medium. Auteurism was largely responsible for redeeming much of Hollywood cinema from the trash bins of disposable popular entertainment to which most of it had previously been consigned. As a measure of the extent to which auteurism took hold of the Hollywood sensibility itself as a way of legitimizing its own activity, one need only consider the case of Play it Again, Sam (1972): written by and starring Woody Allen, based on his own stage play, and clearly employing his own comic persona, the film was nevertheless listed in the opening credits as "A Herbert Ross film," since Ross directed it. And if, as now seems clear, classical auteurism had its serious limitations in both theory and practice, it should be remembered that it was ultimately responsible as well for shifting critical concern from overt theme to mise-en-scene -- that is to say, from the social importance of subject to the felicities of style. As well, it was none other than Sarris who suggested that an auteur may be discovered by locating "the tension between a director's personality and his material"[4] -- an attitude that has led to the subsequent ideological deconstruction of classic Hollywood films, a critical activity that has characterized much recent significant writing on the cinema.

The 1960s also witnessed both the crumbling of the Hollywood studio system and the critical and commercial success of a number of bold, exciting films by independent feature filmmakers that seemed to connect with the concerns of the nation's young people more seriously than the youth exploitation movies that preceded them. As a result of these developments, American film, for so long dismissed as mere entertainment, began to be viewed with a new critical attentiveness. And, too, European "art" films, such as those of Ingmar Bergman, Jean-Luc Godard, Federico Fellini, and Michelangelo Antonioni, began appearing more often (at least in large cities) on American screens. The distaste for the movies voiced by established critics like H.L. Mencken and Edmund Wilson -- even by highbrow film critics like Dwight Macdonald and John Simon -- seemed now crusty and outdated compared

10

to the rapt enthusiasm of Pauline Kael.

At the same time, a number of scholars began to devote their attention to the popular media. An important teacher of media education and former scholar of medieval literature, Professor Gerald O'Grady of the State University of New York at Buffalo, embraced the utopianism of Buckminster Fuller and the "expanded cinema" approach of Gene Youngblood, proclaiming that in his research activity he had dropped the "eval" in order to emphasize the "media". The popularization of Marshall McLuhan's ideas in particular helped cultivate a new awareness of film and other forms of popular culture as media with their own distinctive properties.

Students were of the first television generation, and the swelling of enrollments in film courses testified to their clear interest in the subject. Consequently, film courses sprang into being in colleges across North America. With stable enrollments, healthy budgets, and active student interest in all the humanities, many institutions experienced little difficulty in establishing courses in film, even though such courses may entail considerable expense (film rentals, projection equipment, and staff fees) and administrative problems (timetabling, adequate screening facilities).

Thus film culture was thriving by the late 1960s. But the study of film did not completely fulfill its promise to become the darling discipline of the 70s. Of course this was in part the result of the steady decline in humanities enrollments during that decade, with the marked shift of students in an increasingly difficult economy toward more job-oriented programs in business and the sciences. Yet there are additional factors with which the serious study of cinema has had to contend.

The unfortunate associations of commercialism and cheap (aesthetically as well as economically) entertainment that often characterized the medium in its early days as vaudeville and peep-show attraction continue to do so for some. "Movies" are still regarded by most people more as a social event and emotion-al diversion than as an intellectual experience. This attitude informs the use of film in the classroom by so many heedless, if not simply bored, elementary and high school teachers. Until quite recently teachers at these levels had not undertaken any study of film and used the medium merely as a substitute for books and lectures. Since film (with the exception, perhaps, of so many of those awful "educational" documentaries with their pompous "voice-of-God" narration) provides an inherent visual interest, many teachers look to movies to do their jobs for them. Movies instead of teaching, I have discovered in my own screen education classes for teachers, is the way teachers think all too often. It is no coincidence that film use in the public schools increases on Fridays and just before holidays, times when both teachers and students begin thinking more about what will happen after class than of what is going on in it.

Students, in turn, are glad when a film is shown in class because it is, first of all, something different; also, they can assume an easy, passive relation to a movie just as they do in the theater or at home when watching television. Nothing in their experience has taught them how to -- indeed, that they must -- look critically at a visual text. When these students enter college, they often consider a course in film as "Mickey Mouse" (itself a cinematic term of reference not without its implications), that is, as an easy subject of study. However, with the greater number of film courses now offered at the college level and with the recent development at some schools of programs in screen education for teachers, this unproductive state of affairs already has begun to change.

Such an uncritical attitude toward film seems even more distressing when one considers the enormous implications of serious film study. We live in a media-saturated culture -- a "wired nation" that continues to colonize the "global village" -- in which film and television play a large and important role. Studies have shown that many young children spend a large percentage of their time watching television and that by the time they reach high school most young people have devoted more hours to television than they have spent in the classroom. As a result, children are socialized to a large extent through the visual media and do not realize the degree to which their values and behavior patterns have been shaped by the images these media generate. Children in our schools are taught to read but almost never to look. As teachers we owe it to our students to show them how the visual media shape one's perceptions of the world,

so that they may think more independently; as concerned individuals we owe it to ourselves to help open the media to the
possibility of alternative ideological points of view. These
are, to be sure, ethical and political arguments, but they are
essential to a serious consideration of what the teaching of
film involves and to the informing philosophy of a liberal arts
education.

The refusal to take film seriously as a mass medium and as
a valid field of critical inquiry is not restricted to the public schools. The common notion among actors in the early part
of the century that film acting was a debasement of their art
may have disappeared with the rise of Hollywood and the star
system, with the lure of fame and fortune, but this view remains essentially that of many elitist intellectuals. It is
true (for reasons too complex to discuss here) that film adaptations of great novels have most often produced inferior works
of cinema, and for many academics trained in literary analysis
this has been sufficient proof of the medium's inherent in-
ability to achieve aesthetic complexity. Forgetting that
great films have been made from mediocre fiction, they consign
the study of film to what they consider the more appropriate
yet distinctly inferior area of popular culture (if, indeed,
they consider that vague, questionable field worthy of serious
study).

As a result of this attitude, and because film incorporates
aspects of so many other disciplines (history, psychology, art,
architecture, sociology, philosophy, politics, drama, photo-

14

graphy), the question of where in the conventional departmental
structure of higher education film might or should be taught has
become particularly problematic. In the anthology of essays on
the teaching of film which I edited for the Modern Language
Association in 1983, Film Study in the Undergraduate Curriculum,
at least five of the seventeen contributors considered this
issue of paramount importance in describing their efforts to
mount a program of film study.[5] The interdisciplinary nature
of many university film programs suggest that in many cases
either administrations have not been particularly eager to
adequately fund these programs, or that the field of study has
not been deemed worthy enough to require full departmental
status. Nevertheless, many film scholars have adopted an interdisciplinary model for their programs simply to get the
subject into the curriculum, although some do prefer it for the
greater flexibility it offers.[6]

Two related issues also emerge as major considerations in
the serious teaching of film. The first is the question of the
text. Because of the nature of the medium, it is impossible
without access to special equipment (analytic projectors,
moviolas) to engage in a close analysis of a film. Without such
equipment, the text remains ephemeral and elusive; the class
must rely on memory -- so often extremely unreliable, as anyone
who has ever taught film can attest. Moreover, while poems,
for example, can be re-read many times before a class discussion,
students will likely have seen the film to be discussed only

once. Under such circumstances, classroom seminars may seem doomed to degenerate into a series of impressionistic, subjective assertions. Thus the teaching of film is seriously suspect for those who value rigorous textual analysis.

However, there are ways around this problem. Students can purchase published screenplays, for example; and while this is not an ideal solution, since they do not detail camera movements, sound effects and other textual elements, it can be enormously helpful. Generally, though, any serious program in film study must have the necessary financial support to allow for the purchase of analytical equipment and the support staff to supervise and maintain it. The introduction of relatively inexpensive, widespread video technology in recent years, and the large number of classic films now available in video format, offers still another possible direction for film programs. And while video viewing should not be practised as a substitute for the experience of the large screen, it is perfectly suited to the task of close analysis which may follow a regular 16mm screening.

The second issue is the relation between theory and practice, film analysis and filmmaking, academic and professional training. While the university context, in my view, should not be geared toward the training of Hollywood professionals, the two areas cannot in fact be so easily separated. Just as teachers of literature (English) programs consider writing (whether analytical or creative, itself a problematic distinction) integral to their activity, so the production of images has enormous value in gaining a critical understanding of them. Most teachers of film criticism, theory, and history agree on the importance of "hands-on" experience and that it can be managed satisfactorily with a minimum of equipment. Lev Kuleshov's post-revolutionary Soviet film workshops even operated without film stock! From a pragmatic point of view, it should be remembered that many students first enter academic programs with vague but optimistic hopes of becoming movie directors; and rather than crush these dreams we can present a more sober, realistic picture of the industry even while encouraging students to devote more time to thinking about the kinds of images they want to make.

By now the study of the cinema has clearly proved itself academically respectable and worthy of administrative support. It is those who resist this who should be on the defensive. Much of the ground-breaking work of the newer critical theories and methods -- structuralism, feminism, semiology, and Marxism -- has taken place in film criticism, often with exciting and productive results. While the expectations for film studies in the 1960s may have failed to materialize fully, the subject nevertheless has found a place -- even if it remains precariously and vaguely defined -- in the post secondary curriculum, and enrollment in film studies has managed, if not to increase, at least to hold its own. Acccording to the American Film

Institute's <u>Guide to College Courses in Film and Television</u>, published in 1978, courses in film and/or television are offered at no fewer than 1,067 colleges and universities in the United States alone.[7] The <u>Guide</u> lists a total of 9,228 courses in film and television, of which 7,015 are at the undergraduate level and 2,133 at the graduate level (the remainder are available for either undergraduate or graduate credit) under the auspices of a wide range of departments (eleven). Taking into account that the AFI's survey was far from comprehensive, these statistics are quite impressive.

There are as well other indications of a new academic respect toward film study. Publishing in the field has increased dramatically in recent years. There are many new scholarly journals dealing exclusively or primarily with film, and a number of publishers, including some major university presses, have been actively developing a film book market. Annual film conferences, where scholarly papers are read and ideas exchanged, are supported by a number of universities (Purdue, University of Wisconsin at Milwaukee, Ohio). Professional societies in the field have become firmly established. The Society for Cinema Studies, for example, has consistently grown since its inception (as the Society of Cinematologists) in 1959 from under 25 to over 600 members in 1987. The organization accordingly has reached a more mature, self-reflexive stage in its development where it now engages in such activites as establishing procedural guidelines for refereed journals and for promotion and tenure review.

Undoubtedly, some will view these developments as an unfortunate co-optation of cinema study by the educational system. The burgeoning shelves of academic publications on cinema, for example, indicate not only a greater intensity of scholarly activity, but is also the result of the academic "publish or perish" syndrome. However, in my view this increase in film-related activity indicates a more healthy film culture generally; and given the pervasiveness of the visual media in contemporary life, and our society's encouragement of the popular view that everyone is a film critic, it can only prove beneficial in the end.

The rapid growth and maturation of film study in the last three decades is startling, especially when one considers that until recently most teachers of film came to the discipline (and some still do) out of personal interest but trained in other fields (most often, literature). The teaching of film had tended, therefore, to define itself under fire rather than to be recollected in tranquility. Still, again until recently, the infrequent literature that has appeard on film pedagogy has rarely risen above the cant of McLuhanesque "open class-room" optimism. But this situation is now changing, largely because academic positions in film are being filled more frequently by young Ph.D.s of graduate film programs. The more experienced teachers, meanwhile, have now had time to re-

19

flect upon what it is they do. The collection of writings in
which this article appears is itself testimony to the continuing
development of film study as a distinct field of scholarly
activity and pedagogical reflection, perhaps one of the most
significant for a liberal arts education in the latter part of
the Twentieth Century.

NOTES

[1] Dudley Andrew, "An Open Approach to Film Study and the Situation at Iowa," in Film Study in the Undergraduate Curriculum, ed. Barry Keith Grant (New York: Modern Language Association, 1983), p. 45.

[2] Ramona Curry, "Twenty Five Years of SCS: A Socio-Political History," Journal of Film and Video, Vol. 38, no. 2 (Spring 1986), p. 44.

[3] Richard Roud, "The French Line," Sight and Sound, Vol. 29, no. 4 (Autumn 1969), pp. 166-171.

[4] Andrew Sarris, "Notes on the Auteur Theory in 1962," Film Culture, No. 27 (Winter 1962/63), p. 7.

[5] See the essays by Dudley Andrew, James Michael Welsh, Jerry Wood, Gerald Mast, and Jack Nachbar.

[6] This is the position taken by Andrew, for example. Op. Cit.

[7] The American Film Institute Guide to College Courses in Film and Television, ed. Dennis R. Bohnenkamp and Sam L. Grogg, Jr. (Princeton: Peterson's Guides, 1978).

II. INTRODUCTION TO FILM STUDIES

Introduction to Film: English 353   Dr. Barbera
Spring 1987

Calendar of Films

INTRODUCTION TO COURSE
Jan 20 Pauline at the Beach (1983, screenplay and direction by
        Eric Rohmer). Discussion of auteur theory and analysis of
        Rohmer's style.

PART I: THE MEDIUM
Jan 27 Two short films: Basic Film Terms (1970) and The
        Director (1975, narrated by Rod Serling, featuring
        excerpts from: Hitchcock's The Lady Vanishes and The 39
        Steps; Truffaut's Two English Girls, Jules and Jim and
        Shoot the Piano Player; Kurosawa's Rashomon and Dodes'ka-
        den; and Bergman's Winter Light, The Seventh Seal, The
        Magician, and All These Women). Discussion of terms to be
        used in the course, types of shot transitions, and the
        "art" of zooming.

Feb 3   Subjective camera ad absurdum: Lady in the Lake (1946,
        directed by and starring Robert Montgomery). Also, The
        Camera (1975, narrated by Rod Serling, featuring excerpts
        from: Cocteau's Beauty and the Beast; Truffaut's Two
        English Girls; Pelissier's The Rocking Horse Winner;
        Hitchcock's The Lady Vanishes; Schoedsack and Pichel's The
        Most Dangerous Game; Bergman's The Silence; and
        Parajanov's Shadows of Forgotten Ancestors). Discussion
        of the effective use and the abuse of subjective camera.

Feb 10 The art of framing: Night of the Living Dead (1968,
        directed by George Romero). Also, The Edited Image (1975,
        narrated by Rod Serling, featuring excerpts from:
        Eisenstein's Potemkin; Dearden's Saraband; Riefenstahl's
        Olympia; Varda's Le Bonheur; Lang's Metropolis & Saville's
        Evergreen; and Welles' Citizen Kane). Discussion of tight
        framing as a convention of horror and suspense films, of
        framing as an aspect of mise-en-scène and of mise-en-
        scène as the "before" to the "after" of editing. Also a
        discussion of aspects of editing: image association, the
        contraction and expansion of time, sequence tempo or
        rhythm, and choice of shot transitions.

Feb 17 Cinematic masterpiece: Citizen Kane (1941, directed by
        and starring Orson Welles, with Dorothy Comingore, Joseph
        Cotton, Everett Sloane, Ray Collins and Agnes Moorehead).
        Discussion of the film's mise-en-scène (with emphasis on
        the use of deep focus photography and extreme camera
        angles), dynamic editing (including varied shot
        transitions), and imaginative sound track.

PART II: FICTIONAL NARRATIVE FORMS

25

Feb 24 Tragedy: The Blue Angel (1930, directed by Josef von Sternberg and starring Emil Jannings and Marlene Dietrich). Discussion of how the film creates the sense that the professor is moving toward his doom.

Mar 3 Comedy: Mr. Smith Goes to Washington (1939, directed by Frank Capra and starring James Stewart, with Jean Arthur, Claude Rains, Edward Arnold and Thomas Mitchell). Discussion of how the film creates the sense that Smith will be vindicated, despite the odds against him.

Mar 10 Spring Break

Mar 17 Allegory: The Seventh Seal (1956, directed by Ingmar Bergman, with Max von Sydow, Bibi Andersson, and Gunnar Bjornstrand). Also Two Men and a Wardrobe (1957, directed by Roman Polanski) and The Fat and the Lean (1963, directed by Roman Polanski). Discussion of how these allegories are effectively communicated by the choice of what is shown and how it is shown.

Mar 24 Satire: The Great Dictator (1940, directed by and starring Charles Chaplin, with Paulette Goddard). Also The Dove (1968). Discussion of satire and of these films as satires.

PART III: TOPICS IN CRITICISM
Mar 31 Defining a Genre: Screwball Comedy. His Girl Friday (1940, directed by Howard Hawks, with Cary Grant, Rosalind Russell and Ralph Bellamy) and Bringing Up Baby (1938, directed by Howard Hawks, with Cary Grant and Katherine Hepburn). Discussion of these films as they exhibit the conventions of screwball comedy, and of various explanations for the screwball comedy as a phenomenon of the 1930s.

Apr 7 Film as an Expression of Culture: Ugetsu Monogatari (1953, directed by Kenji Mizoguchi). Discussion of what is Japanese about the film and what is universal about it.

Apr 14 Film as an Expression of Culture: Invasion of the Body Snatchers (1956, directed by Don Siegel, with Kevin McCarthy, Dana Wynter and Carolyn Jones). Discussion of the film as an expression of American anxieties during the McCarthy era.

Apr 21 Narrative Conventions: The Gothic Film. Picnic at Hanging Rock (1975, directed by Peter Weir). Discussion of the film's Gothic conventions as a clue to its riddle.

Apr 28 Free Discussion: The Night of the Shooting Stars (1983, directed by Paolo & Vittorio Taviani).

Above is the syllabus for the spring of 1987. The course
meets one day a week for four hours, during which a film or
films is shown and discussed. The most important texts for the
course are the films, but there are some required readings: in
the Spring of 1987 these were Jack Finney's novel, Invasion of
the Body Snatchers; Ingmar Bergman's screenplay for The Seventh
Seal; a list of basic film terms; Glen Johnson's essay on
Invasion of the Body Snatchers from the Journal of Popular
Culture; and Andrew Sarris's essay on "The Sex Comedy Without
Sex" from American Film (March 1978). In addition, Giannetti's
Understanding Movies is recommended, as well as Kael's Citizen
Kane Book and other readings.

In other semesters I have varied the content somewhat,
using Lord of the Flies as an example of allegory, for example,
and looking at It Happened One Night and Holiday as examples of
Screwball Comedy. Often, under "topics in criticism," I've
included a category I call "moral criticism": I've shown
Freaks and asked whether it is compassionate or exploitative,
and I've had students argue for and against saying A Boy and
His Dog is sexist -- always paying attention to what is shown
and how it is shown.

INTRO TO THE FILM Eng 368 A. Fall, 1987. Professor Lou Giannetti

Course has a $15 lab fee to help defray costs of film rentals.
Payable at Cashier's Office in Adelbert Main. Return receipt
to instructor. Be sure to sign sign-in sheet at Film Society
desk. Non-payment of lab fee will result in a grade of I.

COURSE OBJECTIVES: A) To understand the language systems and
aesthetic components of the films of the course; B) To provide the
student with the ability to analyse how any film works as a
complex aesthetic entity.

COURSE REQUIREMENTS: Responsible attendance, occasional quizzes,
midterm, final, term paper (8-10 typed pages). Late papers will
be penalized. Excessive absences will result in a lowered grade:
5 unexcused absences lower your grade one full level.

REQUIRED TEXT: Understanding Movies, by Louis Giannetti. Prentice-
Hall, 1987. FOURTH EDITION, in paperback.

REQUIRED FILMS: All shown by CWRU Film Society in Strosacker
Auditorium.

Aug. 25.	Top Hat (USA, 1935), Mark Sandrich, director.
Aug. 28.	Crocodile Dundee (Australia, 1986), Peter Faiman.
Sept. 5.	Salvador (USA, 1986), Oliver Stone.
Sept. 8.	The Lift (Netherlands, 1985), Dick Maas.
Sept. 12.	The Color of Money (USA, 1986), Martin Scorsese.
Sept. 15.	The Wall (Turkey, 1983), Yilmaz Guney.
Sept. 18.	Peggy Sue Got Married (USA, 1986), Francis Ford Coppola.
Sept. 22.	Oedipus Rex (Italy, 1967), Pier Paolo Pasolini.
Oct. 3.	Sid and Nancy (USA, 1986), Alex Cox.
Oct. 6.	Rouge Baiser (France, 1986), Vera Belmont.
Oct. 16.	Platoon (USA, 1986), Oliver Stone.
Oct. 20.	Signal 7 (USA, 1983), Rob Nilsson.
Oct. 23.	Tin Men (USA, 1987), Barry Levinson.
Oct. 30.	Angel Heart (USA, 1987), Alan Parker.
Nov. 3.	Portrait of Teresa (Cuba, 1979), Pastor Vega.
Nov. 7.	Radio Days (USA, 1987), Woody Allen.
Nov. 10.	Jules and Jim (France, 1961), Francois Truffaut.
Nov. 17.	The Times of Harvey Milk (USA, 1984), Robert Epstein.
Nov. 21	Vertigo (USA, 1958), Alfred Hitchcock.
Nov. 24.	Gap Toothed Women (USA, 1987), Les Blank.
Dec. 1.	Cries and Whispers (Sweden, 1972), Ingmar Bergman.
Dec. 4.	Eraserhead (USA, 1978), David Lynch.
Dec. 8.	Night and Fog in Japan (Japan, 1960), Nagisa Oshima.

INTRODUCTION TO FILM
01: 354: 201: 08 (D/C)
Fall 1987

Miriam Hansen
Off.: 43 Mine St.
Tel.: 932-7355

LECTURES: M6, W6   Hickman 210
SCREENINGS: M7,8,9   Art History 200
READINGS: Bordwell/Thompson, Film Art: An Introduction (= BT)
             Xeroxes on reserve at Douglass Library

REQUIREMENTS: 1. Attendance at both lectures and screenings is considered
essential to this course. Students who miss more than five (5)
classes will fail the course unless a note from the Dean's Office can
satisfactorily explain the cause of absence. Keep in mind that
screenings cannot be repeated outside the time scheduled for them and
that the quality of your written work will crucially depend upon
first-hand knowledge of each film. Use of video tapes is encouraged
(insofar as the films are available on tape), but VCR-viewing cannot
become a substitute for main screenings.
    2. Readings. Students are expected to have completed the
readings before the meetings for which they were assigned.
    3. Papers. One short paper (2-3pp.), due October 5, and one
slightly longer paper (4-5pp.), due Nov. 18. Late papers will be
penalized and cannot be accepted without prior consultation.
Papers should be typed, but not on onion skin or corrasible bond.
    4. Exams. A midterm (Oct. 14) and a 3-hr. final (December 15).

Sept. 2:   INTRODUCTION

I. WAYS OF READING A FILM

Sept. 9:   ELEMENTS OF FILM ANALYSIS
             Reading: BT, 22-43, 82-99

Sept. 14-16: NARRATIVE; EDITING
             Reading: BT, 286-295, 199-210

             The Lady Vanishes (Hitchcock/GB, 1938; 97 min.)

Sept. 21-23: THE SHOT: FRAMING, MISE-EN-SCENE
             Reading: BT, 119-135, 162-174

             The Lady Vanishes (second viewing required)

Sept. 23:   Uncle Josh at the Moving Picture Show (in class)
             Reading: Plato, "Parable of the Cave" (handout)
                      Barthes, "Upon Leaving the Movie-Theater" (handout)

II. THE INSTITUTION OF CINEMA

Sept. 28-30: EXHIBITION PRACTICES, TYPES OF FILM AND THE CREATION OF A
             FILM SPECTATOR
             Reading: BT, 3-19, 120-121, 345-49
                      Gunning, "Cinema of Attractions" (reserve)

Sept. 28:   Before the Nickelodeon (Musser, 1982; 60 min.) [in class]

             Edison kinetoscope films (US, 1893-1898)
             Lumière films (France, 1895-1898)
             Trip to the Moon (Méliès/France, 1902)
             Uncle Josh at the Moving Picture Show (Porter/Edison, 1902)
             Grandpa's Reading Glass (Biograph, 1902)
             The Gay Shoe Clerk (Porter/Edison, 1903)

Sept. 30:   Correction, Please: Or, How We Got Into Pictures (Burch/GB,
             1979; 60 min.) [in class]

Oct. 5:   FIRST PAPER DUE

Oct. 5-7:   THE RISE OF NARRATIVE

Oct. 5:   The "Teddy" Bears (1907) [in class]
             Reading: BT, 349-353

             The Great Train Robbery (Porter/Edison, 1903)
             Life of an American Fireman (Porter/Edison, 1903)
             The "Teddy" Bears (Porter/Edison, 1907)
             A Corner in Wheat (Griffith/Biograph, 1909)
             Easy Street (Chaplin, 1917; 20 min.)
             Cops (Keaton, 1922; 20 min.)

Oct. 7:   Life of an American Fireman (1903) [in class]
             Reading: Musser, "The Early Cinema of Edwin Porter" (reserve)

Oct. 12-14: EDITING: ALTERNATION, CONTINUITY
             Reading: BT, 210-220
                      Altman, "The Lonely Villa and Griffith's Paradigmatic
                      Style" (reserve)

Oct. 12:   The Lonedale Operator (1911) [in class]

             The Lonely Villa (Griffith, 1909)
             The Lonedale Operator (Griffith, 1911)
             The Musketeers of Pig Alley (Griffith, 1912)
             Hell's Hinges (Hart/Ince, 1915; 59 min.)

Oct. 14:   MIDTERM

III. MODES OF FILM PRACTICE:

Oct. 19-21: NARRATIVE, HISTORY, IDEOLOGY
             Reading: Wollen, "The Semiology of the Cinema" (reserve)
                      Rogin, "The Sword Became a Flaming Vision" (optional)

             The Birth of a Nation (Griffith, 1915; 155 min.)

Oct. 19:   The Birth of a Nation, reel two or tape [in class]

30

Oct. 26-28:   THE MISE-EN-SCENE OF THE FANTASTIC: GERMAN EXPRESSIONISM
              Reading: BT, 119-126, 133, 353-355

              The Cabinet of Doctor Caligari (Wiene/Germany, 1919; 50 min.)
              Nosferatu: A Symphony of Horror (Murnau/Germany, 1921; 88 min.)

Nov. 2-4:   THE MISE-EN-SCENE OF THE EROTIC: "WOMAN" IN CLASSICAL HOLLYWOOD FILM
              Reading: BT, 119-150, especially 122-131
                       Berger, Ways of Seeing, chs. 2 & 3 (reserve)

              Shanghai Express (Sternberg & Dietrich, 1932; 84 min.)

Nov. 9-11:   ALTERNATIVES TO CONTINUITY EDITING: SOVIET MONTAGE
              Reading: BT, 220-231

              Battleship Potemkin (Eisenstein/USSR, 1925; 60 min.)

Nov. 11:   Man with a Movie Camera (Vertov, 1929), reel one [in class]

Nov. 16-18:   FRAMING AND THE LONG TAKE; POLITICS AND FORM
              Reading: BT, 174-191, 330-335

              The Crime of Monsieur Lange (Renoir/France, 1935; 84 min.)

Nov. 18:   SECOND PAPER DUE

Nov. 23-25:   SOUND AS NARRATIVE DEVICE
              Reading: BT, 232-260

              M (Lang/Germany, 1931; 99 min.)

Nov. 25:   M, reel one or tape [in class]

Nov.30/Dec.2: SOUND AND CINEMATIC SPACE; THE MUSICAL
              Reading: Williams, "The Musical Film and Recorded Popular Music"
                       (reserve)

              Gold Diggers of 1933 (LeRoy, 1933; 96 min.)

Dec. 7-9:   STYLE, AUTHORSHIP, SELF-REFLEXIVITY
              Reading: BT, 261-265, 277-284, 100-116; 151-198 (repeat)

              Citizen Kane (Welles, 1941; 119 min.)

Dec. 7:   Citizen Kane, reel one or tape [in class]

Dec. 9:   REVIEW

Dec. 15:   FINAL

INTRODUCTION TO FILM
01: 354: 202: 05 (D/C)
Spring 1987

Miriam Hansen
Off.: Murray 047 (CAC)
Tel.: 932-7332

LECTURES: T6, Th6   Language Building 001
SCREENINGS: Th7,8,9   D/C Art History 100
TEXTS: Bordwell/Thompson, <u>Film Art: An Introduction</u> (= BT)
             Xeroxes on reserve at Douglass Library

REQUIREMENTS: 1. <u>Attendance</u> at both lectures and screenings is considered
             essential to this course. Students who miss more than five classes
             will fail the course unless a note from the Dean's Office can
             satisfactorily explain the cause of absence. Keep in mind that
             screenings cannot be repeated outside the time scheduled for them and
             that the quality of your written work will crucially depend upon
             first-hand knowledge of each film. Use of video tapes is encouraged,
             but should not become a substitute for main screenings.
                   2. <u>Readings</u>. Students are expected to have completed the
             readings before the meetings for which they were assigned.
                   3. <u>Papers</u>. One short paper (2-3pp.), due February 17, and one
             slightly longer paper (4-5pp.), due April 14. Late papers will be
             penalized and cannot be accepted without prior consultation. Papers
             should be typed, but not on onion skin or corrasible bond.
                   4. <u>Exams</u>. A midterm (March 12) and a 3-hr. final (May 11).

Jan. 20:   INTRODUCTION; ASPECTS OF CLASSICAL NARRATIVE CINEMA
             Reading: BT, 346-353, 364-367; 7-8, 82-99 (narrative)

Jan. 22/27: <u>Only Angels Have Wings</u> (Howard Hawks, 1939; 121 min.)

Jan. 29/   GENRE: THE WESTERN
   Febr. 3: Reading: Schatz, <u>Hollywood Genres</u>, 4-10
                      Tudor, "Genre"
                      BT, 23-41

             <u>She Wore a Yellow Ribbon</u> (John Ford, 1949; 103 min.)

Febr. 5/10: GENRE AND AUTEUR THEORY; SCREWBALL COMEDY
             Reading: Wollen, "The Auteur Theory"
                      BT, 19-20; 199-220 (editing)

             <u>Bringing Up Baby</u> (Howard Hawks, 1938; 102 min.)

Febr. 12/17: GENRE AND STYLE: DETECTIVE THRILLER/FILM NOIR
             Reading: Place, in: Kaplan, ed. <u>Women in Film</u> Noir, 35-65
                      BT, 119-141, 146-150 (mise-en-scene), 168-174, 261-265

             <u>The Maltese Falcon</u> (John Huston, 1941; 101 min.)

Febr. 17:   FIRST PAPER DUE

32

Febr.19/24: STARS AND DIRECTORS; THE POLITICS OF "THE LOOK'
            Reading: Dyer, Stars, 142-149, 177-178
                     Abel, "Notorious: Perversion par Excellence"
                     BT, 292-295; 196-197 (point-of-view shot)

            Notorious (Alfred Hitchcock, 1946; 101 min.)

Febr.26/   REFLECTIONS ON CLASSICAL AMERICAN CINEMA: THE FRENCH NEW WAVE
March 3:   Reading: BT, 373-376; 220-228

            Breathless (Jean-Luc Godard, 1960; 89 min.)

March 5/10: SELF-REFLEXIVITY, STYLE, AUTHORSHIP
            Reading: BT, 100-116, 277-284; 151-181, 188-191, 198

            Citizen Kane (Orson Welles, 1941; 119 min.)

March 12:   MIDTERM

March 12/24: THE MUSICAL: SELF-REFLEXIVITY AND THE MYTH OF ENTERTAINMENT
            Reading: BT, 232-249 (sound)
                     Feuer, "The Self-Reflective Musical and the Myth of Entertainment"

            Singin' in the Rain (Gene Kelly/Stanley Donen, 1952; 102 min.)

March 26/31: FILM TECHNOLOGY IN THE 1950s; CINEMASCOPE & COLOR—A EUROPEAN RESPONSE
            Reading: BT, 152-153, 163-166, 181, 196
                     Morrison, "3D: High, Wide and Handsome"
                     Neale, "Color and Film Aesthetics"

            Lola Montes (Max Ophuls, France/West Germany 1955; 140 min.)

April 2/7: TRADITIONS OF NATIONAL CINEMA: ITALIAN NEO-REALISM
            Reading: BT, 371-373, 119-120, 147-148
                     Bazin, "An Aesthetic of Reality"

            Open City (Roberto Rossellini, 1945; 101 min.)
April 7:   (in class) Paisan (Rossellini, 1946; segment)

            NON-NARRATIVE TYPES OF FILM

April 9/14: DOCUMENTARY (I)
            Reading: BT, 55-62, 144-145, 232-233
                     Nichols, "Modes of Address"

            The Battle of San Pietro (John Huston, 1945; 35 min.)
            Land without Bread (Luis Buñuel, 1932; 25 min.)
            Union Maids (Jim Klein/Julia Reichert, 1976; 55 min.)

April 14:   SECOND PAPER DUE

April 16/21:   DOCUMENTARY (II)
               Reading: BT, 314-321

               Night and **Fog** (Alain Resnais, France, 1955; 31 min.)
               The **Titicut** **Follies** (Frederick Wiseman, 1967; 85 min.)

April 23/28:   AVANT-GARDE (I)
               Reading: BT, 355-359; 62-72, 220-222

               The **Smiling** **Mme**. **Beudet** (Germaine Dulac, France 1924; 20 min.)
               Entr'acte (RenéClair, France 1924; 16 min.)
               Ballet **Mécanique** (Fernand Leger and Dudley Murphy, 1924; 12 min.)
               An **Andalusian** **Dog** (Buñuel/Dali, France 1928; 16 min.)
               La **Jetée** (Chris Marker, France 1964; 28 min.)

April 30:   AVANT-GARDE (II); ANIMATION
               Reading: Sitney, "Meshes of the Afternoon"
                        Brakhage, from "Metaphors of Vision"

               Meshes **of** **the** **Afternoon** (Maya Deren/Alex. Hammid, 1943, 12 min.)
               Ritual **in** **Transfigured** **Time** (Deren, 1946; 15 min.)
               Water **Window** **Baby** **Moving** (Stan Brakhage, 1959; 17 min.)
               Asparagus (Suzan Pitt, 1978; 19 min.)
               Betty **Boop** **in** **Blunderland** (Max Fleischer, 1933; 7 min.)

May 11:   FINAL

CINEMA STUDIES IN AN ENGLISH DEPARTMENT

Charles J. Maland
University of Tennessee

In a university without a Cinema Studies Department, where ought film be taught? This question has confronted many institutions in the last two decades, and it has been answered in a variety of ways. Since film is such a hybrid art, a strong case for including film can be made by a variety of departments: theater, broadcasting, communications, modern languages, art history, even history, business, and philosophy.

Yet it may be that in the Humanities, film study most often takes place in English Departments. At the University of Tennessee, which has no Film Department but which does have an interdisciplinary Cinema Studies Program, more courses in film studies are taught in the English Department than in any other department. Focusing especially on narrative films, the courses are offered at the sophomore, upper-division, and graduate level.

This is partly for economic reasons. The English Department has been willing to provide the funds necessary to rent and purchase films. It has also hired faculty trained in Cinema Studies whose primary responsibility is to teach film courses. The financial commitments have led to the regular teaching of the series of courses listed below. It may be appropriate to add that the program is supported by a large collection of videotapes in the University Library's Non-Print Department, as well as extensive facilities for both individual and group videotape showings. Although the English Department courses show nearly all the required films in 16mm, this videotape collection is heavily used for student papers. It enables the students doing critical analyses of films the chance to see a film as many times as they wish while they are preparing their papers.

* * * * * * * * * *

INTRODUCTION TO FILM STUDIES

This sophomore level course runs parallel to a variety of introductory genre courses in the English Department, like Introduction to Poetry, Introduction to Drama, and Introduction to the Novel. It is the only lecture/discussion course of the film offerings (all others run in sections no larger than 32 students). In general, the course is composed of three sections of 30 students each term it is offered. All the students meet for lectures on Monday and screenings on Wednesday, then the discussion sections meet separately with discussion leaders on Fridays. While the film screenings have at times been organized historically, beginning with Lumiere/Melies/Griffith, note that in the syllabus below the films were chosen to coincide with the issue of film aesthetics focussed on in any particular week. The syllabus gives a clear idea of the goals, structure, and requirements of the course.

Introduction to Film Studies
English 2690

M 2:20-3:10 Lecture
W 2:20-4:15 Screening
F 2:20-3:10 Discussion Groups

The task which I am trying to achieve is above all to make you see.
D.W. Griffith
The cinema is a ribbon of dreams.
Orson Welles
Film is a fascinating way to discover the world and to develop an understanding of its politics, its psychology, its structure, its language.
James Monaco
That's the great thing about the movies. You're giving people little, tiny pieces of time that they never forget.
Jimmy Stewart

* * * * * * * * * * * * * *

Introduction to Film Studies is designed to introduce students to the history of narrative film and to the fundamentals of how film as an art form communicates. It also aims to train students to watch films more closely so that their viewing will become more active and hence richer. By the end of the course you should be able to:

1. Trace the major developments in film history, relating the films we see this term to the periods and places in which they were made.
2. Discuss in considerable detail Bordwell and Thompson's concept of film form, break down the concept into its various aspects of narrative and style, and define film terms associated with film form.
3. Identify the various elements of film style when you see or hear them.
4. Analyze and evaluate each of the films we see this term and compare their styles and narratives with those of others we see.
5. Distinguish between various types of narrative and non-narrative films.

If you are able to do these things and are a more knowledgeable, sensitive, and perceptive viewer of films when the course in over, it will have been a success.

REQUIRED BOOKS:
Film Art, by David Bordwell and Kristin Thompson
Film Study Guides by Carringer, et al.

EXAMS:

Everyone will take a midterm and a final exam.

PAPERS:

Each student will write two typewritten critical analyses of 1000-1500 words. Each essay should be carefully organized and contain a clearly articulated main idea in the opening paragraph. Essays should also reveal your growing understanding of the cinema as an art form and medium of expression. We will provide more specific instructions about the papers about ten days before each paper is due.

GRADING:

Each exam and paper will count 25% of your grade. Your performance on any quizzes will be considered in deciding borderline grades. In addition, while your participation in class discussions will not lower your grade, it could raise a borderline grade.

COURSE STRUCTURE:

Generally, the course will run as follows: on Monday we will lecture on film aesthetics and history, largely to prepare you for the film we see on Wednesday and to discuss issues raised by our readings in Bordwell and Thompson. On Friday we will divide the class into three discussion groups, each one led by a discussion leader.

NON-PRINT:

The Non-print Department of the library is located on the second floor of the Hodges Library. It has a large collection of classic feature films, including most of the films you will have the chance to write on. (To write good analytical papers on films, it is necessary to see the film at least twice, for in most cases it is difficult to notice film style on first viewings.) You may see videotapes at Non-print by going to the second floor of Hodges and turning your ID to the staff on duty at the Non-print counter.

OUTSIDE READINGS ON FILM:

The new library has extensive holdings in film history, theory, and criticism. The bibliography sections at the end of chapters in Film Art can lead you to sources for further reading. We would also be happy to suggest other books if you get interested in a subject and would like to explore it further.

Topics, Reading, and Viewing Schedule

FA = Film Art   C = Carringer, ed. Film Study Guides

SEPTEMBER
  25: Introduction to course: the Prehistory of Movies

  28: Film Production (Technological and Social); the Concept of Film Form; FA, ch. 1, pp. 345-53
  30: See TOOTSIE (Sydney Pollack, 1982)
OCTOBER
   2: Discussion of TOOTSIE in discussion groups.

   5: Film Form and the Analysis of Narratives: FA, Chs. 2, 4.
   7: See HIS GIRL FRIDAY (Howard Hawks, 1940); FA, 353-67
   9: Discuss HGF--meet in discussion groups; FA, 287-300

  12: Film Style I: Mise-en-Scene: FA, Ch. 5; C, 58-72.
  14: See THE SEVENTH SEAL (Ingmar Bergman, 1957)
  16: Discuss THE SEVENTH SEAL

  19: Film Style II: Framing: read FA, Ch. 6.
  21: See THE 400 BLOWS (Francois Truffaut, 1959); FA, pp. 373-80.
  23: Discuss THE 400 BLOWS.

26: Film Style III: Editing--FA, Ch. 7
28: See NORTH BY NORTHWEST (Alfred Hitchcock, 1959); C, 73-91
30: Discuss NORTH BY NORTHWEST

2: Film Style IV: Sound, and Putting it All Together, FA, Chs. 8-9
4: See CITIZEN KANE (Orson Welles, 1941); FA, pp. 364-67
6: Discuss CITIZEN KANE; C, pp. 28-45.

9: Mid-term Exam
11: See BICYCLE THIEVES (Vittorio De Sica, 1947)--FA, pp. 325-42, 367-73
13: Discuss BICYCLE THIEVES; C, p.46-57.

16: Silent Film Comedy: Charlie Chaplin. Read FA, review pp. 349-53. See The Rink and The Immigrant (the latter may be shown at the start of class on Wednesday).
18: Silent Film Comedy: Buster Keaton. See Sherlock, Jr.
20: Discuss Chaplin and Keaton

23: Non-Narrative Film Form: See TANGO; FRANK FILM. FA, Ch. 3
25: Non-Narrative Film Form, II: Documentary Films, Parodies; FA, 314-20
27: No Class: Thanksgiving Break

30: Recent Independent Narrative Cinema: see EL NORTE (NOTE: Special Showing--2:20-4:15) FA, 287-8; 325-42
DECEMBER
1: Discuss EL NORTE; class review

7: Final Exam: Monday, 2:20-4

                * * * * * * * * * *

Professor Gerald Mast
Eng 280/480 GS HUM 201/310 ArtDes 251
Introduction to Film I
G. Mast (G-B 319; Wed 1:30-3; Thurs 10-11:30)

BOOKS (in Bookstore under ENG 280)

Mast, Gerald   A Short History of the Movies, 4th edition (SH)
Mast, Gerald, ed.   The Movies in Our Midst (MM)
Mast, Gerald and Marshall Cohen, eds. Film Theory and Criticism (MC)
Giannetti, Louis   Understanding Movies, 3rd edition (GI)
          all books are also on reserve in Regenstein under ENG 475

DATE	TOPIC	READINGS	SCREENINGS
Jan 6	Introduction to the Introduction		
8	Invention and Primitives	SH, chaps 1,2 MM, pp. xv-39	
13	From Porter to Biograph: 1903-1907	SH, chap 3 MM, pp. 41-56 GI, chaps 1,2	for screenings
15	Griffith at Biograph	SH, chap 4 MM, pp. 56-99 GI, chaps 3,4	see
20-22	The Birth of a Nation	MM, pp. 99-153 MC, pp. 7-22, 243-78	separate
27-29 Feb 3	The Tramp	SH, chap 5 MC, pp. 535-58 MM, pp. 157-76	schedule
5	The Lubitsch Touch	SH, chap 6 MM, pp. 176-236	
10-12	Jacques Tati's Playtime	GI, chaps 5,6 MC, pp. 23-27, 123-39	
17-19 24	German Expressionism	SH, chap 7 MC, pp. 28-32, 279-87	
26- Mar 3-5	Soviet Montage	SH, chap 8 MC, pp. 77-122	
10-12	Documentary to Dada	MC, pp. 33-44 GI, chaps 9,10	

Eng 280/480 GS HUM 201/310 ArtDes 251
Introduction to Film I
G. Mast (G-B 319; Wed 1:30-3; Thurs 10-11:30)

SCREENINGS

Tues, Jan 6 & 7 PM Films of the 1890s (USA, Edison, 1894-99)
Wed, Jan 7   "   Lumiere Program (France, Lumiere, 1895-1900)
                       Jupiter's Thunderbolts (France, Melies, 1903)
                       The Mermaid (France, Melies, 1903)
                       The Magic Lantern (France, Melies, 1904)
                       A Trip to the Moon (France, Melies, 1903)

Sat, Jan 10 & Noon Life of an American Fireman (USA, Porter, 1903)
Mon, Jan 12   7 PM The Great Train Robbery (USA, Porter, 1903)
                       Rescued from an Eagle's Nest (USA, Porter, 1907)
                       Personal (USA, McCutcheon, 1904)
                       Rescued by Rover (GB, Hepworth, 1905)
                       The Black Hand (USA, McCutcheon, 1906)
                       Her First Adventure (USA, McCutcheon, 1908)

Tues, Jan 13 & 7 PM The Adventures of Dollie (USA, Griffith, 1908)
Wed, Jan 14   "   An Awful Moment (USA, Griffith, 1908)
                       The Lonely Villa (USA, Griffith, 1909)
                       A Corner in Wheat (USA, Griffith, 1909)
                       The Lonedale Operator (USA, Griffith, 1911)
                       The Two Paths (USA, Griffith, 1911)
                       The Musketeers of Pig Alley (USA, Griffith, 1912)

Sat, Jan 17 & Noon The Birth of a Nation (USA, Griffith, 1915)
Mon, Jan 19   7 PM

Sat, Jan 24 & Noon Kid Auto Races (USA, Lehrman, 1914)
Mon, Jan 26   7 PM The Rounders (USA, Chaplin, 1914)
                       The New Janitor (USA, Chaplin, 1914)
                       The Tramp (USA, Chaplin, 1915)
                       The Pawnshop (USA, Chaplin, 1916)

Tues, Jan 27 & 7 PM Easy Street (USA, Chaplin, 1917)
Wed, Jan 28   "   A Dog's Life (USA, Chaplin, 1918)

Sat, Jan 31 & Noon City Lights (USA, Chaplin, 1931)
Mon, Feb 2   7 PM

Tues, Feb 3 &   7 PM The Marriage Circle (USA, Lubitsch, 1924)
Wed, Feb 4   "

Sat, Feb 7 &   Noon Playtime (France, Tati, 1967)
Mon, Feb 9   7 PM

Sat, Feb 14 & 11 AM The Cabinet of Dr. Caligari (Germany, Wiene, 1919)
Mon, Feb 16   7 PM   Metropolis (Germany, Lang, 1926)

41

Tues, Feb 17 & Wed, Feb 18	7 PM "	The Last Laugh (Germany, Murnau, 1924)
Sat, Feb 21 & Mon, Feb 23	Noon 7 PM	Sunrise (USA, Murnau, 1927)
Tues, Feb 24 & Wed, Feb 25	7 PM "	Strike (USSR, Eisenstein, 1924) Mother (USSR, Pudovkin, 1926)
Sat, Feb 28 & Mon, Mar 2	Noon 7 PM	Potemkin (USSR, Eisenstein, 1925)
Sat, Mar 7 & Mon, Mar 9	Noon 7 PM	Nanook of the North (USA, Flaherty, 1922)
Tues, Mar 10 Wed, Mar 11	7 PM "	Entr'acte (France, Clair, 1922) Return to Reason (France, Ray, 1924) Ballet Mecanique (France, Leger, 1924) Un Chien andalou (France, Dali-Bunuel, 1929)

COURSE REQUIREMENTS

1) Short Essay. Examine a single short film (not seen in class) or a single scene from a feature film (seen inside or outside class) in detail, using the films and viewing equipment available in the Film Study Center across the hall (Cobb 407-09). Write an essay (8-12 typewritten, double-spaced pages) which is a detailed explication of the inter-relation of style and content in the sequence, the relationship of cinema devices (framing, blocking, editing, lighting, costume, decor, acting, gesture, camera angle, camera movement, etc.) to the effects and information of the sequence.

Some suggestions:

a) You need to make appointments to use the Center in advance; there are sign-up sheets on the door. As the days dwindle down to a precious few before the essay is due, it gets more and more difficult to get an appointment. MORAL: do your film research as early as possible.

b) A major difficulty of this essay is gathering what you will discover to be an immense amount of data into a coherent discussion. You should not merely list everything you see in the sequence in chronological order. You need to select, organize, and focus your data to produce a coherent essay. One thing to remember to aid your organization is that you need not analyze a whole scene or even a whole short film; you can define your sequence, your unit, as a fragment of a larger whole.

c) If you need some help with the assignment—or with any other of the course's materials and issues—it is readily available. In this course,

relief is spelled Arthur Knight. You can make an appointment with him to
discuss any matters of the course or essay--difficulties in analyzing films,
understanding terminology and issues, looking closely at fragments of film,
organizing your observations into a coherent essay structure. You can even
write practice paragraphs, develop an outline, or submit a whole essay for
Arthur's comments before you submit the essay.

The short essay is DUE: TUESDAY, FEBRUARY 24.

2) Final Exam (for UNDERGRADUATES) and Term Paper (for GRADUATE STUDENTS).

      A) The final exam for undergraduates will be in two parts. There
will be a take-home essay, handed out the final day of class (March 12). And
there will be an in-class exam, scheduled during the Final Exam period
(Thursday, March 19, 1:30-3:30 PM). The in-class exam will be composed of
two major parts: an "objective" section composed of identifications related
to film history; and short essays. The take-home exam will be due at the
same time as the in-class exam (NO LATER THAN 3:30 PM ON THURSDAY, MARCH 19).

      B) The term paper for graduate students will be on a general problem
of pre-1927 film history, theory, or criticism, developed in conference with the
instructor. It is due NO LATER THAN 4:30 PM ON TUESDAY, MARCH 17. It is
expected that this paper will require additional reading and/or viewing of
books on reserve in Regenstein and films available in the Study Center.

Professor Gerald Mast

Eng 280/480 GS HUM 310 ArtDes 251
Introduction to Film II
G. Mast (G-B 319)   W 1:30-3, Th 1-2

BOOKS (in Bookstore under Eng 280)

Mast, Gerald   <u>A Short History of the Movies</u>, 3rd edition (SH)
Mast, Gerald, ed.   <u>The Movies in Our Midst</u> (MM)
Mast, Gerald and Marshall Cohen, eds. <u>Film Theory and Criticism</u> (M&C)
Kawin, Bruce   <u>How Movies Work</u> (K)
     all books are also on reserve in Regenstein under ENG 475

DATE	TOPIC	READINGS	SCREENINGS
Mar 31-Apr 2	The Coming of Sound	SH, chap 9 MM, pp. 238-313 MC, 215-34 K, 120-200	see
Apr 7-9	Ernst Lubitsch	SH, chap 11 to p. 246 MM. pp. 315-45 K, 201-85	separate
14-16	Jean Renoir's <u>Grand Illusion</u>	SH, chap 10 MC, pp. 124-39	screening
21-23	Orson Welles's <u>Citizen Kane</u>	SH, chap 11 to end MM, pp. 345-83 K, 97-117	schedule
28-30	American Genre: the Western	MM, 383-48 MC, 434-50 K, 288-409	
May 5-7	American Auteur: Howard Hawks	MC, 527-71 MM, 441-88	
12-14	Visions of the Fifties: Hitchcock, Sirk	SH, chap 12 MM, 448-64 K, 410-521	
19-21	European "Art Film": <u>Red Desert</u>	SH, chaps 13, 14 MM, 604-93	
26-28	American and European "art-genre" film: <u>Breathless</u> <u>Chinatown</u>	SH, chaps 15, 16, 17 MC, pp. 139-63, 503-20	
June 2-4	American Independent Cinema	MM, 693-749 MC, pp. 31-41, 51-76	

Eng 280/480 GS HUM 310 ArtDes 251
Introduction to Film II
G. Mast (G-B 319)   W 1:30-3, Th 1-2

SCHEDULE OF SCREENINGS

Tues, Mar 31, 7 PM Wed, Apr 1, 7 PM	Applause (USA, Rouben Mamoulian, 1929)
Sat, Apr 4, 1 PM Mon, Apr 6, 7 PM	Monte Carlo (USA, Ernst Lubitsch, 1930)
Tues, Apr 7, 8 PM Wed, Apr 8, 7 PM	Trouble in Paradise (USA, Ernst Lubitsch, 1932)
Sat, Apr 11, 1 PM Mon, Apr 13, 7 PM	Grand Illusion (France, Jean Renior, 1937)
Sat, Apr 18, 1 PM Mon, Apr 20, 7 PM	Citizen Kane (USA, Orson Welles, 1941)
Sat, Apr 25, 11 AM Sun, Apr 26, 1 PM Sat, Apr 25, 1 PM Sun, Apr 26, 3 PM Sat, Apr 25, 3 PM Mon, Apr 27, 7 PM	Stagecoach (USA, John Ford, 1939) Red River (USA, Howard Hawks, 1948) The Searchers (USA, John Ford, 1956)
Sat, May 2, 1 PM Sun, May 3, 3 PM Sat, May 2, 3 PM Mon, May 4, 7 PM Sun, May 3, 1 PM Mon, May 4, 9 PM	Only Angels Have Wings (USA, Howard Hawks, 1939) His Girl Friday (USA, Howard Hawks, 1941) The Big Sleep (USA, Howard Hawks, 1946)
Sat, May 9, 1 PM Sun, May 10, 3 PM Sat, May 9, 3 PM Mon, May 11, 7 PM Sun, May 10, 1 PM Mon, May 11, 9 PM	Rear Window (USA, Alfred Hitchcock, 1954) Vertigo (USA, Alfred Hitchcock, 1957) Imitation of Life (USA, Douglas Sirk, 1959)
Sat, May 16, 1 PM Mon, May 18, 7 PM	Red Desert (Italy, Michelangelo Antonioni, 1964)
Sat, May 23, 1 PM Mon, May 25, 7 PM Sat, May 23, 3 PM Mon, May 25, 9 PM	Breathless (France, Jean-Luc Godard, 1959) Chinatown (USA, Roman Polanski, 1975)
Sat, May 30, 1 PM Mon, June 1, 7 PM	Meshes of the Afternoon (USA, Maya Deren, 1943) Fireworks (USA, Kenneth Anger, 1947) Scorpio Rising (USA, Kenneth Anger, 1963) Mothlight (USA, Stan Brakhage, 1963) Wavelength (USA, Michael Snow, 1967)

Eng 280/480 GS HUM 310 ArtDes 251
Introduction to Film II
G. Mast (G-B 319)   W 1:30-3, Th 1-2

COURSE REQUIREMENTS

1) Select any sound-film in the Film Library not studied in class.
Choose a single scene (or section, or sequence, or portion) of the
film and study it in detail on the moviola. Write an essay (8-12
typewritten, double-spaced pages) which is a detailed explication of
the specific segment and its relationship to the film as a whole.
Your treatment of the segment might include discussion of camera
angles and movement, framing, lighting, editing, music, sound, dialogue, blocking, color--whatever seems expressively important in the
section. You should then relate the function of the section (the
information it provides about characters, events, themes, images,
style) to the film as a whole. Why is the segment important to the
film as a whole? What does it do and how?

For advice, consultation, organization, and fretting about the paper,
Arthur Knight will provide guidance, assistance, suggestions, criticism,
and assurance. He will schedule appointments with the desireous or
the needy as the quarter unfolds. ESSAY DUE: MAY 19.

2) A Final Take-Home examination or a term paper (Graduate Students
MUST write a paper, undergraduates have the option). The term paper,
devised in consultation with the instructor, can be a study of a
single filmmaker studied during the course, or of an American film
genre, or a style of filmmaking, an historical issue related to film
(like the Hollywood Code or Blacklisting), a theory related to some
group of films, a technique or theme you have observed in several
different films or filmmakers, etc. The take-home exam, for those who
would rather not devise their own topic, will require the writing of
three essay questions.

ALL WORK FOR THE COURSE IS DUE BY 5 PM ON TUESDAY, JUNE 9.
FOR GRADUATING SENIORS, BY 5 PM ON TUESDAY, JUNE 2.

Popular Culture 250

Introduction to Popular Film   Fall, 1987

Instructor: Jack Nachbar
Office: Popular Culture House (Corner of Wooster and South College)
Office Hours: 1:30-2:30; 3:30-4:30 M & W; 3-4 T & R and by appointment. (You
are welcome to see me any time I'm in. Just call and make sure I'm there.)

Texts: KINKOS NOTES (Buy at Kinkos)
         THE MAKING OF THE WIZARD OF OZ by Aljean Harmetz
         JAMES DEAN: THE MUTANT KING by David Dalton

Course Requirements:

No class attendance will be kept. Come and go as you please. BUT, you are TOTALLY
responsible for everything that happens in class (including the showing of films)
and for all class assignments. If you miss class borrow someone's notes. All
parts of the course must be completed for you to pass.

There will be six units in the course:
         a. Introduction   d. Movie Genres
         b. The Hollywood Studio Years   e. The Movie Industry NOW.
         c. Censorship and its effects   f. Movie Stardom

1. At the end of every two units, there will be a 90 minute test. All three
tests will be the short essay type.

2. There will also be two short papers. Some brief research may be needed for
these, but the main emphasis on the papers will be class materials.

Each of the five items will count for 20% of your class grade. In the case of
borderline grades, a bit more weight will be placed on the final test and the
second paper.

Purpose and Direction of the Course:

Most Introductory Courses on Movies stress the ART of the motion picture. This is
usually done by concentrating on the development, history and imagery of "classic"
films.

This course is different. Although it uses some historical perspectives, PC 250
is unlike most introductory movie courses in the movies it looks at and the
reasons why they are studied. PC 250 studies movies not because they are works
of art (although many of them are) or because they are influential in the
historical development of the motion picture, but because they are representative
of a POPULAR entertainment form. (until television, the most popular entertainment
form the world has ever known). Therefore, "quality" will not be a major issue
in the course. Our major concerns are:
         1. What makes popular movies popular?
         2. Why are these elements of popularity appealing?
         3. What influences on Hollywood determined the forms popular movies took on?
         4. Are popular movies moving in new directions or are they evolving into
             essentially new forms?

An incidental but perhaps important objective of the course is your increased
appreciation of popular movies. Ideally, by understanding them better your
perspective for enjoyment will also be broadened.

Part I INTRODUCTION TO THE ELEMENTS OF MOVIE POPULARITY

Week One

| Thur. Aug. 27 | General Introd. to course
The Five Basic Elements of Movie Popularity | Assign: | Pick up books |

Week Two

| Tue. Sept. 1 | Film: TOP GUN with Tom Cruise and
Kelly McGillis | Assign: | Kinky
Wizard, Chapter
1 |

| Thur. Sept. 3 | The elements of popularity in TOP GUN
The Origins of the Elements of Popularity | Assign: | Kinky
Wizard, Chapter
2-3 |

Part II THE HOLLYWOOD STUDIO YEARS

Week Three

| Tue. Sept. 8 | The Coming of Vertical Integration and
the Hollywood Assembly Line | Assign: | Kinky
Wizard, Chapter
4 |

| Thur. Sept. 10 | A typical Year for the Movies: 1939 | Assign: | Kinky
Wizard, Chapter
5-7 |

Week Four

| Tue. Sept. 15 | Film: THE PURPLE VIGILANTES (1937)
Why B Movies? | Assign: | Kinky
Wizard, Chapter
8 |

| Thur. Sept. 17 | Film: THE WIZARD OF OZ | Assign: | Finish Wizard |

Week Five

| Tue. Sept. 22 | How is Wizard a Studio Years movie?
Final thoughts on Studio Years.
Q and A for upcoming test | Assign: | Study for Test |

| Thur. Sept. 24 | Test # One |

Part III HOLLYWOOD CENSORSHIP AND ITS EFFECTS ON THE ELEMENTS OF POPULARITY

Week Six
Tuesd. Sept. 20   (Note: For today you should have read Kinky's, 33-42)
                                Censorship, 1905-1934
                                Assign: Kinky's, 43-44.

Thursd. Oct. 1   Film: GOLDDIGGERS OF 1933 (1933) starring all kinds of folks
                                Assign: Kinky's, 45-52.

Week Seven
Tuesd. Oct. 6   GOLDDIGGERS and the Code
                                Censorship, 1934-present
                                Assign: FIRST PAPER ASSIGNED

Thur. Oct. 8   Film: BLUE VELVET (through my tears) with Dennis (nutball)
                                  Hopper
                                Assign: Relax from the shock of the movie (Happy Dreams)

Part IV RITUALISM, PART ONE: POPULAR MOVIE GENRES

Week Eight
Tue. Oct. 13   Film: THE MALTESE FALCON (1941) with Bogie and Mary Astor
                                Assign: Crank that paper into high gear.

Thur. Oct. 15   BLUE VELVET and the New Freedoms
                                An Introduction to Popular Film Genres
                                Assign: Kinky's, 87-96.
Week Nine
Tue. Oct. 20   The Hard-Boiled Detective Genre
                                Assign: Have you thought about that paper lately?

Thur. Oct. 22   Film: CHINATOWN (1974) with Jack Nicholson and Fay Dunaway
                                Assign: Kinky's, 100-103

Week Ten
Tue. Oct. 27   Film: SWING TIME (1936) with Fred and Ginger
                                Assign: Kinky's, 97-99; finish paper

Thur. Oct. 29   Discuss CHINATOWN
                                The Hollywood Musical Genre   PAPER NUMBER ONE IS DUE
                                Kinky's, 81-86

Week Eleven
Tue. Nov. 3   Film: SINGING IN THE RAIN (1952) with Kelly, O'Connor and
                                  Reynolds
                                Kinky's, 53-62

Thur. Nov. 5   Compare SWINGIN and SINGIN
                                An Introduction to the Modern Film Industry
                                Assign: Study for Test

Week Twelve
Tue. Nov. 10   TEST NUMBER TWO
                                Assign: Kinky's, 63-80 (Skim 68-72)

Popular Culture 250   Fall, 1987
Schedule for Parts V and VI

Part V (Cont.) The modern Film Industry and Its Effects

Week Twelve (Cont.)
Thursd., Nov. 12   The Evolution of the Modern Movie Industry
                        Assign: Get caught up on Kinky's Readings

Week Thirteen
Tue. Nov. 17   Film: TOOTSIE (1982) with Dustin Hoffman and Jessica Lange

Thur. Nov. 19   The Modern Movie Industry and Its Effects on the Movies
                        TOOTSIE as a Contemporary Hollywood Film.
                        Assign: PAPER NUMBER TWO ASSIGNED

Part VI MOVIE STARDOM

Week Fourteen
Tuesd. Nov. 24   Film: CASABLANCA (1942) with Bogie, Ingrid Bergman and
                           Paul Henreid.
                        Assign: Kinky's, pp. 104-112; MUTANT KING, Beginning to 117

Thur. Nov. 26   Turkey Time (Yay!!!!!) No Class

Week Fifteen

Tue. Dec. 1   An Introd. to Movie Stardom
                        Bogart as Star
                        Assign: Kinky's, 113-119; MUTANT KING, 118-217.

Thur. Dec. 3   The Essential Appeal of Movie Stars
                        An Introduction to James Dean as Star
                        Assign: MUTANT KING, 220-263.

Week Sixteen

Tue. Dec. 8   Film: REBEL WITHOUT A CAUSE (1956) with James Dean, Nt.
                           Wood and Sal Mineo.
                        Assign: Finish MUTANT KING; finish papers

Thur. Dec. 10   James Dean as a Movie God   SECOND PAPERS DUE!!!!
                        Final Thoughts about Popular Movies
                        Course Evaluation
                        Assign: Study for Test

FINALS WEEK

Thursday, Dec. 17   3:30-5:30   Third Test

50

METRO-GOLDWYN-MAYER PICTURES

C U L V E R — C I T Y
CALIFORNIA

October 6, 1938

To: The Kid
From: L. B. Mayer
Re: Your request for our special effects department to send you back to the future.

I think its OK, Kid. I checked with my special effects boys and they tell me we can fix up your funny little car any way you want. And since I know the fellows pretty well in city hall in downtown L.A., we should be able to get all the power we need. You'll be back in 1987 before you know it! But nothing is free in this world, kid. Believe me, I know. Garbo, Gable, Crawford -- they cost me a fortune. Anyway, I do you a favor, then you do me a favor.

Here's the problem, Kid. A new kid movie, THE WIZARD OF OZ, is scheduled to start shooting next week. What a headache. The picture is budgeted at 2 million, and I have a hunch it might cost lots more than that. That damned Nick Schenck is on the phone ten times a day from New York yelling that all the money is going to put us in the poorhouse. And who is handling all that dough? Mervyn LeRoy and Art Freed, that's who. Neither of those guys has produced anything. The wolf is at the door, Kid, and I'm counting on you to chase him away. Don't get me wrong. I love the idea for the movie. God, I saw the last few pages of the script the other day and I cried like a baby. But tears ain't dollars, Kid, and what counts out here is dollars.

I want for you to prepare me a report. This report has to tell me how to make THE WIZARD OF OZ into a winner. Not some time in the future, but NOW, today, get it!!!? Tell me how to save some money on the production, and how to get more people into the theaters. I'll pass the ideas along to our wonder boy producers before its too late and we all lose out shirts.

You say you already know some things about how the movie went in the near future. Well, you better. Write me a detailed report of about 1200 to 1500 words. Think about it for a couple of weeks, but I need it before the production gets too far along. Make sure it's in the hands of my administrative assistant Nachbar no later than October 29th. And, Kid, this memo BETTER BE GOOD. My future may be at stake here. New York Nick is just waiting for his chance to put me in the toilet. And your future is at stake for sure. If your ideas are nothing but dishwater, you get no trip back to 1987. If you want out of here, you better put four things in the report:
      a. Writing skills (This is business, after all)
         1) Grammar   2) Good organization
      b. Creativity. (Good ideas are where it's at, Kid, past or future)
         1) In your writing   2) In ideas on the problem
      c. Accuracy.(Do you really know about the movies in 1938 like you say?)
      d. Proof.   (No vague stuff, Kid. I need to be convinced.)
Remember when you told me about that Popular Culture movie course you were taking? I suggest you use that stuff. The lectures, the readings, all that stuff.

Do good, Kid.

Please retain
Please review

English 3500
Introduction to Film
Spring 1989

Structure and Purpose of the course:

1. Kinds of Films (and practice in-class writings)

> Fictional
> Documentary
> Experimental

2. Expressiveness of Film Techniques (films about the techniques
of cinema and clips to illustrate them)

> Cinematography
> Editing
> Sound
> Subjects: settings, performers, composition

3. Viewer Responses

> Fantasies
> Meanings and Symbols
> Evaluations

The course will introduce you to a wide variety of films--
fictional, documentary, experimental, feature-length and short,
live action and animated. The course will also give you a better
understanding of how cinematic techniques add to the total impact
of films and how and why viewers respond to films as they do.

"Introduction to Film" has no prerequisites and is designed for
students in any major.

Class meetings: T & Th 4:40-6:40
Television Learning Center, Turlock
and off campus in Stockton, Sonora, Dos
Palos, Castle Air Force Base, and Manteca

Texts: William H. Phillips, Analyzing Films
duplicated materials available from the bookstore

On Reserve in the Library:
scripts for UN CHIEN ANDALOU, PSYCHO, WOMAN IN THE DUNES,
THE SEVEN SAMURAI, and CITIZEN KANE

Course requirements:

-for a letter grade or credit grade: course points

    a.   regular and punctual attendance (if you
          miss roll call, let me know you are
          present before you leave class that day) -10 to +2
    b.   in-class writing exercises   10
    c.   quizzes on the readings, class presentations,
          and films but mainly the readings. All but
          one of the quizzes will be counted toward
          the course grade. No make-up quizzes will
          be given   20
    d.   one 500-1,000 word essay on the expressiveness
          of a film technique   20
    e.   one 500-1,000 word essay on the meanings of
          a film studied in the course, or a systematic
          evaluation of a film studied in the course   20
    f.   take-home final examination essay(s)   30

    -for audit credit (meaning that your transcript will show
    that you audited this course): regular class attendance

Since it is only fair to apply the same requirements to all
students, please do not ask for an exemption from the
requirements listed above.

Bonus points:

    After each student's course score is added up, scores will
be correlated with letter grades for the course (for example, it
could work out that 88-100 would be an "A" for the course, 78-87,
a "B," etc.); then 1-3 bonus points for corrections or
constructive suggestions on how to improve Analyzing Films or the
duplicated material written by the instructor will be added to
final course scores.
    It is also possible to earn 1-5 additional bonus points for
a concise and carefully-done 500-word book report on one of the
film books in the CSUS library. If you do the book report, first
browse through the film books in the CSUS library, choose one of
interest to you, check it out, read it carefully, then in your
500-word report answer the following questions: What does the
book cover? How well does it do so and why do you say so? No
more than half of your report should be description of the book.
On the final draft of your report include your social security
number but not your name.
    Some students will probably earn a higher course grade as a
result of bonus points. For instance, if it happens that an 88
is an "A-" for the course and a student has a course score of 86
and 3 bonus points, then that student will earn an "A" for the
course. Students who do not earn bonus points are not penalized
by this policy: bonus points do not affect the grades of those
who do not earn them.

Grades:

Option 2 = A,B,C,D,F, or Credit/No Credit. A = excellent; B = good; C = satisfactory; D = unsatisfactory; F = failure; CR = credit or at least "C" work; NC = no credit or below "C" work. Students wanting to take the course Credit/No Credit must give me the appropriate filled-out forms by _____.

Instructor:

   Dr. William H. Phillips / Cal. State Univ., Stanislaus /
      Turlock, CA 95380
   Office: Classroom 237-B
   Telephone: (209) 667-3683
   Office hours until __/__:
      and by appointment
   Papers and notes may be left in Library 110
   Messages may be called in to (209) 667-3361

Class Schedule

KINDS OF FILMS

1.	introduction to course 3 short films: fictional, documentary, experimental	3 short films again and discussion

----

2.	CITIZEN KANE	analysis of C.K.

3.	NANOOK OF THE NORTH	analysis

----

4. a program of short experimental films

THE EXPRESSIVENESS OF FILM TECHNIQUES

5. cinematography: clips and analysis

----

6. editing: clips and analysis

----

7. sound: clips and analysis

----

8. subjects: settings, performers, composition
    PSYCHO
    First Essay Due

VIEWER RESPONSES

9. fantasies
   A TRIP TO THE MOON
   2001: A SPACE ODYSSEY

   ---

10. meanings and symbols
    WOMAN IN THE DUNES
    Take-home Final Exam Handed Out

    ---

11. evaluations
    THE SEVEN SAMURAI (complete version)

----

12. CITIZEN KANE: expressiveness of techniques and viewer
    responses
    Second Essay Due

    ---

13. discussion   conferences on final exam,
    course review   requirements, reading
    films evaluation   assignments, other
    course evaluation   film courses, or ???

   / : Final Exams Due in Library 110 or Classroom 237-B

Professor Thomas B. Sobchack

A CRITICAL INTRODUCTION TO FILM   Film/English 214

General Information: The purpose of this course is to introduce the student to the
aesthetic elements of film. The cinema is a material art and depends upon its
combination of visual and aural devices to create its effects. The class will
concentrate on the narrative film for examples of of camera work, sound, editing,
and direction. By watching films, reading the text, participating in class
discussions, and writing tests and papers, students will increase their ability to
make critical judgements about the movies. Attendance at film screenings and
discussions is vital.

Written Work: Two concise, analytical papers, one on a topic chosen from material
in Ch. 1-4 in the text, and one on material from Ch. 5-8. (See Ch. 9 for details on
the form and content of papers.) All written assignments will be typewritten,
double spaced with proper margins. The mid-term exam will be short answer
identifications; the final exam will include short answer identifications and essay
questions. Final grade is derived from grades on papers and exams as well as class
participation.

Text: Sobchack & Sobchack, An Introduction to Film , 2nd. ed.

Class Schedule:

Week of:	Reading	Topic	Film Title
9/29	Ch. 1	The Hollywood Standard	THE STUNTMAN
10/6	Ch. 2	Film Space	THE THIRD MAN, Basic Film Terms
10/13	Ch. 3	Film Time	POTEMKIN, OWL CREEK BRIDGE
			Gunsmoke Editing, Film Graphics
10/20	Ch. 4	Film Sound	CITIZEN KANE, Understanding
10/27	First Paper Due		Movies
10/27	Ch. 5	Genre Comedy	HIS GIRL FRIDAY
10/29	MID-TERM QUIZ		
11/3	Ch. 5	Genre Melodrama	LITTLE CAESAR
11/10	Ch. 6	Auteurs & Genre	STAGECOACH
11/17	Ch. 6	Non-genre	WILD STRAWBERRIES
11/24	Ch. 6	Non-Genre	SEVEN SAMURAI
12/1	Ch. 7	Documentary	NANOOK OF THE NORTH, TRIUMPH
12/8	Second Paper Due		OF THE WILL, CITY OF GOLD
12/8	Ch. 8	Experimental, Avant-	THE FRONTIER, LA JETEE, NIGHT
		Garde, Animation	MAIL, FRANK FILM, UN CHIEN
			ANDALOU, BOOGIE DOODLE, ETUDE,
			CAT'S CRADLE, CLOSED MONDAYS

Theater Arts 80D: The Film Experience   Fall 1987
Tu Th 2:00-4:45 pm (Lecture & Screening) Thimann 3   Vivian Sobchack
W 7:30 pm (Screening) Thimann 3   D124 Porter

REQUIRED TEXTS (On 2-hour reserve at McHenry Library; on sale at Bay Tree
   Bookstore)

Cook, Pam, ed. The Cinema Book New York: Pantheon, 1985

Sobchack, Thomas and Vivian C. An Introduction to Film, Second Edition Boston:
   Little, Brown, 1986

FEES: There is a $15.00 screening fee to cover part of the cost of film
rentals and wear and tear on Theatre Arts videotapes. Unless the fee is
paid, you will not receive credit for TA 80D and will not be able to
register for Winter Quarter. You will be billed by mail after instructor
has received your name, current mailing address, Social Security number, and
student ID number. Please pay promptly or you will be assessed a late fee.
Upon receipt of the above information, the instructor will give you a "Class
Pass" which can be used as your admission to the Wednesday night screenings.
You are able and encouraged to see the films twice; just remember to bring your
"Class Pass" with you!

SCREENINGS: Films will be screened in the afternoon class, the Wednesday
evening series, and most of them can also be viewed for study purposes on
video at the McHenry Library (go to Recordings). All films must be seen at
least once! They are, after all, the primary texts of the course. However,
some films may not be available other than at a single in-class or evening screening. The syllabus will indicate which films are available and on reserve in
video, but be advised that you must reserve screening time at McHenry well in
advance of when you want to use the facility.

DISCUSSION SECTIONS: In addition to the large class meetings/screenings, you
will also be required to sign up for and attend a discussion section which
will meet one hour per week. In section, you will discuss films, readings,
lectures, and develop your analytic and critical skills. You must attend a
particular section regularly; no "floating" allowed. At the moment, all sections
are scheduled to meet in Porter D140. Tentative times are listed in the class
schedule but will be altered as student demand and scheduling allow.

PAPERS: Written work for the course will consist of three critical papers
(6 pages minimum). The papers should demonstrate your ability to analyze
cinematic construction in particular class film(s). These will be due in
your discussion section in the weeks indicated below. You must write about
films shown in class, although other films may be discussed in conjunction
with class films. (Any exceptions must be cleared with your Teaching Assistant
in advance, or the paper will be deemed unacceptable.) In regard to all papers,
you are to read and refer to Chapter 9 of An Introduction to Film. Called
"Writing College Papers About Film," it is a handy guide to critical questioning
and thinking, topic selection, and proper manuscript preparation. As well,

it includes examples of and from real student papers. Please note that Teaching
Assistants have been instructed that manuscripts are to be typed and that late
papers are not acceptable.

READINGS & SCREENING BY CLASS MEETING: Readings listed are due on the date
specified and related to the films you'll be seeing. (A word on the two tests--
you'll be reading all of the Intro book, but only portions of the Cook book;
the latter might present problems for some of you given its basically theoretical emphasis, but do please try to stay with it despite--and, indeed,
because of--its theoretical/technical concepts and language.) Evening screenings are also indicated--as are those films on reserve (on video) in McHenry.
You are encouraged to come to the evening screenings, but please remember to
bring your Class Pass and be advised that no seats are guaranteed; arrive before
7:30 pm. Film titles are indicated below by capital letters and are followed
by the director's name, the film's general release date, whether the film is
in black-and-white or color, the country of its origin, and the approximate
running time.

TH 10/1   Introduction to Cinematic Literacy: An Experiment in Seeing
           DUCK AMUCK (Chuck Jones, 1953, Color, USA, 5 min.)
           AN OCCURRENCE AT OWL CREEK BRIDGE (Robert Enrico, 1962, B/W, France,
           27 min.) On reserve as LA RIVIERE DU HIBOU with LA JETEE.
           A MOVIE (Bruce Conner, 1958), B/W, USA, 12 min.) On reserve as
           Bruce Conner compilation tape (which has other Conner films);
           Note: There is another copy of A MOVIE--under that title, but it
           was badly taped; the above version is better.

T 10/6   The Hollywood Standard: Narrative and Vision Reading Due: Sobchack,
           Chap. 1 ("The Hollywood Standard"), (pp. 3-42; Part III ("Mainstream
           Narrative Film"), pp. 204-221;)
           Cook ("Technology"), pp. 25-31; Recommended: Cook ("The
           Studios"), pp. 10-25.
           A NICKEL FOR THE MOVIES (James Naremore, 1984, Color, USA. 21 min.)
           THE PURPLE ROSE OF CAIRO (Woody Allen, 1985, Color, USA, 82 min.) On reserve.
                 *** SECTION SIGN-UP AT END OF CLASS***

W 10/7   7:30 pm Screening: THE PURPLE ROSE OF CAIRO

TH 10/8   Reading: Cook ("History of Narrative Codes"), pp. 208-215 and
           ("Melodrama"), pp. 73-84; Sobchack, Part V ("A Guide to Film Analysis
           and Criticism"), pp. 412-421--although whole chapter should be read
           before you do your 1st paper!
           BASIC FILM TERMS: A VISUAL DICTIONARY (Sheldon Renan, 1970, Color,
           USA, 15 min.)
           CAUGHT (Max Ophuls, 1949, B/W, USA, 83 min.) On reserve.

T 10/13 The Moving Image: Space in the Cinema
          Reading: Sobchack, Part II ("The Elements of Film"), pp. 44-53;
          Chap. 2 ("Film Space"), pp. 54-103.
          THE COLOR PURPLE (Steven Spielberg, 1985, Color, USA, 155 min.)
          On reserve.

W 10/14 7:30 pm Screening: THE COLOR PURPLE

TH 10/15 Reading: Cook ("Italy and Neo-realism"), pp. 36-39; ("Authorship
          and Cinema"), pp. 114-116, 118.
          LA STRADA (Federico Bellini, 1954, B/W, Italy, 107 min.)
          In Library's own collection.

T 10/16 Reading: Sobchack, Chap. 6 ("Nongenre Narrative and Its Makers"),
          pp. 284-333.
          DIRECTORS AT WORK: THE DIRECTOR AND THE IMAGE (Carl Workman, 1982,
          Color, USA, 27 min.)
          SUGAR BABY (Percy Adlon, 1985, Color, Germany, 86 min.)
          On reserve.

W 10/21 7:30 pm Screening: SUGAR BABY

TH 10/22 The Moved Image: Time in the Cinema
          Reading: Sobchack, Part II ("Elements of Film"), pp. 104-111.
          INTERPRETATION AND VALUES: "GUNSMOKE" EDITING FILM (American
          Society of Cinema Editors, 30 min.)
          FILM GRAPHICS: ABSTRACT ASPECTS OF FILM EDITING (14 min.)
          A STUDY IN CHOREOGRAPHY FOR THE CAMERA (Maya Deren, 1943, B/W, USA,
          3 min.) On Reserve on Maya Deren compilation tape.
          OLYMPIA: "Diving Sequence" (Leni Riefenstahl, 1938, B/W, Germany,
          5 min.) On reserve with Bruce Conner's A MOVIE which is a separate
          tape from Bruce Conner compilation,
          NIGHT AND FOG (Alan Resnais, 1955, B/W, Color, France, 31 min.) On
          reserve as above title or NUIT ET BROUILLARD

T 10/27 ***FIRST PAPER DUE IN SECTION THIS WEEK!
          Montage
          Reading: Sobchack, Chap. 3 ("Film Time"), pp. 112-162;
          Cook ("Authorship and Cinema"), pp. 119-120, 132-133, 226.
          CITIZEN KANE (Orson Welles, 1941, B/W, USA, 119 min.) On reserve.

W 10/28 7:30 pm Screening: KOYAANISQATSI (Godfrey Reggio, 1983, Color,
          USA, 87 min.)

TH 10/29 Reading: Cook ("Film Narrative and the Structuralist Controversy"),
          pp. 222-225; 228-231 (at least try this last!)
          KOYAANISQATSI. On reserve.

T 11/3   Mise-en-Scene
          Reading: Cook ("Authorship and Cinema"), pp. 165-166, 196.
          RED PSALM (Miklos Jancso, 1972, Color, Hungary, 88 min.)

W 11/4   7:30 pm Screening: RED PSALM

TH 11/5   STEAMBOAT BILL, JR. (Buster Keaton, 1927, B/W, USA, 80 min.)
          On reserve.

T 11/10 The Aesthetics of Sound
          Reading: Sobchack, Part II ("Elements of Film"), pp. 163-169;
          Chap. 4 ("Film Sound"), pp. 170-202.
          DODES' KA-DEN (Akira Kurosawa, 1970, Color, Japan, 140 min.)
          On reserve.

W 11/11 7:30 Screening: DODES' KA-DEN

TH 11/12 THE MOVIES LEARN TO TALK ("Twentieth Century," 1960, B/W, USA,
          26 min.)
          BEGONE DULL CARE (Norman McLaren, 1949, Color, Canada, 3 min.)
          ETUDE (1972, Color, USA, 8 min.)
          FRANK FILM (Frank & Carolyn Mouris, 1973, Color, USA, 9 min.)
          LA JETEE (Chris Marker, 1962, B/W, France, 30 min.) On reserve.

T 11/17 ***SECOND PAPER DUE IN SECTION THIS WEEK!

          Genre Film
          Reading: Sobchack, Chap. 5 ("Genre Films"), pp. 222-283.
          SINGIN' IN THE RAIN (Stanley Donen & Gene Kelly, 1952, Color, USA,
          103 min.) On reserve.

W 11/18 7:30 pm Screening: PENNIES FROM HEAVEN (Herbert Ross, 1981, Color,
          USA, 108 min.)

TH 11/19 Reading: Cook ("Genre") pp. 58-64; 106-112; ("Levi-Strauss" &
          "Propp"), pp. 232-236.
          PENNIES FROM HEAVEN. On reserve.

T 11/24 Experimental, Independent & Animated Film
          Reading: Sobchack, Part IV ("The Alternative Film"), pp. 374-383;
          Chap. 8 ("Experimental, Independent, and Animated Film"), pp.
          384-410; Cook, ("Alternative Narrative System"), pp. 216-220.
          UN CHIEN ANDALOU (Luis Bunuel & Salvador Dali, 1928, B/W, France
          15 min.)
          MESHES OF THE AFTERNOON (Maya Deren, 1943, B/W, USA, 15 min.)
          On reserve on Maya Deren compilation tape.
          OFFON (Scott Bartlett, 1967, Color, USA, 10 min.)
          WINDY DAY (John & Faith Hubley, 1968, Color, USA, 12 min.)
          DAVID HOLZNAN'S DIARY (Jim McBride, 1968, B/W, USA, 78 min.)

W 11/25 No Screening

TH 11/26 No class: HOLIDAY

T 12/1   Non-Fiction Film
          Reading: Sobchack, Part IV ("The Alternative Film"), pp. 336-345;
          Chap. 7 ("The Documentary Film"), pp. 346-373.
          PRELUDE TO WAR (Frank Capra, 1942, B/W, USA, 54 min.)
          On reserve.
          THE LIFE AND TIMES OF ROSIE THE RIVETER (Connie Field, 1981, Color,
          USA, 60 min.) On reserve.

W 12/2   7:30 pm Screening: REAL LIFE: AN AMERICAN COMEDY (Albert Brooks,
          1979, Color, USA, 99 min.) This is the only screening of this film,
          but it is on reserve.

TH 12/3   LAND WITHOUT BREAD (Luis Bunuel, 1932, B/W, Spain, 28 min.) in Library
          collection.
          NO LIES (Mitchell Block, 1973, Color, USA, 17 min.)
          HIGH SCHOOL (Frederick Wiseman, 1968, B/W, USA, 75 min.)

T 12/3   *** LAST PAPER DUE IN SECTION THIS WEEK!

          Finale: Against Classification, For Interpretation
          Reading: Cook ("Barthes" & "Narrative and Audience"), pp. 238-250,
          ("Counter-cinema and cultural practice"), pp. 196-198.
          SANS SOLEIL (Chris Marker, 1982, Color, France, 100 min.)

W 12/9   7:30 pm Screening: SANS SOLEIL

TH 12/10 Reading: Cook ("Authorship and the Cinema"), pp. 126-129, 183.
          THE CRITIC (Ernest Pintoff & Mel Brooks, 1963, Color, USA, 3 min.)
          REAR WINDOW (Alfred Hitchcock, 1954, Color, USA, 112 min.)
          On reserve.

                        TH-TH-THAT'S ALL FOLKS!

III. DIRECTORS

<u>D. W. Griffith</u>

Readings:

There is a "professor publishing" text for this class at Kinko's on the hill.
It should include Dixon's <u>The Clansman</u> and <u>The Leopard's Spots</u>, the MOMA
shot-by-shot analysis of <u>Intolerance</u>, the special issue of <u>Film Culture</u> on <u>BOAN</u>,
Henderson's biography, excerpts from Henderson's books on the Biograph films,
"The Chink and the Child" (source of <u>Broken Blossoms</u>), DCC handouts, etc.
    In Norlin, the DWG microfilm collection bears the catalog #3953.

Papers and Exams:

There will be at least one paper (to be determined when the class size stabilizes),
and there will be a final exam. Attendance at all class meetings is mandatory,
and no repeat showings will be possible for any reason.

Showings:

1. F(riday) S(ept) 5: [1920]
        Way Down East (standard version with musical score)
2. M(onday) S 8: [1895-1909]
        Lumiere premier program (1895), <u>A Trip to the Moon</u> (Melies, 1902),
        <u>The Magic Lantern</u> (Melies, 1903), <u>The Great Train Robbery</u> (Porter, 1903),
        <u>Rescued by Rover</u> (Hepworth, 1904 and 1905 versions), <u>Rescued from an
        Eagle's Nest</u> (Porter/Edison, 1908, dir. J. Searle Dawley; rel. 1/16/08),
        <u>The Dream of a Rarebit Fiend</u> (Porter, 1906), <u>At the Crossroads of Life</u>
        (Biograph, July 1908, dir. Wallace McCutcheon, ph. G. W. ("Billy") Bitzer
        and Arthur Marvin; scr. & st. DWG), <u>The Adventures of Dollie</u> (Biograph,
        6/18/08; rel. 7/14/08, dir. DWG, ph. Marvin), <u>Those Awful Hats</u> (Biograph,
        1/11/09; rel. 1/25/09, dir. DWG, ph. Bitzer; DWG's 66th Biograph film).
3. F S 12: [1909]
        What Drink Did, <u>The Guerilla</u> (if available), <u>Her First Biscuits</u>,
        <u>The Lonely Villa</u>, The Son's Return, <u>Mrs. Jones's Lover or "I Want My
        Hat!"</u>, The Country Doctor, <u>The Mended Lute</u>, <u>Pippa Passes</u>, <u>A Corner
        in Wheat</u>, The Redman's View.
4. M S 14: [1910]
        The Way of the World, The Unchanging Sea, <u>Ramona</u> (if available), <u>Over
        Silent Paths</u>, The Usurer, The Sorrows of the Unfaithful, <u>In Life's
        Cycle</u>, Rose o' Salem Town, His Trust, <u>What Shall We Do With Our Old?</u>
5. F S 19: [1911]
        The Lonedale Operator, Was He A Coward?, The Broken Cross, <u>The Chief's
        Daughter</u>, Enoch Arden I & II (if available), <u>The Last Drop of Water</u>,
        <u>Swords and Hearts</u> (if available), Her Awakening, <u>The Battle</u>.
6. M S 22: [1912]
        The Girl and Her Trust, The Lesser Evil, An Unseen Enemy, <u>The Painted
        Lady</u>, The Musketeers of Pig Alley, The New York Hat, <u>Love in an
        Apartment Hotel</u>.
            [1913]
        The Mothering Heart, The Lady and the Mouse, <u>The Switchtower</u>.
7. F S 26: [1914]
        The Battle at Elderbush Gulch (prod. 1913), <u>Judith of Bethulia</u>,
        <u>Regeneration</u> (1915, dir. Raoul Walsh).

8. M S 29: [1914]
       Home Sweet Home, The Avenging Conscience
9. F O(ctober) 3: [1915]
       The Birth of a Nation, first half
10. M O 6:
       The Birth of a Nation, second half
11. F O 10: [rivals, 1915-16]
       The Italian (1915, dir. Barker, prod. Ince), Civilization (1916, dir.
       West & Willat, prod. Ince)
12. M O 13: [1915-1919]
       The Mother and the Law, The Fall of Babylon (unreconstructed MOMA version)
13. F O 17: [1916]
       Intolerance
14. M O 20: [1974]
       The Godfather, Part II (dir. Coppola)
15. F O 24:
       The Three Ages (1923, dir. Keaton & Cline), Intolerance
16. M O 27: [1918]
       Hearts of the World
17. F O 31: [1919]
       A Romance of Happy Valley, Traffic in Souls (1913, dir. Tucker)
18. M N(ovember) 3: [1919]
       True Heart Susie, Tol'able David (1921, dir. King)
19. F N 7: [1919]
       Broken Blossoms
20. M N 10: [1931]
       The Struggle
       What Drink Did, The Musketeers of Pig Alley [repeated]
21. F N 14: [1919]
       Scarlet Days, The Greatest Question
22. M N 17: [1920]
       Way Down East (restored version)
23. F N 21: [1921]
       Orphans of the Storm
24. M N 24: [1924]
       America
25. M D(ecember) 1: [1924]
       Isn't Life Wonderful
26. F D 5: [1925]
       Sally of the Sawdust
27. M D 8: [1930]
       Abraham Lincoln
28. F D 12: [1921]
       Dream Street

Useful abbreviations:

prod = producer (if a name) or year produced/shot
dir = director
ph = cinematographer
ed = editor
scr = screenwriter
st = star or featured player
b/o = based on
rel = release date
DWG = David Wark Griffith
AB = American Mutoscope and Biograph Company; American Biograph, Biograph
BOAN = The Birth of a Nation
MOMA = The Museum of Modern Art

67

Take-home final exam, D. W. Griffith
Due 7:30 A.M., Friday, December 19, 1986

Length: No restrictions
Number of questions answered: No restrictions
Format: Typed--and free of typos
Dates and film titles must be complete and exact
Influence on grade: Unquantifiable

1. Trace and comment upon this sequence: A ROMANCE OF HAPPY VALLEY, BROKEN
   BLOSSOMS, TRUE HEART SUSIE, THE GREATEST QUESTION, WAY DOWN EAST.

2. Comment on the contributions to Griffith's work made by one or more of the
   following:

   A. Bitzer
       Sartov
   B. Lillian Gish
       Mae Marsh
       Miriam Cooper
       Carol Dempster
       Mary Pickford
   C. H. B. Walthall
       Bobby Harron
       Richard Barthelmess

3. Bitzer vs. Sartov and/or Gish vs. Dempster

4. The range and limits of Griffith's vision
   --to be answered in general terms or, specifically, in terms of:
       Cinematic structure
       Politics
       Human relationships
       The film business
       Personal and public expression
       Words and pictures
       Ideology
       History
       His best (and/or worst) film

5. Compare (in terms of structure, excellence, emotional impact, range, etc.)
   THE MOTHER AND THE LAW and INTOLERANCE.

6. Griffith's use of sources (re. Dixon, Burke [B. Blossoms & Dream Street],
   research, etc.).

7. A theme in Griffith's work--how he used it, how its treatment varied through
   his career, and what he appears fundamentally to have thought about it:

War	City vs. country values
Race	Physical cruelty and violence
Sexuality	Parenting (including childbearing)
Temptation	Fidelity and perseverance
Worldliness	Audience manipulation & rooting interest
Religion	Fall/death and redemption/life
Comparisons and Contrasts	"Links in the system"
Money	Alcohol

8. The use of "chase cutting" and the last-minute rescue in the dramatic and emotional and thematic structures of Griffith's films.

9. Griffith's use and development of:

Screen acting	Animals (esp. in characterization)
Intertitles	Camera movement
Tinting and toning	Camera placement
Music	Comparisons and contrasts

10. The rivals of Griffith (perhaps including Griffith)

ENGLISH 347
Winter 1985
Larry Landrum

This course is designed to make students more aware of the ways visual
imagery is created and effected through film. Contrasted in the course will
be films selected from the works of Stanley Kubrick and Martin Scorsese. The
two filmmakers are concerned with common themes, but their styles and specific
subject matters are quite different. While Kubrick often adapts his films
from literary works and contrives elaborate sets to express his ideas and
interpretations, Scorsese tends to shoot on location from scripts which are
often reworked as the scenes develop. Each director is meticulous in his
attention to detail, evolving highly complex and interwoven texts. Our first
concern will be to learn to "read" the films as film or cinema texts; our
second concern will be to examine the larger social and cultural meanings of
the films. It is important to remember that filmmaking is a collaborative
art. A director is an auteur, or author only in the sense that within the
limitations of the economic and political hegemony of the industry, he or she
has ultimate responsibility for what appears on the screen. The director
works with script writers, set designers, actors, cinematographers, production
managers, editors, laboratory technicians and people with many other kinds of
skills. The contributions of these personnel must be taken into account in
any final evaluation of films, and it is partly a matter of convenience that
we refer to Scorsese's or Kubrick's films. Each frame, then, reflects and
bears evidence of a wide range of skills. If you keep this fact in mind when
viewing the films, you will be alerted to details that you might ordinarily
overlook. And to grasp the full meaning of the text it is necessary to note
details. Since there are twenty-four frames appearing on the screen each
second in the films we will see this term, close attention is advised.

Each film will be considered individually in lecture-discussions
following the screening and in separate, optional discussion sessions. Since
it is difficult to understand films based on one viewing, and particularly to
remember the details necessary to write effectively about them, the course
will involve two screenings for each film. Ordinarily, discussion following
the first viewing will focus on the structure of the film and my remarks will
attempt to place the film in a broader cinematic and cultural context.
Discussion following the second viewing will focus more on details within the
film. You might, if your schedule allows, delay the readings for each film
until you have seen it at least once in order to form your own impressions,
then read the assigned materials before the second viewing. In addition,
optional discussion sessions will include, when possible, viewing and
discussion of especially significant sequences from the films. This will also
be an opportunity to clear up any questions you have that have not been
adequately answered. I will be available during my office hours for further
consultation. Feel free to stop by and talk.

It should be noted that attendance at both the Monday and Wednesday
screenings is required. Note the running times of the films so that you will
be able to plan your evening around the class; some of the films will run
longer than two hours and you will be expected to remain until the film has
ended. Plan to arrive on time for class; you may not be permitted to enter
the screening room after the film has begun. During the screening, please
respect others' concentration. A brief intermission will follow each
screening to allow you to stretch, gather your thoughts, or leave for the
evening. You are not required to remain for the discussion following the
screening, although I recommend that you do remain.

Text:

No adequate text containing all the information needed for the course is
currently available. Therefore, I have assembled materials for the course
which include both articles and chapters from books. These materials and
others are available on half hour and overnight loan from Assigned Reading
(Main Library, first floor near the East Wing elevators).

Requirements:
Papers (2 papers, 5 pp. each)   60%
Final Exam   40%

Calendar:
**Please note: * indicates REQUIRED READING (on Assigned Reading). The rest of
the material is recommended, and unless otherwise indicated, allusions in
lectures to these authors will refer to this material.**

Week of January 7-13: *Paths of Glory

*Kolker, Robert Philip. A Cinema of Loneliness. NY: Oxford University Press,
1980. Pp. 69-138.
Nelson, Thomas. Kubrick: Inside a Film Artist's Maze. Bloomington: Indiana
University Press, 1982. Pp. 37-53.
De Vries, Daniel. The Films of Stanley Kubrick. Grand Rapids: Eerdmans,
1973. PN 1998 .A3 K737. Pp. 17-23.
Kagan, Norman. The Cinema of Stanley Kubrick. NY: Holt, 1972. Ungr PN 1998
.A3 K753. Pp. 47-67.
Phillips, Gene D. Stanley Kubrick: A Film Odessey. NY: Popular Library, 1975.
Ungr PN 1998 .A3 K746. Pp. 43-60.
Walker, Alexander. Stanley Kubrick Directs. NY: Harcourt, 1972. Ungr PN
1998 .A3 K75 1972. Pp. 82-155.

**Week of January 14-20: *Dr. Strangelove, or How I Learned to Stop
Worrying and Love the Bomb** (Kubrick, 1964)

*Walker, Alexander. Stanley Kubrick Directs. NY: Harcourt, 1972. Ungr PN
1998 .A3 K75 1972. Pp. 158-221.
*Ciment, Michel. Kubrick. NY: Holt, Rinehart, Winston, 1983. PN 1998 .A3
K736513. Pp. 205-211.
*Wolfe, G. K. "Dr. Strangelove, Red Alert, and Patterns of Paranoia in the
1950's," Journal of Popular Film and Television. 5:1 (1976) 57-61.
*Maland, C. "Dr. Strangelove (1964): Nightmare Comedy and the Ideology of
Liberal Consensus," American Quarterly. 31:5 (1979) 697-717.
De Vries, Daniel. The Films of Stanley Kubrick. Grand Rapids: Eerdmans,
1973. PN 1998 .A3 K737. Pp. 34-44.
Kagan, Norman. The Cinema of Stanley Kubrick. NY: Holt, 1972. Ungr PN 1998
.A3 K753. Pp. 111-144.
Nelson, Thomas. Kubrick: Inside a Film Artist's Maze. Bloomington: Indiana
University Press, 1982. PN 1998 .A3 K743. Pp. 79-98.
Phillips, Gene D. Stanley Kubrick: A Film Odessey. NY: Popular Library, 1975.
Ungr PN 1998 .A3 K746. Pp. 107-125.

Week of January 21-27: *Lolita (Kubrick, 1962).

*Nelson, Thomas. Kubrick: Inside a Film Artist's Maze. Bloomington: Indiana
University Press, 1982. PN 1998 .A3 K743. 54-78.
De Vries, Daniel. The Films of Stanley Kubrick. Grand Rapids: Eerdmans,
1973. PN 1998 .A3 K737. Pp. 27-33.
Kagan, Norman. The Cinema of Stanley Kubrick. NY: Holt, 1972. Ungr PN 1998
.A3 K753. Pp. 81-109.
Phillips, Gene D. Stanley Kubrick: A Film Odessey. NY: Popular Library, 1975.
Ungr PN 1998 .A3 K746. Pp. 83-102.

Week of January 28-February 3: *Taxi Driver (Scorsese, 1976)

*Kolker, Robert Philip. A Cinema of Loneliness. NY: Oxford University Press,
1980. Pp. 206-269.
*Taylor, Bella. From "Martin Scorsese," in Jon Tuska, ed., The Contemporary
Director. Scarecrow, 1981. Pp. 342-360.
*Moss, R. F. "The Brutalists: Making Movies Mean and Ugly," Saturday Review.
7 (October 1980) 14-18.
*Rice, J. C. "Transcendental Pornography and Taxi Driver," Journal of Popular
Film. 5:2 (1976) 109-123.
*"The Conversation: John Gregory Dunn and Paul Schrader: On Fame, Guilt, and
the Wars of Hollywood," Esquire. (July 1982) 85-88, 90, 92-93, 95.
Jacobs, Diane. Hollywood Renaissance. Pp. 123-148.
Thompson, R. "Screen Writer: Taxi Driver's Paul Schrader," Film Comment. 12
(March/April 1976) 6-11.

**Week of February 4-10: *Mean Streets (Scorsese, 1973) First paper due
Feb. 4.**

Jacobs, Diane. Hollywood Renaissance. Pp. 123-148.
*Taylor, Bella. From "Martin Scorsese," in Jon Tuska, ed., The Contemporary
Director. Scarecrow, 1981. Pp. 321-330.
*Kelly, Mary Pat. Martin Scorsese: The First Decade. Pleasantville, NY:
Redgrave, 1980. Pp. 85-101. [Special Collections—Library]

Week of February 11-17: *A Clockwork Orange (Kubrick, 1971).

*Nelson, Thomas. Kubrick: Inside a Film Artist's Maze. Bloomington: Indiana
University Press, 1982. PN 1998 .A3 K743. Pp. 133-164.
*Sobchack, Vivian C. "Decor as Theme: A Clockwork Orange," Literature/Film
Quarterly. 9:2 (1981) 92-102.
Ciment, Michel. Kubrick. NY: Holt, Rinehart, Winston, 1983. PN 1998 .A3
K736513. Pp. 151-163.
De Vries, Daniel. The Films of Stanley Kubrick. Grand Rapids: Eerdmans,
1973. PN 1998 .A3 K737. Pp. 57-68.
Kagan, Norman. The Cinema of Stanley Kubrick. NY: Holt, 1972. Ungr PN 1998
.A3 K753. Pp. 167-187.
Phillips, Gene D. Stanley Kubrick: A Film Odessey. NY: Popular Library, 1975.
Ungr PN 1998 .A3 K746. Pp. 157-170.
Walker, Alexander. Stanley Kubrick Directs. NY: Harcourt, 1972. Ungr PN
1998 .A3 K75 1972. Pp. 41-53.

Week of February 18—24: *Spartacus (Kubrick, 1960)

*Neale, Steve. "Masculinity as Spectacle: Reflections on Men and Mainstream
  Cinema," vf
De Vries, Daniel. The Films of Stanley Kubrick. Grand Rapids: Eerdmans,
  1973. PN 1998 .A3 K737. Pp. 23—26.
Kagan, Norman. The Cinema of Stanley Kubrick. NY: Holt, 1972. Ungr PN 1998
  .A3 K753. Pp. 69—80.
Phillips, Gene D. Stanley Kubrick: A Film Odessey. NY: Popular Library, 1975.
  Ungr PN 1998 .A3 K746. Pp. 65—78.

Week of February 24—March 3: *Barry Lyndon (Kubrick, 1975).

*Nelson, Thomas. Kubrick: Inside a Film Artist's Maze. Bloomington: Indiana
  University Press, 1982. PN 1998 .A3 K743. Pp. 165—196.
*Stephenson, W. "The Perception of 'History' in Kubrick's Barry Lyndon,"
  Literature/Film Quarterly. 9:4 (1981) 251—60.
Berenson, Marisa. Discusses her role in Barry Lyndon, her work with Kubrick,
  and other matters on NBC tv, 12/16/75. 8 min. Voice Library, M2151 bd.3.
Ciment, Michel. Kubrick. NY: Holt, Rinehart, Winston, 1983. PN 1998 .A3
  K736513. Pp. 167—179, 213—216.
Phillips, Gene D. Stanley Kubrick: A Film Odessey. NY: Popular Library, 1975.
  Ungr PN 1998 .A3 K746. Pp. 175—180.

Week of March 4—10: *New York, New York (Scorsese, 1977). **Second paper
due March 4.**

*Rafferty, T. "Martin Scorsese's Still Life," Sight & Sound. 52:3 (1983)
  186—192.

Final Exam: Monday, March 11, 8—10 pm, B-104 Wells.

LITERATURE AND FILM

The Films of Alfred Hitchcock, 1954-1976
Spring, 1987

English 347, Section 1   Office Hours: M 12:55-2:55
Dr. Lunde, 289 Bessey   TT 12:10-1:10 &
Graduate Assistant: Mr. Raber   by appointment
                                                Phone: 5-7668

Required Reading:

   Donald Spoto, The Art of Alfred Hitchcock: Fifty Years of His Motion Pictures,
   Doubleday, paper.

   Donald Spoto, The Dark Side of Genius: The Life of Alfred Hitchcock,
   Ballantine, paper

Recommended Reading:

   Marshall Deutelbaum and Leland Poague, A Hitchcock Reader, Iowa State
   David Freeman, The Last Days of Alfred Hitchcock, Overlook
   Michael Haley, The Alfred Hitchcock Album, Prentice-Hall
   Robert Harris & Michael Lasky, The Films of Alfred Hitchcock, Citadel
   Albert LaValley, Focus on Hitchcock, Prentice-Hall
   Gene Phillips, Alfred Hitchcock, Twayne
   William Rothman, Hitchcock: The Murderous Gaze, Harvard
   John Russell Taylor, Hitch: The Life and Times of Alfred Hitchcock, Pantheon
   Francois Truffaut, Hitchcock, Simon and Schuster
   Robin Wood, Hitchcock's Films, Paperback Library

Class, Screening, Reading and Assignment Schedule:

   April   2: Introduction to Alfred Hitchcock
           7: A "Pleasant" Diversion: Screening of Dial "M" for Murder
           9: Commentary and discussion: Dial "M" for Murder; read The Art, 3-4,
               228-235, 501-516; The Dark Side, 3-82, 364-369, 617-639.
          14: The "Perfect" Film: Screening of Rear Window.
          16: Commentary and discussion: Rear Window; read The Art, 236-249;
               The Dark Side, 369-378.
          21: A "Light" Entertainment: Screening of To Catch a Thief.
          23: Commentary and discussion: To Catch A Thief; read The Art, 250-
               257; The Dark Side, 373-381.
          28: The Documentary Experience: Screening of The Wrong Man.
          30: Commentary and discussion: The Wrong Man; read The Art, 282-289;
               The Dark Side, 395-410.
   May   5: Hitch, a reassessment.
           7: Hour Examination.
          12: A Question of Identity: Screening of Vertigo.
          14: Commentary and discussion: Vertigo: read The Art, 290-337; The
               Dark Side, 410-435, paper due.
          19: The Suspense/Thriller par excellence: Screening of North by
               Northwest.
          21: Commentary and discussion: North by Northwest; read The Art
               338-353; The Dark Side, 435-447.
          25: HOLIDAY (no office hours)
          26: The Triumph of the Master: Screening of Psycho.
          28: Commentary and discussion: Psycho; read The Art, 354-381; The
               Dark Side, 447-463.

June 2: Final Coda: Screening of <u>Family Plot</u>.
         4: Commentary and discussion: <u>Family Plot</u>; read <u>The Art</u>, 446-494;
             <u>The Dark Side</u>, 557-583; summation.
         9: Final Examination: 8:00-10:00 p.m.

Paper Assignment:

There will be a requirement of <u>one</u> report essay of approximately 1600 words
which will be due on May 14. The assignment will be an analysis of a
specific theme, technique, characterization or symbol drawn from one or more
of the assigned Hitchcock films. Extensions will be granted only with prior
approval of the instructor and with good cause. You may refer to the
question sets for topic suggestions. <u>Failure to complete the paper or to
take both examinations will automatically result in a course grade of 0.0.</u>

All papers are to be clearly written, neat in appearance, persuasive in
organization and supported with strong evidence. Papers <u>not</u> meeting these
criteria will <u>not</u> be accepted. More announcements on papers will be
forthcoming.

Other Announcements:

Announcements on grading policies, examinations, class presentations, reading
assignments, reserve reading lists, optional classes will be forthcoming.
There will be additional handouts periodically this term.

Note on adaptation:

For your information, the following assigned films are based on adaptations
of literary works: Dial "M" for Murder, on a play by Frederick Knott; <u>Rear
Window</u>, on a long short story by Cornell Woolrich; <u>To Catch a Thief</u>, on a
novel by David Dodge; <u>Vertigo</u>, on a novel by Pierre Boileau and Thomas
Narcejac, D'entre les morts; Psycho, on a novel by Robert Bloch; <u>Family Plot</u>,
on a novel by Victor Canning, <u>The Rainbow Pattern</u>.

FEATURE FILMS*

April 7: <u>Dial "M" for Murder</u> (Warner Brothers,1954) (88 minutes)
      14: <u>Rear Window</u> (Paramount, 1954) (112 minutes)
      21: <u>To Catch a Thief</u> (Paramount, 1955) (97 minutes)
      28: <u>The Wrong Man</u> (Warner Brothers, 1956) (105 minutes)
May 12: <u>Vertigo</u> (Paramount, 1958) (120 minutes)
      19: <u>North by Northwest</u> (MGM, 1959) (136 minutes)
      26: <u>Psycho</u> (Paramount, 1960) (109 minutes)
June 2: <u>Family Plot</u> (Universal, 1976) (120 minutes)

*The announced running times of these films may vary a bit; this depends on the
print available.

Questions for Rear Window
Professor Lunde - English 347

1. Comment on the theme of voyeurism, as explored both verbally and visually in the film. For example, there is much discussion of "rear window ethics," "peeping Toms," and the like.

2. How does Rear Window explore the theme of love? Notice how the situations in each of the apartments surrounding the courtyard represent different variations of romantic relationships and the like.

3. Explore how visual and verbal references to "hot" and "cold" suggest the emotional status of the characters.

4. Again, Hitchcock welcomed the challenge of a constricted setting to tell his story. Hence, the camera and its movements are restricted with few exceptions to set-ups inside the Jefferies apartment. How does this enhance the point-of-view of major characters in the story? When do the shots move outside the apartment?

5. What is the significance of Jeff's profession as a roving photographer?

6. How is Jeff as guilty as the villain Lars Thorwald? How is he especially compassionate?

7. Comment on the character of Lisa Freemont. How does she represent an independent, mature spirit? Notice how and when she often turns on the lamps in the apartment. How is she in this fashion an angel of light or a "life-giver?"

8. Comment on the character of Stella. How is she a responsible, practical person, despite her lack of sophisticated credentials?

9. Comment on the themes of isolation and community in the film. How does the scene where the couple discovers that their dog has been killed reflect a sense of communal love or the lack thereof?

10. Hitchcock loved the live theatre. What are the verbal and visual references to theatre in the film? Notice how each of the apartment settings could be viewed as sets in a play. What is the significance of all this?

11. Hitchcock was, of course, born a Catholic to lower middle class parents in England. How does this story suggest powerful themes of marital fidelity, sin, redemption and private confessionals?

12. Hitchock was trained in the days of silent cinema. Comment on the number of sequences which depend almost solely on visuals to move the story forward.

13. Explore the resolutions at the end of the story. How are Jeff and Lisa now reconciled with one another? How is there still tension in the relationship?

14. Why is Jeff so reluctant to commit himself to the "perfect" Lisa? What are his basic insecurities? How does he represent the traditional Hitchcock male hero, who is at first isolated and immature? How does he mature in the story, moving from a passive to an activist stance?

15. Hitchcock believed deeply in the power of editing (sometimes called "montage") as the essence of filmmaking. Comment on the editing in the film. Notice the use of a large number of fade-outs as transitional devices.

16. Comment on the effectiveness of images of light and darkness.

17. What does the film say about a person's capacity to see?

18. Explore the character of Lars Thorwald. How is he still a sympathetic character despite the monstrous act he commits? What does one really know about him? How is he a haunted figure, like other Hitchcock villains?

19. What is the significance of Lisa's wearing Mrs. Thorwald's ring?

20. Comment on the character of Tom Doyle, the police detective. How is he at first obtuse, like other Hitchcock authority figures? How is he a sympathetic character?

21. Comment on the role of music -- pop tunes, instrumental and the like--in this film.

22. What is the significance of the framed photographs featured in Jeff's apartment?

23. How do the dangerous events of the story draw Lisa and Jeff together?

24. Comment on the visual and verbal references to food.

25. How does Lisa's expertise in fashion help solve the crime?

English 347   Professor Lunde
Questions for Psycho

1. Comment on the verbal and visual references to birds. Note the pictures
    of birds (including ducks) in Marion's motel room, the stuffed birds in
    Norman's office, Marion's last name (Crane). What structure resembles a
    bird's nest? When does the camera angle take a bird's eye view? How do
    Norman's and Marion's mannerisms seem birdlike? How does the camera
    movement at the beginning suggest a bird in flight? How do the dissolves
    during Marion's journey suggest the flight of a bird? Recall that
    Hitchcock's next film is entitled The Birds.

2. Comment on water images in the film. Note the rainstorm, the watery bog,
    the shower water, among other references.

3. Comment on the interplay of light and darkness in the film.

4. What is the MacGuffin of the story?

5. Compare and contrast the Bates motel with the Bates house, both in terms
    of appearance and theme.

6. How does the title Psycho refer to Marion as well as to Norman?

7. Explore the significance of names in the film: for example, Marion Crane,
    Marie Samuels, Fairvale, Norman Bates, Gorman (town in California),
    "California Charlie" (the used car salesman), Dr. Richman (the
    psychiatrist).

8. Explore the significance of numbers in the film: for example, Marion's
    second set of license plates reads "NFB 418."

9. How are themes of resurrection and of redemption indicated here?

10. Comment on the images of eyes in the film: note the treatment of Norman's
    eyes, Marion's eyes, the California patrolman's eyes, Cassidy's eyes,
    the eyes of the stuffed birds, Mother Bates' eyes, Milton Arbogast's
    eyes, among others. How do these images suggest themes of blindness and
    of new vision?

11. Examine the theme of voyeurism in the film. How does this theme repre-
    sent the theme of the violation of privacy?

12. Explore the meaning of the various reflected images in the film.

13. Analyze the famous sequence where Marion takes a shower at the motel.
    Why would Marion feel safe here? Comment on the shifting perspectives
    and camera angles which occur during the sequence.

14. Trace the significance of circular images in the film.

15. Analyze the significance of the pictures behind Marion and Caroline in
    the real estate office.

16. Comment on the function of the following characters: Sheriff Al Chambers, Mrs. Chambers, Dr. Richman, Cassidy, Mr. Lowery, Caroline, Milton Arbogast.

17. How does Psycho resemble a so-called silent film?

18. During what time of year does the story take place? Why is this important?

19. Why does the headline of Marion's newspaper include the designation "OKAY"?

20. Trace the significance of verbal and visual references to food in the film.

21. Compare and contrast Norman Bates with Sam Loomis.

22. Compare and contrast Marion Crane with her sister Lila.

23. What does the film imply about the power of darkness, the power of irrational forces?

24. How do the principal characters—Sam, Norman, Marion—display immature qualities? What are signs of their maturity?

25. Comment on the significance of the Bates house. What significant details does Lila discover when she investigates Norman's and his mother's bedrooms?

26. What do Marion's room in Phoenix and Sam's hardware store say about their socio-economic status?

27. Comment on the film's treatment of "small town America" with its portrait of Fairvale.

28. What are instances of black humor in the film?

29. Comment on the effectiveness of Bernard Herrmann's musical score.

30. What images of the film suggest perceptions derived from Freudian psychology?

31. Analyze the visual and verbal detail of the parlor scene where Marion and Norman share some their private emotional turmoil. How does each person seem threatened by the other? How does Norman help Marion resolve her problems?

32. What does the film say about the theme of appearance and reality?

33. How is this film existential in vision?

34. How is this a story of children without parents?

35. How are the principal characters—Sam, Marion, Lila, Norman—all haunted by the past?

36. How does the film involve the audience directly in its events?

37. Why is the last shot a symbol of rebirth and of restoration?

38. How and why are many of the film's principal characters--Sam, Norman, Lila, Marion--consumed with such emotions as fear, self-doubt and guilt?

39. How is Sam typical of a Hitchcock male hero? How is he atypical?

40. Trace the significance of the dissolves in the films.

A CLOSER LOOK:

FILMS BY COPPOLA, WELLES, WAJDA, AND CHAPLIN

Chuck Maland   Topics in Film Studies

                                      English 4090

D.W. Griffith, prominent early American film director, once described his goal as a filmmaker this way: "My task is above all to make you see." If I might modify his phrasing, the goal in this course is to help students see, hear, and understand four challenging and important feature films--made by four important directors and their talented collaborators--as completely as possible. We will try in the course of ten weeks to master these films and learn about film art by taking a closer look.

The idea of the course stems from an observation that one rarely has enough time in a film course to examine really carefully how film narrative, style, and theme interact in individual films. Instead of spending a week on each film, as is common in film courses, we will use between two and two-and-a-half weeks for each film, much of the time discussing individual scenes or even individual shots with the aid of a videotape and a videodisc machine. This close analysis will be supplemented by reading a book on film aesthetics (Film Art), a book on the production of a single film, and a collection of essays related to film history, film analysis, and the particular films we are seeing. I will also suggest some outside reserve reading.

By the end of the term students should know the system of film form described in Film Art, as well as the concepts and terminology associated with it. They should also know the films so well that Vito Corleone, Charles Foster Kane, Mateus Birkut, Chaplin's Tramp, and other lesser characters in the four films are like old friends. Finally, students should have a firm sense of how the collaborative nature of film production requires the talents of a wide variety of people. During the term students will apply what they learn about film form by writing a critical essay on another film (see below). In a more general sense, however, I hope students will leave the course better able to see and hear films, as well as more sensitive to the rich artistic possibilities of cinematic expression.

REQUIRED READINGS:

Film Art, by David Bordwell and Kristin Thompson
The Making of Citizen Kane, by Robert Carringer
Topics in Film Studies: Selected Readings

EXAMS:

All students will take a midterm and a final exam.

PAPER:

All students will do a typewritten essay of 1500-2500 words. The papers will graded by the same standards of clarity, organization, and stylistic effectiveness as any other 4000 level English course. (Graduate students will do a more substantial essay on a topic worked out with Dr. Maland.)

The paper should be a close formalist analysis of one of the following films: Coppola's _The Godfather, Part Two_, Hitchcock's _Psycho_, Tati's _Mon Oncle_, or Kurosawa's _Ikiru_. (All are available in Non-Print in Hodges Library.) Your paper should both define what you understand as the central concern(s) of the film and discuss how elements of narrative and cinematic style function to create the film's form and communicate its meaning. Use Bordwell and Thompson's analyses of _Citizen Kane_ as a model, though you will not be able to go into as much detail as they do because of space limitations. You may do library research for the paper; be sure to document your sources properly.

GRADING:

The paper and the two exams will each count 30%. The quality of your classroom participation and your performance on other brief activities--both in class and out of class--will count 10% and will be especially important in deciding borderline grades.

READING AND VIEWING SCHEDULE

JANUARY

6: Introduction to Course

8: _Film Art_ (FA), Chs. 1-2

COPPOLA AND _THE GODFATHER_ (1972)

11: Introduction to _The Godfather_: _Selected Essays_ (SE), #1;

13: View _The Godfather_

15: Narrative analysis: BT, Ch. 3, SE, #2-#3

18: No Class--Martin Luther King's Birthday

20: Mise-en-scene and Sound: BT, Chs. 5, 8

22: Framing and Editing: BT, Chs. 6-7

25: MID-TERM EXAM

WELLES AND _CITIZEN KANE_ (1941)

27: View _Citizen Kane_. Read Carringer (C), Chs. 1-2

29: Themes and Narrative (review BT, ch. 3)

FEBRUARY

1: Mise-en-scene (production design): C, ch. 3

3: Cinematography and editing: C, ch. 4

5: Post Production (Including sound): C, chs. 5-6

WAJDA AND <u>MAN OF MARBLE</u> (1976)

8: Cinema and the Roots of Solidarity--an Introduction to <u>Man of Marble</u>: SE, # 4-5

10: View <u>Man of Marble</u>

12: Narrative Structure: SE, 6-7

15: Political Perspective

17: Film Style, I

19: CRITICAL ESSAY DUE: Film Style, II

CHAPLIN AND <u>CITY LIGHTS</u> (1931)

22: Chaplin and Charlie: View Chaplin Short

24: View <u>City Lights</u>. Read SE, #8

26: Theme and Narrative

28: Film Style, I

MARCH

2: Meet in Hodges 252 for viewing of <u>The Unknown Chaplin</u>

4: Film Style, II

7: Course Summary

9: Final Exam

Reserve Reading

I have placed a number of books relevant to the course on reserve. They should provide you the opportunity to do outside reading on the ideas, films, and filmmakers treated in the course. I have placed them on overnight reserve. See me for other recommendations for outside reading.

GENERAL

Bordwell, David. Narration in the Fiction Film

Bordwell, David, Kristin Thompson, and Janet Staiger. The Classical Hollywood Cinema

Kawin, Bruce. How Movies Work

Nichols, Bill, ed. Movies and Methods

THE GODFATHER

Johnson, Robert K. Francis Ford Coppola

Kolker, Robert. A Cinema of Loneliness

Rosow, Eugene. Born to Lose

Zuker, Joel. Francis Ford Coppola: A Guide to References and Resources

CITIZEN KANE

Carringer, Robert. The Making of "Citizen Kane"

Cowie, Peter. The Cinema of Orson Welles

Kael, Pauline, ed. The "Citizen Kane" Book

Higham, Charles. The Films of Orson Welles

Leaming, Barbara. Orson Welles

McBride, Joseph. Orson Welles

Naremore, James. The Magic World of Orson Welles

MAN OF MARBLE

Ascherson, Neal. The Polish August

Blazynski, George. Flashpoint Poland

Liehm, Mira and Antonin. The Most Important Art

Michalek, Boleslaw. The Cinema of Andrzej Wajda

Singer, Daniel. The Road to Gdansk

CITY LIGHTS

Chaplin, Charles. My Autobiography

Huff, Theodore. Charlie Chaplin

Kerr, Walter. The Silent Clowns

Lyons, Timothy. Charles Chaplin: A Guide to References and
Resources

Mast, Gerald. The Comic Mind

Molyneaux, Gerard. Charlie Chaplin's "City Lights"

Robinson, David. Chaplin: His Life and Films

ENGLISH 347 - WOODY ALLEN
Professor Pogel

COURSE DESCRIPTION & REQUIREMENTS

Textbook List:
1. Allen, Woody, Four Films of Woody Allen. New York: 1982.
2. Allen, Woody, Three Films of Woody Allen New York: 1987
3. Pogel, Nancy, Woody Allen Boston: 1987
3. Course Packet for Eng. 347 - (includes study questions, term paper
    directions and topic suggestions, Language Lab. hours, grade log
    sheet, and reserve reading list)

Course Objectives:

This course is designed to heighten your critical understanding of
film through the study of Woody Allen's films and writings. Allen is a
major American director whose work suggests a number of important issues
for film students. Allen would like to see himself as a popular filmmaker
who nevertheless challenges the mainstream and "takes risks." He has been
criticized by some critics, however, for making films that are too narciss-
istic or apolitical and for making films that merely reaffirm conventional
wisdom. Allen's early major films such as Take the Money and Run, Bananas,
or Sleeper are primarily "funny" spoofs, and they reflect the influence of
his early parodic essays and stories as well as his background as a joke
writer and stand-up comic. The films following Annie Hall experiment
with serio-comedy and drama and deal more explicitly with Allen's concerns
in a serious manner. Allen has acknowledged that the movement from a
primary interest in jokes to more serio-comedies and drama involved formal,
dramatic and thematic problems. Critics and audiences have frequently
chided Allen for abandoning his earlier "wilder comedy" for the later
serio-comic and "heavy" style.

This course deals with Allen's development, the controversies and
questions that arise from that development; therefore, the course has
several additional, more specific objectives:

1) To examine stylistic and structural problems and consequences of
Allen's development from the earlier to later films such as
    a) the transition from cartoon figures to more human, multi-
        dimensional characters
    b) from films in which visual style is the servant to the joke to
        films which are visually more attractive and complex.
    c) from joke-centered, episodic structures to a greater variety of
        strategies and structures in which jokes are more
        integral to the narrative, dramatic, and thematic directions of
        the films
    d) from comic defenses to explicitly serious themes and dialogues

2) To trace the evolution of Allen's consciously intertextual, reflexive
style; to examine the use of allusions to American and European films,
literature, painting, and popular culture, particularly as these pertain to
Allen's dialogues with influences, and his developing treatment of memory
and the past.

3) To explore the development of Allen's "little man and woman" figures as they are the focus for a series of thematic and/or stylistic dialogues and as they reflect upon ethnic and gender issues.

4) To explore the tensions between Allen's attempts to create films that present (limited?) alternatives to dominant cinema while also remaining accessable to a broad audience and financially successful.

By the end of the course you will be expected to recognize the characteristics and problems associated with Allen's particular development, to understand his major concerns and recognize how his visual and narrative strategies relate to themes in his films, to his audiences, and to the industry and milieu within which he works. You should have some understanding of how his films are responses to and critiques of our culture and times, and you should be able to see the deconstruction that occurs within the films and be able to gain enough distance on those films to discover their own difficulties and contradictions. To respond sensitively to the texts of this course it is necessary to "read" Allen's films attentively.

Class Organization and Methods:

This four credit class meets for regularly scheduled times four hours a week and for two additional arranged hours. Ordinarily, you will see a film on Monday nights during the regularly scheduled classtime from 7:00 to 9:00. Since Allen films generally run between 85-95 minutes, about a half hour remains for introductory remarks, class business etc. On two occasions, you will be asked to stay for an extra hour to see required films. You are compensated for this additionally scheduled time because you will seldom have to remain for a full two hours on Tuesdays.

Although most showings are on Monday, some films will be shown only once during the arranged hours on Tuesday afternoons. On some occasions, the "two hours arranged" will be used to show the Monday films a second time. Tuesday arranged times are from 4:00 to 5:45.

Wednesday night classes will generally be devoted to video-assisted lectures and class discussions of the films.

You are advised to attend both scheduled and arranged classes regularly. For those who wish to see Allen films several times, who cannot make an arranged class, who wish to see an Allen film not included in this course, or a film to which an Allen film refers, video tapes are available in the Language Laboratory. Laboratory hours are listed in your course packet.

Requirements to Obtain a Final Grade:
1. Attend class regularly; see all films; participate in discussions
2. Take two examinations, each worth 25% of the final grade
3. Write a proposal and tentative outline for the term paper (10%) and hand it in by the due date. [See instructions and sample, course packet]
4. Hand in an 8 page minimum term paper, double-spaced and typed (40%) by the due date.
5. Record all grades on the "Grade Log Sheet" in your course packet; collect all graded papers and an up-to-date Grade Log Sheet in a large manilla envelope with your name on it. Hand in the last day of class.

<u>Materials</u> <u>on</u> <u>Reserve</u> <u>at</u> <u>Main</u> <u>Library</u>:

A number of books and periodical articles by and about Woody Allen and/or his films are on reserve in the assigned reading section on the first floor, Main Library. The reserved materials include both assigned readings (see class calendar) and readings that will help you with the term paper. Multiple copies of required readings are available. Because the reserved readings constitute a significant portion of most days' assignments, you are advised to plan your schedules in order to avoid the library's congested hours. All assigned items are on two hour/in-library reserve.

<u>Bibliography</u>:

A bibliography of books and articles by and about Woody Allen appears in your text, <u>Woody</u> <u>Allen</u> Boston: Twayne, 1987 (several copies also on reserve). For additional articles see indexes listed in the MSU Libraries Subject Guide #25 - "Film Literature," in your course packet.

ENGLISH 347 - Woody Allen/ Fall, 1987
Professor Pogel

<u>CLASS CALENDAR</u>

Please Note: In addition to the required reading assignments listed below,
          you should look at the appropriate set of study questions
          (in the Course Packet or handouts) before seeing the films.

M 9/28   Introduction to the Course (Goals, Issues, Requirements)
             Purchase all texts and materials before next class
             Read: WA, Ch. 1, 2 and pp. 33-39 of Ch. 3
             Read: Robert Stam, <u>Reflexivity</u> in <u>Film</u> and <u>Literature</u>,
                "Introduction," pp. 1-27, [on reserve]

T 9/29   See <u>Take the Money and Run</u>
             Read: "Spring Bulletin," and "A Look at Organized
                Crime" in <u>Getting Even</u> [on reserve]
             Pauline Kael, "Against Spoofing," in <u>The National</u>
                <u>Society of Film Critics On Comedy</u>, pp. 104-
                107 [on resere]

W 9/30   Discuss <u>Take the Money and Run</u>
             See excerpts from <u>Dillinger</u>, <u>The Hustler</u>, and <u>Cool Hand</u>
                <u>Luke</u>

M 10/5   See <u>Bananas</u>
             Read: "Viva Vargas", p. 92 in <u>Getting Even</u> [on reserve]
                and WA, 39-54

T 10/6   See <u>Sleeper</u>
             Read: WA, Ch. 4, p. 57-58, 65-70
             Read: Christopher Lasch, <u>The Culture of Narcissism</u>,
                "Preface" and "Chap. 1," pp. xiii - 30 [on
                reserve]

W 10/7   Discuss <u>Bananas</u> and <u>Sleeper</u>
             See excerpts from <u>Viva Zapata</u>,<u>Modern Times</u>, <u>1984</u>,
                <u>Clockwork Orange</u>, <u>Valley of the Giants</u>, <u>The Blob</u>

M 10/12   See <u>Everything You Always Wanted to Know About Sex</u>
             Read: WA, Ch. 4, pp. 58-70

T 10/13   See <u>Love and Death</u>
             Read: "My Philosophy," in <u>Getting Even</u> [on reserve]
                and WA, Ch. 4, p. 70-78

W 10/14   Discuss <u>Everything You Always Wanted to Know</u>... and <u>Love and Death</u>
             See excerpts from <u>Blow-Up</u>, <u>Fantastic Voyage</u>, <u>The Court</u>
                <u>Jester</u>, <u>War and Peace</u>

M. 10/19 See <u>Annie Hall</u>
             Read: <u>Four Films</u>, p. 3-109 and WA, Ch. 5
                Maurice Yacowar, <u>Loser Take All</u>, Ch. 14 [on
                reserve]

T. 10/20 Second showing of Annie Hall/ Discuss Exam #1
                   Read: Molly Haskell, "The Age of Ambivalence," in From
                          Reverence to Rape, 2nd ed. [on reserve]
                          Thomas Schatz, Old Hollywood/New Hollywood, pp.
                          1-28, 45-66, 189-241 [on reserve]

W. 10/21 Discuss Annie Hall and readings
                   See excerpts from Bringing Up Baby and Adam's Rib

M. 10/26 TAKE EXAM #1

T. 10/27 See Interiors
                   Read: Four Films, 113-178 and WA, Ch. 6
                   Read: Mark Schechner, "The Failure of the Therapeutic," in
                          From Hester Street to Hollywood [on reserve]
                          Jack Kroll, "The Inner Woody," in Newsweek 7 Aug.,
                          1978 [on reserve]

W. 10/28 Second showing of Interiors
                   TERM PAPER PROPOSAL & OUTLINE DUE
                   Read: Ira Halberstadt, "Scenes from a Mind," in Take One
                          [on reserve]
                          Peter Cowie, Ingmar Bergman, pp. 276-282 [on reserve]
                          Paisley Livingston, Ingmar Bergman and the Rituals of
                          Art, pp. 232-253 [on reserve]

M. 11/2   Discuss Interiors
                   See excerpts from Cries and Whispers

T. 11/3   See Manhattan and A Midsummer Night's Sex Comedy
                   Read: Four Films, p. 179-276 and WA, Ch. 7 & Ch. 9
                   Read: Robert T. Moss, "Creators on Creating: Woody Allen,"
                          Saturday Review 7 [on reserve]
                          Natalie Gittelson, "The Maturing of Woody Allen," in
                          The New York Times Magazine [on reserve]
                          Joan Didion, "Review of Annie Hall, Interiors, and
                          Manhattan," in New York Review of Books 16 [on
                          reserve]
                          Robert Benayoun, Beyond Words, pp. 98-113 [on reserve]

W. 11/4   Discuss Manhattan and A Midsummer Night's Sex Comedy
                   See excerpts from Midsummer Night's Dream (Reinhardt),
                   Smiles of a Summer's Night, A Day in the Country

M. 11/9   See Stardust Memories / Quiz #1 returned
                   Read: Four Films, p. 277-387 and WA, Ch. 8
                          Pauline Kael, "The Frog Who Turned into a Prince/ The
                          Prince Who Turned into a Frog," in New Yorker (27
                          Oct. 1980) [on reserve]

T. 11/10   See 8 1/2
                    Read: Ted Perry, Filmguide to 8 ½, pp.1-9, 17-68 [on
                               reserve]
                          Robert Stam, Reflexivity in Film and Literature "The
                               Genre of Self-Consciousness," pp. 127-166, and
                               "Reflexivity and the Specifically Cinematic," pp.
                               255-266 [on reserve]

W. 11/11   Discuss Stardust Memories and 8 ½

M. 11/16   See Zelig
                    Read: Three Films, pp. 3-141 and WA, Ch. 10

T. 11/17   Second showing of Zelig
                    Read: Michiko Kakutani, "How Woody Allen's Zelig Was Born in
                               Anxiety and Grew into Comedy," in New York Times
                               18 July, 1983 [on reserve]
                          Stewart Brand, Kevin Kelly, and Jay Kinney, "Digital
                               Retouching: The End of Photography as Evidence of
                               Anything," Whole Earth Review, July, 1985 [on reserve]
                          Bruce Kawin, "Time and Stasis in La Jetée," in Film
                               Quarterly 36 [on reserve]
                          William Johnson, "Orson Welles: Of Time and Loss," in
                               Film Quarterly 21 [on reserve]

W. 11/18   Discuss Zelig
                    See excerpts from Citizen Kane, La Jetée

M. 11/23   See Broadway Danny Rose
                    Read: Three Films, pp. 144-316 and WA, Ch. 11, p. 189-200
                          Fred Ferretti, "How Woody Allen's Old World Inspired
                               His New Film," New York Times 19 Feb., 1984 [on
                               reserve]
                          Phil Berger, "The Business of Comedy," New York Times
                               Magazine, 9 June, 1985 [on reserve]

T. 11/24   See The Purple Rose of Cairo/ Discuss Quiz #2
                    Read: Three Films, pp. 318-473 and WA, Ch. 11, p. 200-213
                          "The Kugelmass Episode" in Side Effects, pp. 41-55 [o
                               reserve]
                    Read: Robert Stam, "The Pleasures of Subversion," in Refle-
                               xivity in Film and Literature, pp. 209-254 [on reserve]

W. 11/25   Discuss Broadway Danny Rose
                    See excerpts from The Godfather and Meet Danny Wilson

M. 11/30   Discuss The Purple Rose of Cairo
                    TERM PAPERS & REVISED OUTLINES DUE
                    See excerpts from "white telephone" films

T. 12/1   Second showing of The Purple Rose of Cairo
                    Complete Student Instructional Rating forms

W. 12/2   TAKE EXAM #2 [Hand in grade log sheet, Exam #1 and graded proposal]

Cinema 469: Film Styles   Instructor: David Shepard
D.W. Griffith   Spring Semester of 1988

Writing in 1940 of Griffith's INTOLERANCE, Iris Barry said "there is so much in it; there
is too much of it . . ." The same might be said of Griffith's career, of his influence, and of
this course. The compression will be severe but the lessons are potentially tremendous.

Like INTOLERANCE, this course will attempt to weave four separate stories into one. We
hope to document the early development of film art in a chronological survey of films by
its most important pioneer; to view the manufacture, distribution and exhibition of films
from the years of the Patents Company to those of the studio through the prism of
Griffith's experience; to consider the emergence of motion pictures as a social influence;
and to study various critical approaches to Griffith's achievements.

Griffith's directing career lasted only twenty-three years, but the output was prodigious:
nearly 500 films for the Biograph Company and 35 features. He also wrote, supervised or
produced but did not personally direct many other films. The manuscript material
available on 38 reels of microfilm in Doheny Library encompasses Griffith's personal
papers, including his unpublished writings, and the business records of his corporations.
There are also scrap books for each of his major films and many reminisences from
associates. There are some two dozen published books and, of course, many articles.

After contemplating all of this, I selected a rather large, yet proportionally very small
collection of materials for study. We will view about 10% of Griffith's Biograph work and
about 25% of his feature film output. We will read one thick biography, D.W. GRIFFITH:
AN AMERICAN LIFE, by Richard Schickel (New York, Simon and Schuster, 1984) and a
fairly formidable anthology comprising studies of individual films, articles completed or
published after Schickel gathered his data, and small amounts of primary source material.

Your responsibilities are to keep current with the assignments, to prepare and present
two ten-minute oral reports during the semester, to write a midterm exam and a final
exam. There is no term paper. As an inspiration to keep current with the readings, there
will be eleven written "reading checks" at the beginnig of class periods, in which you will
be asked to respond briefly to one or two rather general questions; each will count 2
points toward the semester grade. Each report weighs in at 10 points, the midterm at 25
points, and the final at 33 points.

On Saturday, February 20th and Saturday, April 9th, I will offer optional supplementary
screenings of non-Griffith films. They are intended to provide contextual reference for
students who have not seen many films from this period, but as they are not mandatory, I
have also attempted to select exceptional and entertaining works. If you are able to
attend, you should find them well worth the Saturdays in the dark!

SCHEDULE

January 13th Films: THOSE AWFUL HATS, THE COUNTRY DOCTOR, IN THE BORDER
              STATES, WHEN A MAN LOVES, THE LONEDALE OPERATOR, THE LONG
              ROAD, A GIRL AND HER TRUST, ONE IS BUSINESS -- THE OTHER

94

CRIME, THE BATTLE AT ELDERBUSH GULCH. (Original advertising broadsides for each of the Biograph films, including a still, detailed synopsis, length and release date, are reproduced in the anthology).

January 20th   Films: (*denotes film not directed by DWG) *AT THE FRENCH BALL, *RESCUED BY ROVER, *HER FIRST ADVENTURE, THE ADVENTURES OF DOLLIE, *I FETCH THE BREAD, THE CURTAIN POLE, A DRUNKARD'S REFORMATION, *A NARROW ESCAPE, THE LONELY VILLA, THE GIRLS AND DADDY, *THE ASSASSINATION OF THE DUKE OF GUISE, THE SEALED ROOM, PIPPA PASSES, CORNER IN WHEAT. Read: Schickel 15-145, also Altman, Adams, Hilenski in antholgy.

January 27th   Films: THE HOUSE WITH CLOSED SHUTTERS, THE USURER, SORROWS OF THE UNFAITHFUL, THE CHIEF'S DAUGHTER, ENOCH ARDEN, FIGHTING BLOOD, THE BATTLE. Read: Schickel 146-183; also Allen, Merritt ("Rescued . ."), Bowser, Gunning, Deutelbaum in anthology.

February 3rd   Films: A WOMAN SCORNED, THE TRANSFORMATION OF MIKE, THE SUNBEAM, A BEAST AT BAY, THE SANDS O' DEE, THE RENUNCIATION, FRIENDS, THE PAINTED LADY, THE NEW YORK HAT. Read: Merritt ("Mr. Griffith . ."), Geduld 32-38 in anthology.

February 10th Films: THE MASSACRE, AN UNSEEN ENEMY, MUSKETEERS OF PIG ALLEY, THE BURGLAR'S DILEMMA, THE LADY AND THE MOSUE, DEATH'S MARATHON, *THE SWITCHTOWER, THE MOTHERING HEART. Read: Schickel 184-203; also Gish, Kepley ("The Musketeers . . "), Simon, Vardac in anthology.

February 17th Films: JUDITH OF BETHULIA, HOME SWEET HOME (excerpt), THE AVENGING CONSCIENCE. Read: Schickel 203-211; also Rothman ("Judith . . ."), Petric ("The Avenging . . ."), Brown in anthology.

February 20th SUPPLEMENTARY FILMS
9:30   THE COWARD, 1915, Directed by Reginald Barker, Produced by T.H. Ince
10:30   THE MATRIMANIAC, 1916, with Douglas Fairbanks, Directed by John Emerson
11:30   YOUNG ROMANCE, 1914, Directed by George Melford
1:30   CARMEN, 1915, with Geraldine Farrar, Directed by C.B. DeMille
2:45   THE ITALIAN, 1915, with George Beban, Directed by Barker, Prod: Ince

February 24th Film: THE BIRTH OF A NATION Read: Schickel 212-250; also Geduld 39-42, Silva, Cuniberti.

March 2nd   MID-TERM EXAMINATION
               Film: THE BIRTH OF A NATION: selected sequences, outtakes and rushes; LET KATIE DO IT (1915, Directed by S.M. and C.A. Franklin, Produced by DWG). Read: Schickel 267-302; also Geduld 43-45, Merritt ("DWG's The Birth . . .), Simcovich, Petric ("Two Lincoln . . .").

March 9th   Film: INTOLERANCE Read: Schickel 303-339; also Geduld 46-55, Merritt ("On First . . ."), Kepley ("Intolerance . . ."), Drew in anthology. Note: This is a two-week reading assignment, due March 16th.

March 16th   Films: INTOLERANCE (sequences), THE MOTHER AND THE LAW (sequences), BY MAN'S LAW (1913 Biograph, Dir: C. Cabanne, Supervised by DWG), THE REFORMERS, CABIRIA (1913, Italy, Dir: G. Pastrone, sequences); GOING STRAIGHT (1916, Directed by S.A. and C.M. Franklin, Written and Produced by DWG).

March 23rd   Films: HEARTS OF THE WORLD, THE GREATEST QUESTION (sequence), WAR ON THREE FRONTS (1916, Frank von Kleinschmidt, sequence). Read: Schickel 340-360; also Merritt ("DWG Directs . . ."), Lyons, Belton, Naremore in anthology.

April 6th   Films: BROKEN BLOSSOMS, TRUE HEART SUSIE. Read: Schickel 377-415; also Kepley ("Broken . . ."), Browne, Lesage, Merritt ("Broken . . ."), Rothman, Merritt ("The Pastorals") in anthology.

April 9th   SUPPLEMENTARY FILMS
9:15   REBECCA OF SUNNYBROOK FARM, 1917, with Pickford, Dir: Marshall Neilan
10:30   THE LAST OF THE MOHICANS, 1920, Directed by Maurice Tourneur
1:00   SCARAMOUCHE, 1921, Directed by Rex Ingram
2:45   FOOLISH WIVES, 1021, Directed by Erich von Stroheim

April 13th   Film: WAY DOWN EAST Read: Schickel 416-507; also Geduld 62-68, Lennig, Kozloff, Vineburg in anthology.

April 20th   Film: ISN'T LIFE WONDERFUL! Read: Schickel 508-605.

as scheduled FINAL EXAMINATION

A
D W GRIFFITH
READER

CNTV 469   Spring 1988
David Shepard
Paris Poirier, T.A.

For January 13:

Biograph Bulletins for THE ADVENTURES OF DOLLIE, THE COUNTRY DOCTOR, IN THE BORDER STATES, FOR HIS SON, THE LONEDALE OPERATOR, THE ETERNAL MOTHER, THE GIRL & HER TRUST, THE BATTLE AT ELDERBUSH GULCH. (all bulletins from E. Bowser, ed., Biograph Bulletins, Octagon Press, 1973)

January 20:

Biograph Bulletins for THOSE AWFUL HATS, THE BOY DETECTIVE, CAUGHT BY WIRELESS, THE MENDED LUTE, THE GIRLS & DADDY, THE SEALED ROOM, PIPPA PASSES, A DRUNKARD'S REFORMATION, THE LONELY VILLA, THE SON'S RETURN, LINES OF WHITE ON A SULLEN SEA, HER FIRST BISCUITS, A CORNER IN WHEAT (Pre-DOLLIE bulletins from K. Niver, ed., BIOGRAPH BULLETINS)
Altman, "THE LONELY VILLA & Griffith's Paradigmatic Style", QUARTERLY REVIEW OF FILM STUDIES 6, 2, 123-134
Adams, "DWG & the Use of Offscreen Space", CINEMA JOURNAL XV, 2, 53-57
Hilenski, "DWG's Version of Browning's 'Pippa Passes'", LITERATURE/FILM QUARTERLY 4, 1, 76-86

January 27:

Biograph Bulletins for THE HOUSE W/CLOSED SHUTTERS, THE USURER, SORROWS OF THE UNFAITHFUL, WHAT SHALL WE DO W/OUR OLD?, ENOCH ARDEN, THE BROKEN DOLL, THE SMOKER, THE SPANISH GYPSY, KNIGHT OF THE ROAD
Allen, "Motion Picture Exhibition in Manhattan 1906-1912", CJ, Spring 79, 2-15
Merritt, "Rescued from a Perilous Nest", CJ, Autumn 81, 2-30
Bowser, "G's Film Career before THE ADVENTURES OF DOLLIE", GRFS 6, 1, 1-9
Gunning, "Weaving a Narrative", QRFS 6, 1, 11-25
Deutelbaum "DWG & the Possibilities of ENOCH ARDEN", QRFS 6, 1, 27-43

February 3:

Biograph Bulletins for THE TRANSFORMATION OF MIKE, IN THE DAYS OF '49, THE ADVENTURES OF BILLY, THE BATTLE, THE NEW DRESS, DEATH'S MARATHON, THE ROSE OF KENTUCKY, THE PAINTED LADY, THE BROKEN CROSS
Merritt, "Mr. G, THE PAINTED LADY & the Distractive Frame" in Deutelbaum, ed., THE IMAGE ON THE ART & EVOLUTION OF FILM, 147-152
Geduld, ed., FOCUS ON DWG 32-38

February 10:

Biograph Bulletins for ONE IS BUSINESS; THE OTHER CRIME, AN UNSEEN ENEMY, THE MUSKETEERS OF PIG ALLEY, THE GODDESS OF SAGEBRUSH GULCH, DWG's LAST BIOGRAPH FILMS
Gish, THE MOVIES, MR. GRIFFITH & ME, 117-130
Kepley, "THE MUSKETEERS OF PIG ALLEY & the Well-Made Sausage", L/A Q 6, 274-284
Simon, "An Approach to Point of View", FILM READER 4, 145-151
Vardac, STAGE TO SCREEN, 199-210

February 17:

Rothman, "JUDITH OF BETHULIA", THE I in CINEMA, unpub.
Petric, "THE AVENGING CONSCIENCE", FILM CRITICISM 6, 5-27
Brown, "The Great D.W.", ADVENTURES W/DWG, 14-49

February 24:

Geduld, "How I Made TBOAN", FOCUS ON DWG, 39-42
Silva, ed., FOCUS ON TBOAN, 22-40
Cuniberti, TBOAN, selected illus.

March 2:

Geduld, "The Rise & Fall of Free Speech in America", FOCUS ON DWG, 43-45
Merritt, "DWG's TBOAN: Forging New Meanings for the Old South" (unpub)
Simcovitch, "The Impact of G's TBOAN on the Modern KKK", JOURNAL OF POPULAR FILM 1, 1, 45-54
Petric, "Two Lincoln Assassinations by DWG", QRFS 3, 345-369

March 9 and March 16:

Geduld, FOCUS ON DWG, 46-55
Merritt, "On First Looking into G's Babylon" & Kepley, "INTOLERANCE & the Soviets", both in WIDE ANGLE 3, 12-27
Drew, "Historical Sources", DWG's INTOLERANCE, 31-139

March 23:

Naremore, "TRUE HEART SUSIE", QRFS 6, 1, 91-104
Merritt, "DWG Directs the Great War", QRFS 6, 1, 45-65
Lyons, "Hollywood & WWI", JPF 1, 1, 15-30
Belton, "The Art of the Melodramatic Style", THE SILENT PICTURE 15, 28-32

April 6:

Geduld, FOCUS ON DWG, 56-62
Rothman, "True Heart Griffith" (unpub)
Kepley, "G's BROKEN BLOSSOMS", QRFS 3, 1, 37-47

Brown, "G's Family Discourse", QRFS 6, 1, 67-80
Lesage, "BROKEN BLOSSOMS Artful Racism, Artful Rape, JUMP CUT 26, 51-55

April 13:

Cadbury, "Theme Felt Life & the Last-Minute Rescue", FILM QUARTERLY, Fall 74, 39-49

April 20:

Geduld, FOCUS ON DWG, 62-68
Lennig, "The Birth of WAY DOWN EAST", QRFS 6, 1, 105-116
Kozloff, "Where Wessex Meets New England", L/F Q 13, 35-41
Vineburg, "The Restored WAY DOWN EAST", FQ 39, 54-57

Winter 1988

HUMANITIES 279
THE EARLY FILMS OF ALFRED HITCHCOCK

"Some films are slices of life, mine are slices of cake."

Instructor: Bill Vincent
Class Hours: 3:00-5:00 p.m. TWTh. Films will be shown Tuesday and Wednesday
afternoons; Thursday afternoons will be devoted to lecture
and discussion.
        Note: The same film will be shown both Tuesday and Wednesday. You
are expected to attend both showings. As Hitchcock him-
self said, his films are meant to be seen at least twice,
since the first time through one tends to get lost in the
plot and miss the nuances.
        Note: Some of the films run longer than two hours: you
must, therefore, be prepared occasionally to stay till 5:30.
Office: 521 S. Kedzie
Office Hours: 11-12 TWTh; 1:30-2:30 W; and by appointment
Phone: 355-9534
Assigned Readings: Francois Truffaut, HITCHCOCK (revised edition)
                 Tom Ryall, ALFRED HITCHCOCK AND THE BRITISH CINEMA
                 Richard Abel, "NOTORIOUS: Perversion Par Excellence"
                 Michael Renov, "From Identification to Ideology: the Male
                    System of Hitchcock's NOTORIOUS"
Grading: Grades will be curved on the basis of total points, with 140 points
possible:

Class Participation:	10	points
2 500-word papers, 10 points each:	20	points
3 quizzes, 10 points each:	30	points
2000-word paper:	30	points
Final Examination:	50	points
TOTAL:	140	points

ASSIGNMENTS

Jan. 6 & 7   Film: THE LODGER (1926)
                 Reading: Truffaut, 11-77

Jan. 12, 13, 14 Film: THE THIRTY-NINE STEPS (1935)
                 Readings: Truffaut, 77-103; Ryall, Chap. 6

Jan. 19, 20, 21 Film: YOUNG AND INNOCENT (1937)
                 Reading: Truffaut, 105-116
                 Quiz: Quiz # 1 will be given on 21 January.

Jan. 26, 27, 28 Film: THE LADY VANISHES (1938)
                 Readings: Truffaut, 116-125; Ryall, chap. 7
                 Short Paper: First 500-word paper due on 28 January

Feb. 2, 3, 4   Film: REBECCA (1940)
                 Reading: Truffaut 127-143

100

Feb. 9, 10, 11   Film: SHADOW OF A DOUBT (1943)
                  Reading: Truffaut, 145-161
                  Quiz: Quiz # 2 will be given on 11 February

Feb. 16, 17, 19   Film: NOTORIOUS (1946)
                  Readings: Truffaut, 163-177; Abel; Renov

Feb. 23, 24, 25   Film: STAGE FRIGHT (1950)
                  Reading: Truffaut, 179-191
                  Short Paper: Second 500-word paper due 25 February

Mar. 1, 2, 3   Film: ROPE (1949)
                  Reading: Truffaut,
                  Quiz: Quiz # 3 will be given on 3 March

Mar. 8, 9, 10   Film: STRANGERS ON A TRAIN (1951)
                  Reading: Truffaut, 193-208, 345-348
                  Long Paper: 2000-word paper due 10 March

Mar. 19   FINAL EXAMINATION (10:00-noon)

                         RATIONALE
These are the basic premises of the class:
    1. In studying Hitchcock's films, we are studying the work of a great artist.
    2. In studying his work, we are concerned with both content and technique.
    3. In studying his art we are studying Hitchcock himself.
    4. In studying this artist, we are studying the whole Art of film.

The great danger in studying Hitchcock's films is that one can get lost in the
plots. Although the plots of his films are exciting, they should not blind us
to the sub-texts of the films. We must be aware of two major sub-texts--the
thematic sub-text and the technique sub-text. Of these two sub-texts, the
second--technique--is employed to intensify the effect of the first--theme.
Like any great artist, Hitchcock knows his medium thoroughly, and he uses its
resources as deftly as Rembrandt used the resources of 17th-century painting.
Hitchcock was famous for exercising control over all aspects of the film--
script, casting, costuming, sets, camera, editing, music, sound, special
effects. Little wonder that the French critics of the 1950s saw "Hitch" as the
perfect exemplar of their "auteur" theory--i.e., that the director is the
film's author.

Among the techniques we shall be considering are these: narrative structure,
characterization, point of view, motifs, mise-en-scene and mise-en-frame,
editing, casting, performance, sets and costumes, sound, special effects.

Among the themes we shall be considering are these: Good versus Evil;
universal guilt; reality versus illusion as revealed in the theatricality of
presentation, acting, and plot; male-female relations; salvation through
involvement; Woman as Eve; international politics; the films as autobiographical statements; the films as fetishes to ward off inner spirits--especially
leath.

When asked what he wanted engraved on his tombstone, Hitchcock suggested, "This
is what happens to bad little boys."

                            101

HUM 279
EARLY FILMS OF HITCHCOCK

LONG PAPER ASSIGNMENT

Length: 2000 words
Due: Last day of class
Topics: Choose a topic from category I or category II.

I. Consideration of a major theme in Hitchcock´s films.
    The purpose of this topic is to do a thematic analysis of Hitchcock´s early
    films. The approach to take is to develop the theme, using the films as
    illustrations and for evidence. What I do <u>not</u> want is for you simply to go
    through the films one by one and discuss the theme as it pertains to that
    film alone. You should have a thesis and develop it: the thesis should
    probably center on Hitchcock´s own view of the world and how that view
    developed--i.e., is there a difference between the first films and the
    later ones?
Possible Themes:
    1) Parent-child relationships (particularly father-daughter or mother-son)
    2) The theatrical element: blurring of the line between reality and illusion
    3) Women in a world dominated by men.
    4) Guilt, innocence, and divine providence.
    5) Other? Check with me.

II. Consideration of Hitchcock´s techniques:
    Here you will want to consider one aspects of Hitchcock´s technique and
    discuss a) his general approach in using this technique; b) variations in
    the way he uses it; c) why he uses it: for what effect. In other words,
    what is expected here is a fairly comprehensive analysis and categorization
    of the particular technical aspect.
Possible Techniques:
    1) Use of sound
    2) Use of unusual angles
    3) Use of tracking shots
    4) Use of the deus ex machina in narrative
    5) Use of diegetic hooks
    6) Editing techniques
    7) Other (consult me)

Sources: All of the films we´ve seen in class (except THE LODGER unless you
    want to), plus one other film from the early period (<u>not</u> the one you did
    your second short paper on). This may be one of the ones on reserve or one
    you get for yourself, but it must be from the period before 1951. Of the
    ones we´ve seen in class, most will be on reserve should you need to check
    something. You will want to use the Truffaut book, but you need not use
        any other secondary sources: the films will be your sources. If you do
        decide to use outside sources, please footnote any material or ideas
        taken from them.
Grading Criteria:
    The paper should be well written, neat--a final copy, not a rough draft.
    It should show 1) familiarity with the films, the lectures, the Truffaut
    book,and the discussion materials; 2) accurate and appropriate use of the
    film material; 3) intelligent development of the thesis; 5) organization
    and writing skills; and 6) originality of approach.

Winter 1988

SHORT PAPER ASSIGNMENTS

Short paper # 1:

Length: 400-500 words
Due: 28 January
Topic: Key Line approach to thematic analysis. Choose a key line from THE
LADY VANISHES. Quote it exactly, describing the exact circumstances in which
it is spoken, by whom and to whom. Discuss some thematic aspect of the film
from the point of view of this line. The more you can work in in terms of
techniques the better. Note: This paper calls for a thematic analysis, not a
plot summary. Assume that the reader knows the plot.

Short Paper # 2:

Length: 400-500 words
Due: 25 February
Topic: Analyze a film other than those seen in class. Possibilities:
BLACKMAIL, MURDER!, THE MAN WHO KNEW TOO MUCH (1934 version), SABOTAGE, JAMAICA
INN, SUSPICION, and MR. AND MRS. SMITH. You may do one of two things:
1. Write about the film in terms of one of the major themes we've been tracking
in class; or 2. write about the film in terms of its techniques.

IV. FILM AND LITERATURE

English 471
AMERICAN FILM AND FICTION AFTER WORLD WAR TWO

I. The War and Masculinity.
Jan. 14:   Introduction. Robert Aldrich/Ralph Meeker: Kiss Me, Deadly
                (1955)

Jan. 21:   Mickey Spillane: I, the Jury (1947).
                [U. S. Army Training Films: The U.S. Serviceman's Code of
                Conduct.]

Jan. 28:   Norman Mailer: The Naked and the Dead (1948)

II. The Cold War.
Feb. 4:   Howard Hawks/Christian Nyby: The Thing (1951)

Feb. 11:   Elia Kazan/Budd Schulberg/Marlon Brando/Eva Marie Saint/Rod
                Steiger/Karl Malden/Lee J. Cobb: On the Waterfront (1954)
                Eric Bentley: Thirty Years of Treason (Selections from
                testimony before the House UnAmerican Activities Committee)

III. Who Is An American?
Feb. 18:   J. D. Salinger: The Catcher in the Rye (1951)
                Ernest Hemingway: The Old Man and the Sea (1952)

Feb. 25:   Nicholas Ray/James Dean/Natalie Wood/Sal Mineo: Rebel
                Without a Cause (1955)

March 3:   James Baldwin: Go Tell It on the Mountain
                            : "The Black Boy Looks at the White Boy"
                (xerox)

March 10:   Joseph Mankiewicz/Sidney Poitier/Richard Widmark: No Way Out
                (1950)
                Norman Mailer: The White Negro
                [A. E. Van Vogt: Slan]

March 17:   Frank Tashlin/Jayne Mansfield/Tom Ewell/Edmond O'Brien: The
                Girl Can't Help It (1957)

IV. The Force of Nature.
March 24:   Elia Kazan/Marlon Brando/Jean Peters/Anthony Quinn: Viva
                Zapata (1952)

VACATION

April 7:   Jack Kerouac. On the Road (1951)
                Allen Ginsberg: Howl (1956)

April 14:   Anthony Mann/James Stewart/Arthur Kennedy/Rock Hudson: Bend
                of the River (1952)

April 21:   Walt Disney Productions: Nature's Half-Acre (1951)
                William Burroughs: Naked Lunch (1959)

107

Professor Leo Braudy

COURSE REQUIREMENTS

This course deals with the shape of a crucial period in American life, from the
end of World War Two to the election of John F. Kennedy as President. My
approach is through the films and fiction that appeared in those years. But
we will also consider some of the problems of American life and culture to
which many of those works addressed themselves and out of which they emerged:
the threat of Russia, the rising political consciousness of black Americans,
juvenile delinquency, the changing social and sexual relations between men and
women, and the expanding consumer economy that promised so much to so many.

There will be two papers required in the course, 5-8 pages in length, and a
final examination. The papers are due on February 18 and April 7. They can
deal with topics suggested by the instructor or on topics devised by the
student in consultation with the instructor that draw on the student's special
interests. Because we can only take a whirlwind tour of the 50s in this course,
it is always open to consider other works of the period--fiction, poetry, drama,
or films--in papers. Please remember to keep a copy of all written work you
turn in.

The films will be shown on the of the week in which they are discussed and it
is crucial that they be seen. Attendance at screenings and participation in
discussions is mandatory, and will be considered in the final grade.

SHORT LIST OF SUGGESTED READING
Alloway, Lawrence. Violent America: The Movies, 1946-1964.
Bentley, Eric, ed. Thirty Years of Treason.
Belfrage, Cedric. The American Inquisition, 1945-1960.
Caute, David. The Great Fear: The AntiCommunist Purge Under Truman and
Eisenhower.
Ciment, Michel. Kazan on Kazan.
Dickstein, Morris. "Cold War Blues," Partisan Review, 41(1974), 30-55.
Dowdy, Andrew. The Films of the Fifties.
Eisinger, Chester. Fiction of the Fifties.
Gow, Gordon. Hollywood in the Fifties.
Haskell, Molly. From Reverence to Rape.
Herndon, Venable. James Dean.
Hoffman, Daniel, ed. The Harvard Guide to Contemporary American Writing.
[since World War Two]
Hofstadter, Richard. Anti-Intellectualism in American Life.
Kanfer, Stefan. A Journal of the Plague Years.
Klein, Marcus, ed. The American Novel Since World War Two.
Levin, Murray. Political Hysteria in America.
Lukacs, John. A New History of the Cold War.
Mailer, Norman. Marilyn.
Meeropol, Michael and Robert. We Are Your Children.
Miller, Douglas T. and Nowack, Marion. The Fifties.
Nizer, Louis. The Implosion Conspiracy.
Rogin, Michael Paul. The Intellectuals and McCarthy: The Radical Specter.
Starobin, Joseph R. American Communism in Crisis, 1943-1957.
Stone, I. F. The Haunted Fifties.
Witter, Lawrence S. Cold War America: From Hiroshima to Watergate.

108

Comparative Literature 466

Spring, 1983
Prof. Keith Cohen

LITERATURE AND CINEMA
TENTATIVE SYLLABUS

<u>Date</u>		<u>Topic</u>	<u>Reading</u>	<u>Film</u> (3:30 and 7pm R. 155 Van Hise)
<u>Jan.</u>				
24	M	Introduction; organization	Panofsky in Mast,	Shorts by Lumière, Méliès, Porter
26	W	Comparing arts; hazards of analogy	p. 243	(Jan. 27)
31	M	Impressionism	*Cohen, p. 13 (whole chapter)	
<u>Feb.</u>				
2	W	Impressionism in art and lit.	Rec.: <u>Madame Bovary</u>, esp. Bk. II, 13; <u>Heart of Darkness</u>	#<u>Last Year at Marienbad</u> (Resnais) (Feb. 3)
7	M	Renaissance perspective; its distortion in <u>Marienbad</u> Art and technology	Benjamin in Mast, p. 406	
9	W	Syntheses of cinema, historically	Eisenstein, *<u>Film Form</u>, pp. 3–27	
14	M	The "novelistic"	Eisenstein in Mast, p. 394	
16	W	Syntheses of cinema, formally	Hauser, *<u>Social History of Art</u>, vol. 4, Chap 8	<u>Un Chien Andalou</u> (Andalusian Dog) (Feb. 17) (Buñuel)
21	M	Fundamentals of narrative, I	Bluestone in Mast, p. 406	
23	W	Artist/spectator; artist/reader	Eisenstein in Mast, p. 85, p. 101.	
28	M	Mimesis	Metz in Mast, p. 169	
<u>Mar.</u>				
2	W	Fundamentals of narrative, II	*Cohen, pp. 79–104	
7	M	EXAM (in class)		
9	W	Subject/object reversal	Stein, <u>Three Lives</u>	<u>Mildred Pierce</u> (Curtiz) (Mar 10)
14	M	Temporal distortions Woman/Stein/Joan Crawford	Humphrey, *<u>Stream of Consciousness</u>, pp. 23–61; Haskell in Mast, p. 505	
16	W	Non-chronological narration	Fuentes, <u>Death of Artemio Cruz</u>	<u>Potemkin</u> (Eisenstein) (Mar. 17)
21	M	Simultaneity	Joyce, <u>Ulysses</u>, Ch. 10 (pp. 219–55); Ch. 11–13 (pp. 256–382)	
23	W	Methods of montage	Eisenstein, <u>Film Form</u>, pp. 72–83	

*= On reserve in H/C/White – College Library
Mar. 26 – Apr. 4: SPRING RECESS

Apr.				
6	W	Narrative perspective	Joyce, <u>Ulysses</u>, Ch. 1-3 (pp. 2-51)	#<u>Persona</u> (Bergman) (Apr. 7)
11	M	Personae SHORT PAPER DUE (3-5 pages)	Faulkner, <u>The Sound and the Fury</u>	
13	W	Subjective visions	Woolf, <u>To the Lighthouse</u>	
18	M	Multiperspectivism	Humphrey, *<u>Stream of Consciousness</u>, pp. 85-111, pp. 1-22	
20	W	Montage of consciousness	Joyce, <u>Ulysses</u>, Ch. 7 (pp. 116-50); p. 74	#<u>Weekend</u> (Godard) (Apr. 21)
25	M	Voice	Joyce/Fuentes/Woolf Esp. Fuentes, p. 13ff. (1941), p. 87ff. (1924), p. 220ff. (1939), p. 242ff. (1955)	
27	W	Sound/image	Robbe-Grillet, <u>Jealousy</u>	#<u>Hiroshima mon amour</u> (Resnais) (Apr. 28)
May				
2	M	Voice; internal speech	Duras, <u>Hiroshima mon amour</u> Eisenstein, *<u>Film Form</u>, p. 84	
4	W	Representation **(Final paper prospectus due)**	Michelson in Mast, p. 617	
9	M	Mimesis (again); reality/ documentary	Robbe-Grillet, *<u>For a New Novel</u>, pp. 15-47,143-56	
11	W	(W)rap-up; lit./cinema/ modernism		

*=On reserve

#=Available on video in 274 Van Hise

BOOKS REQUIRED
Mast + Cohen, <u>Film Theory and Criticism</u>
Stein, <u>Three Lives</u>
Joyce, <u>Ulysses</u>
Faulkner, <u>The Sound and the Fury</u>
Woolf, <u>To the Lighthouse</u>
Robbe-Grillet, <u>Jealousy</u> (<u>La jalousie</u>)
Fuentes, <u>Death of Artemio Cruz</u> (<u>Muerte de</u> . . .)

BOOKS RECOMMENDED
K. Cohen, <u>Film and Fiction</u>
Eisenstein, <u>Film Form</u>
Hauser, <u>Social History of Art</u>, Vol. 4
Humphrey, <u>Stream of Consciousness in the Modern Novel</u>

Comparative Literature 466   Prof. Keith Cohen

		TOPIC	READING	FILM
September				
R	3	Intro; organization		
T	8	Impressionism	Panofsky in Mast, pp. 215–33	Marienbad (Resnais)
R	10	Renaissance perspective	Cohen, *Film & Fiction, pp. 13–37	(Wed. Sept. 9)
T	15	Impressionism–Art & Lit; Art & Technology	Rec: Heart of Darkness (Conrad)	Shorts by Lumiere, Meliès, Porter (Wed. Sept. 16)
R	17	Synthesis of cinema, historically	Benjamin in Mast, pp. 675–94 Eisenstein, *Film Forum, pp. 3–27	
T	22	The "novelistic"	Eisenstein in Mast, pp. 370–80	Metropolis (Lang)
R	24	Synthesis of cinema, formally	Hauser, *Social History of Art, in Mast Vol. 4, Chap. 8	(Wed. Sept. 23)
T	29	Fundamentals of Narrative, I	Bluestone in Mast, pp. 381–89	
R October	1	Artist/Spectator: artist/ reader	Eisenstein in Mast, pp. 90–123	
T	6	Mimesis	Metz in Mast, pp. 164–76 Fell, *Film & The Narrative Tradition	
R	8	Fundamentals of Narrative, II	*Cohen, pp. 79–104	
T	13	EXAM (in class)		
R	15	Subject/object reversal	Stein, Three Lives	
T	20	Temporal distortions	Humphrey, *Stream of Consciousness, pp. 23–61	Mildred Pierce (Curtiz) (Wed. Oct. 21)
		Woman as Narrator, Woman as object	Mulvey in Mast, pp. 803–16	
R	22	Non-chronological narration	Fuentes, Death of Artemio Cruz	
T	27	Simultaneity	Joyce, Ulysses, Ch. 10 (pp. 219– 55); Ch. 11–13 (pp. 256–382)	Potemkin (Eisenstein) (Wed. Oct. 28)
R	29	Methods of montage	Eisenstein, *Film Form, pp. 72–83	
November				
T	3	Narrative perspective	Joyce, Ulysses, Ch. 1–3 (pp. 2–51)	Persona (Bergman) (Wed. Nov. 4)
R	5	Personae SHORT PAPER DUE IN CLASS		
T	10	Subjectivity	Woolf, To the Lighthouse	
R	12	Multiperspectivism	Humphrey, *Stream of Consciousness, pp. 85–111, pp. 1–22	

T	17	Montage of Consciousness	Joyce _Ulysses_, Ch. 7 (pp. 116-50)	_Une Femme mariée_ (Godard)
R	19	Internal speech in cinema		(Wed. Nov. 18)
T	24	Voice	Eluard, _Capitale de la douleur_ Fuentes, _Artemio Cruz_, p. 13 ff., p. 87 ff., p. 220 ff., p. 242 ff.	
T	December 1	Sound/image	Simon, _Tryptich_	_Alphaville_ (Godard)
R	3	Poetry and Cinema; science fiction		(Wed. Dec. 2.)
T	8 10	Voice/internal speech Representation	Baumbach, _Chez Charlotte and Emily_; Duras, _Hiroshima mon amour_; Comolli in Mast, pp. 741-60	_Hiroshima mon amour_ (Resnais) (Wed. Dec. 9)
T	15	Intertextuality	Puig, _Kiss of the Spiderwoman_	

BIBLIOGRAPHY

1.   Gertrude Stein, Lectures in America
2.   Robbe-Grillet, Pour un nouveau roman (trans.) Toward a new novel
3.   Sergei Eisenstein, Film Form and Film Sense
4.   George Bluestone, Novels into Film
5.   Jean Mitry, Histoire du cinéma, vol. 1
6.   Henry James, The Art of the Novel, ed. R.P. Blackmur; The Future of the Novel, ed. Leon Edel
7.   Christian Metz, Essais sur la signification au cinéma, vols. 1 and 2
8.   Jean Mitry, Esthétique et psychologie du cinéma, vols. 1 and 2
9.   Rudolf Arnheim, Film as Art
10. Béla Balázs, Theory of the Film (trans. Edith Bone)
11. Maurice Bardèche and Robert Brasillach, The History of the Motion Pictures (trans. Iris Barry)
12. Roland Barthes, "Rhétorique le l'image" in Communications 4 (1964): 40-51
13. André Bazin, What is Cinema? (trans. Hugh Gray)
14. Joseph Warren Beach, The Twentieth Century Novel
15. Walter Benjamin, Illuminations (trans. H. Arendt)
16. La Revue des Lettres Modernes, 36-8 (Summer 1958)--(Special no. on Cinéma et roman)
17. Film: A Montage of Theories, ed. R.D. MacCann
18. Film: An Anthology, ed. Daniel Talbot
19. Cahiers du cinéma, 185 (Christmas, 1966) (Special no. on Film et Roman)
20. Joseph Frank, "Spatial Form in Modern Literature" in The Widening Gyre
21. Norman Friedman, "Point of View in Fiction: the Development of a Critical Concept," PMLA, 70 (1955) 1160-84.
22. Arnold Hauser, The Social History of Art, vol. 4
23. Robert Humphrey, Stream of Consciousness in the Modern Novel
24. Intelligence du cinématographe, ed. Marce L. Herbrer
25. Siegfried Kracauer, Theory of Film
26. Vachel Lindsay, The Art of the Moving Picture
27. Claude-Edmonde Magny, L'age du roman américain
28. Hans Meyerhoff, Time in Literature
29. Edgar Morin, Le Cinéma ou l'homme imaginaire
30. Edward Murray, The Cinematic Imagination
31. Robert Richardson, Literature and Film
32. Marie-Claire Ropars-Wuilleumier, De la littérature au cinéma

33. Francoise Van Rossum-Guyon, "Point de vue ou perspective narrative" _Poétique_ 4 (1970): 476-97

34. Peter Wollen, _Signs and Meaning in the Cinema_

35. A. Nicholas Vardac, _From Stage to Screen_

36. A. A. Mendilow, _Time in the Novel_

Professor Linda Dittmar

Narrative Art in the Novel and Film

"Narrative Art in the Novel and Film" is an advanced undergraduate English Major course which also counts towards a "Film Concentration" within UMB's Communication Certificate. Classes meet twice a week for a total of 5-6 credit hours. Some sophomore level preparation in English is a prerequisite, and about a quarter of the class has taken "Film Analysis" and occasionally other film courses. The expectation is that students will be careful writers and experienced readers, but not specialists in the novel, film, narrativity, or twentieth century art movements. They are mature, self-supporting, commuting adults (average age is twenty five), who bring to the course diverse life experiences.

"Narrative Art" guides students towards close scrutiny of increasingly difficult novels and films as these raise complex questions about representation and verisimilitude. It questions the "transparency" assumed by realist practices and highlights, instead, the shaping activity that sustains narrative. Putting the notion of "truth" in crisis, the course posits subjectivity and frank artifice as valid narrative concerns that fit in with broader aesthetic, philosophical, historic, and political developments. Its ongoing comparison of novels and films sustains this emphasis, in that the comparative study of the two media helps uncover issues of authorial intervention and audience reception. Thus, with one exception ("An Occurrence at Owl Creek Bridge"), the course does not concern adaptations; it uses its one adaptation only to foreground questions of formation and rhetoric as more central to its concerns than questions of fidelity.

Novels and films are the course's primary materials. Secondary readings include Giannetti's <u>Understanding Movies</u>, Forster's <u>Aspects of the Novel</u>, and a quantity of xeroxed materials. (See "Bibliographic Note" below.) With the exception of Giannetti and Forster, students tend to find the secondary readings difficult even when they are not current "state of the art" theory. Some of these readings get in-class attention, some are optional, and even the rest are reassuringly defined as "secondary." The course aims to familiarize students with such writing, but its main goal is to help them become critical readers of difficult novels and films, and to make them aware of their own activity while doing so. Thus, for all the historic and national diversity of its materials, the course sequences its formal and thematic considerations tightly. Taught successfully since 1970, its syllabus has undergone only modest changes. Some reflect a need for variety while others test new propositions (e.g. the use of <u>The Other Francisco</u> to replace <u>Last Year in Marienbad</u>). At one point the course had a unit on documentary; later on it acquired a feminist unit (work by Duras, Deren, Dulac, and Woolf) to counterbalance the predominantly masculinist orientation of the material. The film version of <u>Kiss of the Spider Woman</u> may be added next. Assigned secondary readings change to reflect these developments as well as the evolution of film and literary theory and criticism.

116

Professor Linda Dittmar
Narrative Art in the Novel and Film

Syllabus

Week 1:   Introduction to the course.

          Film Screening: Pather Panchali (Ray 1956).

          Reading: 1)   Start Giannetti's Understanding Movies. (The dates
                         below pace you, but try to read faster and finish by
                         week 4).

                         Discussion of Pather Panchali.

                    2)   Forster, Aspects of the Novel.

Week 2:   Film Screening: Rashomon (Kurasawa 1951).

          Fiction: Akutagawa, "In a Grove" and "Rashomon" (in Rashomon and
                    Other Stories, New York: Liveright, 1970).

          Reading: 1)   Kaminsky, "On Literary Realism."

                    2)   (Halperin) Giannetti through Chapter 3.

                    3)   Bluestone, "The Limits of the Novel and the Limits
                         of Film."

                    4)   Chatman, "What Novels Can Do That Films Can't,"
                         (Critical Inquiry).

Week 3:   Fiction: Henry James, The Turn of the Screw (1898).

          Reading: 1)   Lubbock, "The Craft of Fiction: Picture, Drama, and
                         Point of View," (Scholes).

                    2)   Booth, "Types of Narration" (Scholes).

          Film Screening: "An Occurrence at Owl Creek Bridge" (Enrico 1963).

          Fiction: Bierce, "An Occurrence at Owl Creek Bridge."

          Reading: 1)   Cunliffe, "An Occurrence at Owl Creek Bridge,"
                         (Barrett and Erskine).

                    2)   Bellone, "Outer Space and Inner Time," (Barrett and
                         Erskine).

                    3)   Erskine, "Language and Theme," (Barret and Erskine).

Week 4:   Film Screening: The Love of Jeanne Ney (Pabst 1927).

          Reading: 1)   Edel, "Novel and Camera" (Halperin).

                    2)   Bazin, "The Evolution of the Language of Cinema."

117

Fiction: Ehrenbourg, Selection from The Love of Jeanne Ney (New York: Greenwood, 1968).

Week 5: Film Screening: Battleship Potemkin (Eisenstein 1925).

Reading: 1) Schorer, "Technique as Discovery" (Scholes).

2) Giannetti through Chapter 5.

3) Giannetti Chapter 11.

Recommended:
1) Shot-by-Shot analysis of Potemkin (Mayer).

2) Barthes, "The Third Meaning and "Diderot, Brecht, Eisenstein."

Week 6: Fiction: Nathanael West, Miss Lonelyhearts (1933).

Fiction: Vladimir Nabokov, Invitation to a Beheading (1938).

Week 7: Film Screening: The Cabinet of Dr. Caligari (Wiene 1919).

Reading: Kracauer , "Caligari."

Recommended: Giannetti Chapters 6-10.

Week 8: Fiction: John Hawkes, The Cannibal (1949).

Recommended: Sontag, "Fascinating Fascism" (NYRB).

Week 9: Film Screening: Hiroshima Mon Amour (Resnais 1959).

Film Script: Marguerite Duras, Hiroshima Mon Amour.

Reading: 1) Bazin, "Marginal Notes on Eroticism in the Cinema."

2) Metz, "Story/Discourse (A Note on Two Kinds of Voyeurism)" and "The Fiction Film and its Spectator."

Recommended: Dittmar, "Fashioning and Re-fashioning" (Mosaic).

Week 10: Fiction: Virginia Woolf, To The Lighthouse (1927).

Recommended: Virginia Woolf, "Professions for Women" (Women and Writing).

Week 11: Film Screening: The Smiling Madame Beudet (Dulac 1923).
Meshes of an Afternoon (Deren 1943).

Reading: 1) Richardson, "Verbal Language and Visual Language", Marcus.

2) Linden, "The Storied Word" (both in Marcus).

3) Abel, "La Souriante Madam Beudet and L'Inondation."

Week 12: Fiction: William Faulkner, <u>The Sound and the Fury</u> (1929).

Week 13: Film Screening: <u>The Other Francisco</u> (Giral 1975).

          Reading: Hillis Miller, "Ariadne's Thread: Repetition and the
                          Narrative Line" (Valdes).

          Recommended: De Lauretis, "Through the Looking Glass: Women,
                          Cinema, and Language."

Week 14: Fiction: Manuel Puig, <u>Kiss of the Spider Woman</u> (1976).

          Recommended: 1) Williams, "White Zombie" (<u>Jump Cut</u>).

                          2) Russo, <u>The Celluloid Closet</u>.

                          3) Barthes, "Introduction to the Structural
                              Analysis of Narrative.

                          4) Barthes, "Upon Leaving the Movie Theater"
                              (<u>Apparatus</u>).

Week 15: Film Screening: <u>Dames</u> (Enright; dance by Busby Berkeley, 1934).

          Reading: 1) Fischer, "The Image of Woman as Image: The
                          Optical Politics of Dames" (Erens).

                      2) Benjamin, "The Work of Art in the Age of
                          Mechanical Reproduction."

Bibliographic Note

In the absence of an anthology of appropriate secondary readings, the course depends on assorted articles assembled from diverse sources. Many have been anthologized; some are chapters in single-author books; some are currently out of print. The following citations concern only secondary readings, not currently available editions of assigned novels and film scripts. (Citations of out of print novels appear parenthetically in the syllabus).

Works Cited

Abel, Richard. <u>French Cinema: The First Wave, 1915-1929</u>. Princeton: Princeton UP, 1984.

Aumont, Jacques. <u>Montage Eisenstein</u>. Bloomington: Indiana UP, 1987.

Barrett, Gerald R. and Thomas L. Erskine, eds. <u>From Fiction to Film</u>: <u>Ambrose Bierce's "An Occurrence at Owl Creek Bridge</u>." Encino: Dickenson, 1973.

Barthes, Roland. <u>Image--Music--Text</u>. New York: Hill & Wang, 1977.

Bazin, Andre. <u>What is Cinema</u>? Berkeley: California UP, Vol. I, 1967 and Vol II, 1971.

Bluestone, George. <u>Novels into Films</u>. Berkeley: California UP, 1966.

Benjamin, Walter. <u>Illuminations: Essays and Reflections</u>. New York: Schocken, 1969.

Bordwell, David. <u>Narration in the Fiction Film</u>. Madison: Wisconsin UP, 1985.

Branigan, Edward. <u>Point of View in the Cinema: A Theory of Narration and Subjectivity in Classical Film</u>. New York, Mouton, 1984.

Chanan, Michael. <u>The Cuban Image</u>. London: BFI; Bloomington: Indiana UP, 1985.

Chatman, Seymour. <u>Story and Discourse: Narrative Structure in Fiction and Film</u>. Ithaca: Cornell UP, 1978.

---. "What Novels Can Do That Films Can't." <u>Critical Inquiry</u> 8 (1980): 121-140.

De Lauretis, Teresa. Alice Doesn't: Feminism, Semiotics, Cinema. Bloomington: Indiana UP, 1984.

Dittmar, Linda. "Fashioning and Re-fashioning: Framing Narratives in the Novel and Film." Film/Literature. George E. Toles, ed. (Winnipeg: MOSAIC, 1983).

Eisenstein, Sergei. The Film Sense. New York: Harvest, 1947.

---. Film Form. New York: Harvest, 1949.

Erens, Patricia. Sexual Stragagems: The World of Women in Film. New York: Horizon, 1979.

Forster, E.M. Aspects of the Novel. New York: Harvest, 1954.

Giannetti, Louis. Understanding Movies. Englewood Cliffs: Prentice Hall, 1987.

Hak Kyung Cha, Teresa, Ed. Apparatus: Cinematographic Apparatus: Selected Readings. New York: Tanan Press, 1981.

Halperin, John, Ed. The Theory of the Novel: New Essays. New York: Oxford UP, 1974.

Kracauer, Siegfried. From Caligari to Hitler: A Psychological History of the German Film. Princeton: Princeton UP, 1947.

Marcus, Fred H., Ed. Film and Literature: Contrasts in Media. Scranton: Chandler, 1971.

Mayer, David. Sergei M. Eisenstein's Potemkin: A Shot-by-Shot Presentation. New York: Grossman, 1972.

Metz, Christian. The Imaginary Signifier: Psychoanalysis and the Cinema. Bloomington: Indiana UP, 1982.

Mitchell, W.J.T. On Narrative. Chicago UP, 1981.

Russo, Vito. The Celluloid Closet: Homosexuality in the Movies. New York: Harper and Row, 1981.

Scholes, Robert, ed. Approaches to the Novel: Materials for a Poetics. Scranton: Chandler, 1966.

Sontag, Susan. "Fascinating Fascism." New York Review of Books (February 6, 1975).

Valdes, Mario J. and Owen J. Miller, Eds. Interpretation of Narrative. Toronto: Toronto UP, 1978.

Waugh, Patricia. Metafiction: The Theory and Practice of Self-Conscious Fiction. New York: Metheun, 1984.

Williams, Tony. "White Zombie--Haitian Horror." Jump Cut 28 (Spring 1983).

LITERATURE AND FILM   Miriam Hansen
01: 354: 310: 01 (CAC)   Off.: 047 Murray
Spring 1985   Tel.: 932-7332

LECTURES: M2, Th2; Murray 116
SCREENINGS: Th7,8,9; Van Dyck 211
TEXTS: Mary Shelley, Frankenstein
                Charles Dickens, A Tale of Two Cities
                James M. Cain, Mildred Pierce
                Joseph Conrad, Heart of Darkness
                William Faulkner, Absalom, Absalom!
                + xeroxes on reserve at Alexander Library

REQUIREMENTS: 1. Attendance at both lectures and screenings is considered essential
                to this course. Students who miss more than five classes will fail the
                course unless a note from the Dean's Office can satisfactorily explain
                the cause of absence. Keep in mind that screenings cannot be repeated (most
                of the films have to be rented from commercial distributors) and that the
                quality of your written work will crucially depend upon first-hand
                knowledge of each film. Films preceded by an * may not be discussed
                extensively in class but are also required.
                     2. Readings. Students are expected to have completed the readings
                before the meetings for which they were assigned.
                     3. Papers. One short paper (3-4pp.), due February 18, and one slightly
                longer paper (5-6pp.), due April 15. Late papers will be penalized and
                cannot be accepted without prior consultation. Papers should be typed, but
                not on onion skin or corrasible bond.
                     4. Exams. A midterm (March 11) and a 3-hr. final exam.

Jan.21-24:   ASPECTS OF NARRATIVE: STORY/DISCOURSE, TIME, POINT OF VIEW

                Mary Shelley, Frankenstein (1818)

Jan.28-31:   FILM VERSIONS OF THE FRANKENSTEIN MYTH: GERMAN EXPRESSIONISM; HOLLYWOOD

                Clips: The Golem(1920), The Cabinet of Dr.Caligari(1919), Metropolis (1926)

                Frankenstein (James Whale, 1931; 71 min.)
                Bride of Frankenstein (Whale, 1935; 80 min.)

Feb. 4-7:   DIFFERENCES BETW. LITERARY & CINEMATIC NARRATIVE; STRATEGIES OF ADAPTATION

                Shelley, Frankenstein

                *The Enigma of Kaspar Hauser (Werner Herzog, Germany 1974; 109 min.)

Feb. 11-14:   DIFFERENCES BETWEEN THE MEDIA; PROBLEMS OF ADAPTATION

                Ambrose Bierce, "An Occurrence at Owl Creek Bridge" (xerox)

                An Occurrence at Owl Creek Bridge (Lehac/Roubaix, France 1962, 26 min.)
                *The Red Badge of Courage ([Stephen Crane] John Huston, 1951; 69 min.)

February 18:   FIRST PAPER DUE

Feb. 18-21:   HOLLYWOOD AND THE CLASSICAL NOVEL; THE POLITICS OF ADAPTATION

               Charles Dickens A Tale of Two Cities (1859)
               John Ellis, "The Literary Adaptation" (xerox)

               A Tale of Two Cities (Jack Conway, 1935; 121 min.)

Feb. 25-28:   HOLLYWOOD AND THE CONTEMPORARY NOVEL; TEXTUAL/SEXUAL COMPLEXITY IN FILM NOIR

               James M. Cain, Mildred Pierce (1941)

               Mildred Pierce (Michael Curtiz, 1945; 111 min.)

March 4-7:   THE ROLE OF THE NARRATOR: MEANING, MEDIATION, COMPLICITY

               Joseph Conrad, Heart of Darkness (1902)

               Apocalypse Now (Francis Coppola, 1979; 150 min.)

March 11:   MIDTERM

March 11-14:   MULTIPLE FLASHBACK NARRATION; MASS MEDIA, MODERNISM AND AUTHORSHIP

               Citizen Kane (Orson Welles, 1941; 119 min.)

March 25-28:   THE STRUGGLE FOR AUTHORITY; NARRATION, REPETITION AND DEFENSE

               William Faulkner, Absalom, Absalom! (1936)

               Citizen Kane

April 1-4:   Absalom, Absalom! cont.; PERSPECTIVISM cont.

               Rashomon (Akira Kurosawa, Japan 1950; 88 min.)

April 8-11:   TIME, SPACE, CONTRADICTION AND AMBIGUITY; NARRATION AS SEDUCTION

               Alain Robbe Grillet, excerpts from For a New Novel (xerox)
               Last Year at Marienbad (Robbe-Grillet/Alain Resnais, France 1961; 93 min.)

April 15:   SECOND PAPER DUE

April 15-18:   BRECHTIAN CINEMA (I): ALIENATION/DISTANCIATION; HISTORY AND DISCOURSE

               Alexander Kluge, "Anita G." (xerox)
               Yesterday Girl (Kluge, Germany 1966; 88 min.)

               Further reading: Benjamin, "What Is Epic Theater?" (xerox)

April 22-25:   BRECHTIAN CINEMA (II): POLITICS, ECONOMY, SEXUALITY, SIGNIFICATION

               Two or Three Things I Know about Her (Jean-Luc Godard, Fr. 1967; 95 min.)

April 29-   THE BRECHTIAN TRADITION AND WOMEN'S CINEMA
  May 2:
               The All-Round Reduced Personality (Helke Sander, Germany 1977; 98 min.)

123

English 940x, FILM NARRATIVE   Annette Insdorf
Mondays, 1:15 - 5, 118 Mathematics Hall (basement)   Fall 1987

Texts: Anthony Burgess, A Clockwork Orange (Ballantine)
           Gunter Grass, The Tin Drum (Vintage)
           Klaus Mann, Mephisto (Penguin)
           Bill Nichols (ed.), Movies and Methods, Vol. II (U. Cal. Press)
           William Shakespeare, King Lear (Signet)

Sept. 14   Introduction to Cinematic Vocabulary:
           THE CONFORMIST, Bernardo Bertolucci

Sept. 21   The Camera as Narrator:
           TOUCH OF EVIL, Orson Welles
     Read Nichols Intro, pp. 1-25, and Patrick Ogle, pp. 58-78

Sept. 28   Lighting, Color and Visual Texture:
           THE LAST PICTURE SHOW, Peter Bogdanovich
     Read Edward Branigan, pp. 121-143, and Laura Mulvey, pp. 303-315

Oct. 5   From Novel to Screen I: (Symbolism)
           THE TIN DRUM, Volker Schlondorff
     Read The Tin Drum

Oct. 12   The Soundtrack:
           THE CONVERSATION, Francis Ford Coppola
     Read Edward Buscombe, pp. 83-92, and Charles Altman, pp. 517-531

Oct. 19   Montage:
           HIROSHIMA, MON AMOUR, Alain Resnais
     Read Ruby Rich, pp. 340-358, and Mary Ann Doane, pp. 565-576

Oct. 26   Literary Adaptation II: (Note: Class will be held at the Orion Screening Room,
           711 5th Ave. 6 floor)
           RAN, Akira Kurosawa
     Read King Lear
     PAPER DUE

Nov. 2   school holiday

Nov. 9   Literary Adaptation III:
           BLOW-UP, Michelangelo Antonioni
     Read Cortazar (xerox), and Gaylyn Studlar, pp. 602-621

Nov. 16   The Actor as Auteur:
           MEPHISTO, Istvan Szabo
     Read Mephisto, and Robin Wood, pp. 649-660

Nov. 23   Voice-over Narration:
           BADLANDS, Terrence Malick
     Read Paul Sandro, pp. 391-407; Stephen Heath, pp. 509-514; Christian Metz,
     543-549

Nov. 30   Literary Adaptation IV: (Music and Stylization)
           A CLOCKWORK ORANGE, Stanley Kubrick
     Read A Clockwork Orange

Dec. 7   Self-Reflexive Cinema:
           THE STATE OF THINGS, Wim Wenders
     Read Dana Polan, pp. 661-672, and Dudley Andrew, pp. 625-632
     PAPER DUE
                              124

Professor Charles J. Maland, University of Tennessee

FILM AND LITERATURE

English Departments (and English Majors) seem to love this
kind of course. It was the only regularly taught film course on the
books when I arrived at Tennessee in 1978. While a course like
this can too easily fall into the trap of demonstrating film's
inferiority as an art form ("let's look at literary classics and
show how inadequately film adapts them to the screen"), the course
below aims to avoid this trap. It is primarily a course in comparative aesthetics, structured around three chronologically presented
units: film and literary language, adaptations, and a comparison
of two accomplished and thematically related works (one prose
fiction, one film).

Film and Literature
English 3445

TR 9-11:30

Film and Literature might be more accurately titled after
an anthology on the subject called Film and/as Literature. Not
only will we spend time comparing and contrasting film with short
stories, novels, and plays, but we will also consider film as a
kind of narrative literature itself, one which communicates through
edited images and sounds to represent and comment on human value
and experience. In effect we will be studying comparative
aesthetics.

The course is divided into three segments. The first but
very important segment will concentrate on how film communicates
in a way different from written literature. We will, in a sense,
learn the "language" of film. The second and longest segment will
focus on adaptations. In it we will consider what happens when
written literature is transformed into film. In the final segment,
a thematic one, we will examine two works dealing with the theme
of approaching death and its impact on life. By the end of the
course you should be able to do the following:

1. to discuss in detail the differences in the way film and
   written literature communicate (in particular, you should be
   able to define film and literary terms and to identify them
   when you encounter them)
2. to compare in careful detail the literary works we read and the
   film adaptations we see this term
3. to compare and contrast how the final two works in the class
   treat a similar theme and use the strengths of their media to
   do so
4. to analyze perceptively works of film and literature, recog-
   nizing the formal similarities and differences of the media

REQUIRED BOOKS:

The American Short Story, Vol. II, ed. Calvin Skaggs
Ordinary People, Judith Guest
The Death of Ivan Ilych and other Stories, Leo Tolstoy
Readings in Film and Literature (On reserve in Hodges Library--
    see below)

RECOMMENDED BOOK:

Film Art, David Bordwell and Kristin Thompson

Film Art and several other texts related to our topic of
study are available on reserve in Hodges Library (see below).

PAPER:

Everyone in the class will write one paper, typewritten and
due February 19, of around 2000-2500 words dealing with how well
one of the following films adapts its literary source. To do
the paper you will need to read the work carefully and see the
film at least twice so you are familiar with the cinematic style
as well as the narrative. You may write on one of the following:
  a. From Skaggs, short stories by Hawthorne, Twain, or
      Gaines.
  b. Alice Walker's The Color Purple and the Spielberg film
      (if the film is available on videotape by then.)
  c. John Fowles' The French Lieutenant's Woman and the 1981
      Karel Reisz film.
  d. Paul Thoreaux's Mosquito Coast or Beth Henley's Crimes
      of the Heart and their recent adaptations. See the films
      soon if your're thinking about these possibilties.
I am open to other possibilities if you have other works you would
like to propose. But please clear your suggestion with me before
moving ahead with the paper.

GRADING:

First short exam: 20%
Paper: 30%
Final exam: 30%
Class participation: 20%

CLASS PROCEDURES:

CLASS ATTENDANCE IS IMPERATIVE. Films will be shown on assigend
dates, and those we have rented must go back immediately to the
distributor. In addition, since we will spend much of our class
time, especially after the first two meetings, in directed discussion, it is important for you to keep up with the assigned reading.
We may have an occasional short quiz at the start of the class (they
may not be made up).

Reading and Viewing Schedule

****MEET IN HODGES LIBRARY for screenings on all the days
that have an asterisk before them below. All other meetings
are in HSS 203.

JANUARY

  8: Introduction: Film and the Other Arts

 13: Film and Literary Language, I--RFL, #1 (recommended:
     Bordwell, Chapters 4-7)
 15: Film and Literary Language, II--See Toys and discuss
     "The Death of the Ball Turret Gunner" (RFL, #2)

 20: Film and Literary Language, III--Occurrence at Owl Creek
     Bridge (RFL, #3)
 22: Short Exam on Film Language; Introduction to Adaptations
     (RFL, #4 and 5)

*27: Narration versus Dramatization: "The Greatest Man in the
     World," (Skaggs, 301-363, and RFL, #6)
*29: Can Film Adapt Psychological Fiction? "The Jilting of
     Granny Weatherall" (Skaggs, 228-300)

FEBRUARY

 *3: Art versus Life: "Paul's Case" (Skaggs, 160-95)
 *5: Faulkner and Film: "Barn Burning" (Skaggs, 374-407)

 10: Film and Drama: Read "Iphegenia in Aulis"
 12: See Cacoyannis' Iphegenia (RFL, #7); begin discussion

 17: Finish discussion of Iphegenia; discuss "The Greatest Gift"
     (RFL, #8)
 19: See Capra's It's a Wonderful Life

 24: Discuss two versions of Wonderful Life
 26: Film and the Novel: read all of Ordinary People (Guest)

MARCH

 *3: View Redford's Ordinary People
  5: Discussion of Ordinary People; read and begin discussing
     "The Death of Ivan Ilych" (Tolstoy)

*10: View Kurosawa's Ikiru
 12: Discuss "Ivan Ilych" and Ikiru; course summary

 17: Final Exam, 10-11:40 a.m. (alternative period)

127

Reserve Reading

I have placed a number of books on reserve in the Dunford
Hall Reserve Reading Room. The books all treat issues
related to film study generally or to the relationship between
film and literature. As you prepare your paper for the class, you
may scan some of the articles or chapters as a way to stimulate
your thinking about the topic you're writing on. (For example,
Mast's book below reprints a prominent essay on film and theater
by Susan Sontag, while Harrington's anthology has sections on film
and drama, film and the novel, and so on.)

Morris Beja, Film and Literature
David Bordwell and Kristin Thompson, Film Art (2nd ed.)
Keith Cohen, Fiction and Film
John Harrington, ed., Film and/as Literature
Gerald Mast and Marshall Cohen, eds., Film Theory and Criticism
    (3rd ed.)
James Monaco, How to Read a Film
Nicholl, Alardyce, Film and Drama
Bill Nichols, ed., Movies and Methods

Assigned Readings on Reserve

The eight documents listed below are required reading for the course
and available in multiple copies in the Reserve Department.

1. Glossary of Film Terms
2. "Death of the Ball Turret Gunner" (R. Jarrell)
3. "Occurrence at Owl Creek Bridge"
4. "Film and Literature" (M. Beja)
5. "Toward a 'Politique des Adaptations'" (C. Eidsvick)
6. "Adaptations" (M. Beja)
7. Iphegenia in Aulis (Euripides)
8. "The Greatest Gift" (P. van Doren Stern)

        * * * * * * * * * *

Proposed Course: Film and the Liberal Arts (4 q.u.) Fred H. Marcus

Catalogue Description: Analytic study of film as a medium conveying messages
        from a range of disciplines and interrelated subject areas.

Expanded Description: The following films, representing the following
        disciplines, will be shown and analyzed.

   History: All the King's Men

            A study in political demagoguery closely paralleling the actual
            life of Huey Long of Louisiana.

            An Occurrence at Owl Creek Bridge

            A short film depicting an episode during the Civil War. It stresses
            the impact of war on men. Technically, it also reveals film's
            ability to manipulate time.

            A Time Out of War

            Another short film focusing on a brief encounter between two Yankee
            soldiers and a Confederate during the Civil War. It delineates the
            conflict between human dignity and the demands of war.

   Political Science: 1 + 1 = 3

            A very short animated film emphasizing that might may make right
            temporarily but it adds the concept that he who lives by the sword
            may also perish by the sword.

            Boomerang

            A feature film focusing on the courage needed to protect human rights
            when they are threatened by circumstantial evidence. It also
            examines the temptations of the political sin of omission.

            Born Yesterday

            A feature length comedy describing corruption in high governmental
            offices; it demonstrates that knowledge and awareness are necessary
            tools in trying to defeat the misuse of political power.

   Literature: Rhinoceros

            A short animated treatment of Ionesco's play about the dangers of
            conformity.

Young Goodman Brown

A short live-action film about American Puritanism and its values. It is useful in assessing the cultural assumptions of an early American society.

The Open Window

A short satirical film mocking the dull inanity of a middle class British family. It also serves as a superb contrast in media for student comparison of story and adaptation.

Pygmalion

A feature length film adapted from George Bernard Shaw's satiric play on the social status accorded people on the basis of external niceties of manner, speech, and appearance.

Music: ### Bolero

A short live-action film studying the preparation for a performance of Ravel's music by the Los Angeles Philharmonic.

Philosophy: ### Plato's Cave
The Cave

Two short films, one live-action and the other animated, depicting Plato's view of the responsibilities of a philosopher to his state and the dangers inherent in that responsibility.

Sociology: ### Two Men and a Wardrobe

A short film by Roman Polanski focusing on the treatment accorded two non-conformists who differ markedly from a violence-prone society.

Run!

A short live-action film examining the pace of a contemporary society and the implications of its rhythms.

Ersatz

A short Yugoslavian film satirizing our plastic society.

The Conference

A contemporary updating of a 2000 year old theme--what happens to a Christ-like figure in a contemporary world?

The Lottery

A short film adapted from Shirley Jackson's sardonic short story examining the dangers of unexamined traditions.

Visual Arts: The Eye of the Beholder

>A short live-action film demonstrating how different people perceive
>reality and how their perceptions stem from both preconceptions and
>assumptions. This film also lends itself to a study of how the
>cinematic medium can be used to manipulate "reality."

Frank Film

>A short animated film examining the life of the filmmaker. The images
>and sound tracks reflect both his and society's values.

In addition to analyzing the films, students will supplement their
viewing with relevant reading. For example, All the King's Men lends itself
to class reports on Huey Long, contrast with the Robert Penn Warren novel, or
newspaper and magazine reports on Huey Long as a political force for good and/or
evil.

Need for the Course:

>There is no parallel multi-disciplinary course combining film with the
>arts and social sciences in this university. Its subject matter makes
>it a rich integration of message and medium.

Support Needs:

>Of the twenty projected films, five will have to be rented. The total
>cost of rentals, insurance, and mailing will be under $200.

Faculty:

>This is a highly specialized course in which the primary faculty
>expertise must be in the area of film analysis and criticism as the
>common thread linking the varied subjects and films. It will be
>taught by Fred H. Marcus, Professor of English.

Facts:

>8 of these films have garnered one or more Academy Awards.
>4 of these films are feature films.
>5 of these films are animated.
>10 of these films are adaptations from a literary source. (1 novel,
>   3 plays, 1 essay, 5 short stories.)

131

ENG 378
Fall 1984

Studies in Popular Culture
Horror and Adventure: Fiction of the 1890s and Films of the 1970s

Professor G. Waller
1259 Patterson
257-1292

Office hours: M-F 9:30-10:30 and by appointment

In this course we will read several works of fiction that first
appeared at the end of the nineteenth century and compare each
work with an American film released during the 1970s. Almost all
of these texts will be adventure or horror stories of one sort or
another. Although the fictional works we will read are all
products of the nineteenth century (in particular, of Victorian
England), these stories have proven to be among the most
influential, well-known, and culturally significant stories of
the twentieth century. By moving back and forth between fiction
and film and between the 1890s and the 1970s we will be able, I
hope, to learn something about both periods and to raise
important questions about the cultural significance of horror and
adventure stories, stories which so often help to define for us
the nature of heroism and vulnerability, the role of men and
women, and the flaws and strengths of our civilization.

Requirements: Class attendance is required. More than four
absences and your final grade will be lowered. Participation in
class discussion is strongly recommended. Written work will
include at least two short essays (approximately 3-6 pages), one
longer essay (approximately 10 pages), and two exams covering the
readings, films, and class discussion. All reading assignments
must be completed by the assigned date. You must see each film
once and preferably twice. Films will be shown only on the dates
and times listed below.

Reading Schedule

Sept. 4 Arthur Conan Doyle, The Hound of the Baskervilles
      18 Rudyard Kipling, Two Tales (Boston: Int. Pocket
            Library)
Oct.   2 H. G. Wells, The War of the Worlds
      16 Bram Stoker, Dracula
Nov.   8 Robert Louis Stevenson, Dr. Jekyll and Mr. Hyde
      27 Joseph Conrad, Heart of Darkness

132

<u>Film</u> <u>Schedule</u>

<u>Date</u>		<u>Film</u>	<u>Time</u>
Sept.	10(M)	DIRTY HARRY	3:30 & 7:30
	24(M)	THE MAN WHO WOULD BE KING	3:30 & 7:30
Oct.	8(M)	INVASION OF THE BODY SNATCHERS (1978)	3:00 & 7:00
	24(W)	DRACULA (PBS–BBC telemovie)	3:00 & 7:00
	29(M)	NIGHT OF THE LIVING DEAD	2:00 & 7:00
Nov.	12(M)	THE HOWLING	2:00 & 7:00
Dec.	3(M)	RAIDERS OF THE LOST ARK	2:00 & 7:00
	5(W)	APOCALYPSE NOW	3:00 & 7:00
	10(M)	APOCALYPSE NOW	2:00 & 7:00

ENG 378
Fall 1987

Studies in Popular Culture
Stories of War: World War II and Vietnam

Prof. G. Waller
1259 Patterson
257-1292

Office hours: TR 11-12 and by appointment

This course will look closely at a number of films, novels,
documentaries, and journalistic accounts that take as their
subject World War II or the Vietnam War. We will consider how
these stories represent, dramatize, celebrate, and/or interpret
these two very different wars: what kind of conventions are found
in war novels and films? What do these films suggest about
heroism, violence, the identity of the enemy, and the relation
between personal action and patriotic values or military
procedures? What political and cultural values do they express
and embody? What do they provide for their viewers and readers?

Texts: Norman Mailer, The Naked and the Dead (Henry Holt)
       Al Santoli, Everything We Had (Ballantine)
       Michael Herr, Dispatches (Avon)
       J. Glenn Gray, The Warriors: Reflections on Men in
       Battle (Harper)

Requirements: Class attendance is required (more than three
absences and your final grade will be lowered) and participation
in class discussion is strongly recommended. Readings must be
completed by the assigned date, and you must see each film at
least once (and preferably twice). Films will be shown only at
the times indicated on the screening schedule. If you can't make
the screenings drop the course. Written work will include short
exercises (and, if necessary, quizzes), one comparative essay (a
minimum of eight pages typed double-space), and two exams
covering the films, readings, and class discussions.

Reading schedule

Sept. 8 (T) The Warriors, pp. 3-95
      15 (T) The Warriors, pp. 131-213
      22 (T) The Warriors, pp. 97-129
      29 (T) The Naked and the Dead

Oct. 22 (R) The Warriors, pp. 215-242
      27 (T) Everything We Had

Nov. 10 (T) Dispatches

134

<u>Screening</u> <u>Schedule</u>

<u>Date</u>   <u>Film</u>   <u>Time</u>

Sept. 2 (W)   AIR FORCE (1943)   2:00 & 7:00
      9 (W)   BATAAN (1943)   2:00 & 7:00
     14 (M)   WAR COMES TO AMERICA (1945)   2:00 & 7:00
     16 (W)   LIFEBOAT (1944)   2:00 & 7:00
     21 (M)   A WALK IN THE SUN (1945)   2:00 & 7:00
     23 (W)   BATTLE OF SAN PIETRO (1945)   3:00 & 7:00

Oct. 5 (M)   SANDS OF IWO JIMA (1949)   2:00 & 7:00
     12 (M)   BEST YEARS OF OUR LIVES (1946)   2:00 & 6:00
     15 (R)   First Exam

     19 (M)   THE GREEN BERETS (1968)   2:00 & 7:00
     21 (W)   HEARTS AND MINDS (1974)   2:00 & 7:00

Nov. 2 (M)   THE DEER HUNTER (1978)   2:00 & 6:00
     16 (M)   APOCALYPSE NOW (1979)   2:00 & 6:00
     23 (M)   WHO'LL STOP THE RAIN (1978)   2:00 & 7:00
     30 (M)   RAMBO: FIRST BLOOD PART II (1985)   2:00 & 7:00

Dec. 7 (M)   DR. STRANGELOVE (1964)   2:00 & 7:00

Be on time for the screenings, don't engage in idle chatter, and
stay until the final credits end.

135

V. WOMEN IN FILM

MODERN WOMEN DIRECTORS
by Diane Carson

Modern Women Directors is designed as an eight week course,
adaptable to either a quarter system or, as it was
originally offered, to a sixteen week semester, meeting
weekly the first or second half of the semester or meeting
biweekly for the entire semester. Offered on a ten or twelve
week quarter system, the course allows time for an
introductory session, exam and/or discussion periods or an
additional film. Because the content and form of the films
are difficult, it is intended for juniors, seniors and
graduate students in media and film studies or in a women's
studies program.

This course explores contemporary trends in feminist cinema
and raises questions about the roles of women in society,
the changes in sexual mores and the nature of women's
relationships with one another. It includes foreign and
American offerings, live action and animation, high cost and
independent productions. Above all else, it calls into
question the dominant mainstream film which reinforces
patriarchal hegemony and, in so doing, recuperates or
punishes women characters who have been sutured into
coherent narratives with conventional form and content.
Through visual and audio manipulation, innovation and
transgression, each of these films, to a greater or lesser
extent and each in its own way, shakes the viewer out of
complacent, passive viewing and challenges the audience to
confront and question Hollywood values and attitudes.

To aid the student in achieving this awareness, the
professor uses lectures, readings and especially
discussions, both large and small group, of the films
viewed. The size of the class determines the viability of
extensive class discussion, but division into groups of five
or six works well with almost any size class, especially if
the instructor has provided the groups with focused
questions. Because the films are demanding and, in some
instances, quite unsettling, it is particularly important
for the students to articulate their emotional as well as
intellectual responses. In this way the instructor learns
exactly how disturbing each film is and the students, in

sharing their reactions, have a more guided movement beyond
rejection and/or confusion to an understanding of the method
and motivation of the confrontational films. In addition,
the professor can better ascertain the theoretical and
emotional level of development to which the students can
comfortably move. Instructors should expect a fair amount
of viewer resistance to the demands of these films. Students
will sometimes argue that nothing happens, at other times
that the film is "stupid" or "weird," or perhaps that they
don't know why, but the film "bothered me." Rather like
interpreting post-modern art, these films need and warrant
careful explanation and benefit from much more prescreening
preparation and explanation than a film class devoted to
Hollywood examples.

Unit One: Lumière directed, written by and starring Jeanne
Moreau. 1976. 95 minutes.

Because this film is a big budget, studio film with an
internationally famous actress, it is more accessible than
the films to come. Therefore, Lumière offers a good
introduction to Modern Women Directors. Lumière can also
serve as a review of fairly conventional uses of sound,
camera angle, lighting, performance, narrative, etc. because
there is enough familiarity for us to feel at home. To
complement this comfortable style, Moreau takes just enough
liberty with each to nudge us into reconsideration of their
import. Students usually respond positively to this film
enhancing the instructor's initiation of the questioning/
analyzing process so essential to this entire course.

In this film Jeanne Moreau shows us a critical week in Paris
in the lives of four actresses into whose personas she has
cloned herself, that is, they can represent different
aspects and periods in her own life. As actresses, they
perform for an audience. Moreau's decision to portray
actresses raises the critical issues for feminist film
analysis since the watershed 1975 Laura Mulvey article,
"Visual Pleasure and Narrative Cinema." Analysis of Lumière
invites a consideration of significant feminist film theory
either separately or as an integral part of the
investigation of the dominant motifs: beds, lights, mirrors,
being on stage, on display--stereotypical thematic motifs
associated with women. Further, in the intentionally
disorienting and voyeuristically staged opening shots,
Moreau signals her intention to make the familiar
sufficiently unusual and provocative for us to recognize our
usually unacknowledged voyeuristic position and complacent
narrative acceptance. For this course Lumière begins the
eight week journey to examine interpersonal relationships
between women and men and among women. It foregrounds

women's "on-stage" existence, her taking direction from men, and in the final scene it refuses toneatly tie things together. It ends at least temporarily questioning whether Moreau is acting or "real" in her emotional breakdown as she reads lines for the film within the film. To further complicate our perspective, technical apparatus is integrated into the narrative, that is, we sometimes see lights and cameras, and this invites discussion of watching the filming within the film, blurring the distinction between our spectatorial position and the usually untroubled film viewing.

This unit is open to as many theoretical issues as time and energy permit. Lumière nicely bridges the gap between mainstream and unconventional cinema. The performances and the story are so strong, the script so insighful and well written that it does a beautiful job of moving the class to the focus for the remaining films.

Readings: Numerous articles on feminist film theory are possible here, especially Laura Mulvey's "Visual Pleasure and Narrative Cinema," Screen (Autumn 1975) 6-18. As time and energy permit, the instructor and students can review or begin an introduction to feminist film theory. Because no one book addresses this diverse and recent group of films, I usually select one or two articles to place on reserve for students to read. I encourage them to read in books listed at the end of this course file and to browse through periodicals such as Wide Angle, Camera Obscura, Film Quarterly, Quarterly Review of Film Studies, Signs, Cinema Journal, Jump Cut, etc.

Specifically addressing Lumière is Carolyn Porter's review in Film Quarterly, Spring 1977, 53-57.

Unit II. Jeanne Dielman, 23 Quai du Commerce--1080 Bruxelles d. by Chantal Akerman 1975 3hours 17min.

Two weeks of the class because of the length of the film and the level of difficulty.

Jeanne Dielman is extremely long and difficult. This is the film about which most students will complain that "nothing happens." But this film is received particularly well when the students have been prepared for the experience. Numerous students then rave about an experience like no other for a Hollywood film. According to Marsha Kinder, Akerman attempts to present the unseen from the seen, "to say the most, you show the least." In so doing, she transgresses almost all Hollywood conventions, the exceptions being that we do have actors and actresses and a story with a beginning, a middle

and an end, though we feel quite often as though we've
dropped into the middle of Jeanne Dielman's life. What we
watch are three days in the life of a Belgian housewife and
part-time prostitute with attention to the minute details of
her routine. For example, we see every step as Jeanne makes
a meatloaf; we observe here daily stop in a local cafe and
the afternoon routine, paid sexual interlude (for
housekeeping money). The disruption of her schedule and the
minute ways in which it is communicated makes a button left
unbuttoned on a housecoat take on earth shattering import.
Students are overwhelmed at the impact of so simple a story
and are astonished at the conclusion.

Jeanne Dielman demands that we change our habitual way of
viewing film and of viewing the world. It provokes
discussion of the nature of most mainstream film: the
content, the pacing, the camera positions, the cutting
patterns--the technical conventions that we take for granted
and which escape rather than question identity. Most
surprisingly, rather than enforcing a boredom with the
quotidien, Akerman's study reinvigorates our existence as we
learn to look at and enjoy the continually overlooked. For
the purposes of this course the most important element is
the "real" existence of the main female character. She is
not sensationalized, sex and nudity are not presented as
titillating, voyeuristically loaded moments, and we learn
much about our heretofore unspoken conditioned expectations.

Class reading: Marsha Kinder, "Reflections on 'Jeanne
Dielman,'" in Sexual Stratagems: The World of Women in Film
ed. Patricia Erens.

Unit Three: Thriller d. Sally Potter 1979 45 minutes and
Murder in a Mist d. Lisa Gottlieb 1980 30 minutes

Thriller is as difficult in its own way as Jeanne Dielman
and works extremely well as the next film because of the
insights into the usual representation of women. Thriller
is Sally Potter's reconstruction of Puccini's opera La
Boheme from a feminist perspective, that is, it deconstructs
the role of woman as romantic victims in fiction by
questioning the entire paradigm. The important elements
include the use of the mirror, the emptiness of the attic,
the two different actresses and their differences as Mimi I
and Mimi II, the questioning voice over, the progress made
in terms of Mimi I's questions and comments in the course of
the film. Potter's film acts as the catalyst to provoke us
to integrate the romantic notion of the eternally attractive
because doomed woman. Mimi I wants to know what causes her
death and psychoanalytically who she is and who it is that
can dare to investigate her own constructed identity. Mimi

Carson

II broadens the issue to one of woman's place in narrative
and this moves into Mimi's role as commodity,
laborer/seamstress.

Sound is of paramount importance in Thriller. As in the 1986
Dutch film directed by Marleen Gorris, A Question of
Silence, laughter is liberating, challenging and distancing.
Its repeated use as disembodied sound destabilizes the
image. There is no way to slip into a comfortable
relationship with these Mimis as Potter probes the darkest
secrets of identity of women in art beyond film constructs.
This film offers so many issues that it alone can take one
entire class. Preparation is essential or the students will
have such difficulty following what is happening that
they'll have no time left to comprehend the complex
theoretical challenge mounted. But again the effort is well
worth the effort. Though it is through film that we look at
opera, more than film is implicated by the scrutiny. The
representation of women in opera and by extension other
narrative art benefits from another, less conventional
perspective.

The second film in this unit comes as a comic relief, quite
necessary at the midpoint in the course. Murder in a Mist is
a parody of film noir. Its cutting humor is gender related,
of course. Because almost every student understands the
film noir stereotype (The Maltese Falcon, The Big Sleep,
Farewell, My Lovely, etc. etc.) they are delighted not only
to understand the usual conventions but to appreicate the
parody in unparalleled ways and in its most tongue in cheek
send up of Hollywood. This film offers necessary comic
relief from intensive intellectual work but is not less
illuminating of the status quo.

Class reading: E. Ann Kaplan. Women & Film: Both Sides of
the Camera. Methuen: New York, 1983. There is an excellent
article which includes a discussion of Thriller.

Unit Four: Daughter Rite 1979, 53 minutes and What You Take
for Granted 1983 75 minutes, both directed by Michelle
Citron

Filmmaker Michelle Citron has made two ground-breaking
films. About Daughter Rite she said, "I wanted to make a
film about women in families, especially the mother/daughter
and sibling/sister relationships. But I wanted to do so in a
provocative way, that is, create a narrative that did not
offer solutions or answers but instead motivated the
audience to think, and possibly change." The film succeeds
on another level as well because it uses the cinema-verite
style, incorporating super-8 "home movies" and interviews

143

with the two actresses, to undermine the conventions of
documentary filmmaking. So what this unit does is extend the
examination byond narrative to documentary film revealing
its conventions and gender based bias as well.

In What You Take for Granted," two disparate characters,
Anna is a worldly wise truckdriver, and Diana is a
middle-class doctor whose more reserved demeanor reflects a
controlled life style. They meet and gradually get to know
one another providing the core for an unusual, intimate and
moving look at women's experiences in jobs traditionally
held by men. A major part of the film consists of interview
with women in unconventional jobs or with experiences which
reveal the chauvinistic nature of work space. Again the
film's imaginative play with conventional narrative goes
beyond content to include filmic style for the actresses are
ordinary looking people, "obviously acting" and sometimes
quite unconvincingly so, as the students see it. These films
bring the more abstract, esoteric dimensions of films like
Thriller much closer to home--these are experiences to which
students can respond, with which they identify. We all know
the myth of the ideal family, the good girl, the working
woman who should know her place. At this point in the
course, the personal application works well. The stereotype
of the ideal family is deconstructed in the first film; the
stereotype of jobs and some relationships in the second. It
questions naturalistic acting and the social mores of
female-male and female-female relationshps.

Class reading: as in Unit Four: E. Ann Kaplan's Women & Film

Unit Five: Variety d. Bette Gordon 1984 100 minutes

Variety is another film about looking, controlling the gaze
and being looked at so we're back to narrative film. It
solidifies the theoretical understanding the students have
gained by this point in the semester in a film very popular
with them. The main character is Christine, a young woman
who sells tickets at an adult movie house who becomes
fascinated by a mysterious older man who returns to the
theater. Christine becomes the one who looks and pursues
him, reversing the usual gender roles and questioning again
the positioning of the female viewer in film as in life and
once again implicating the film process in the narrative.
Sexual fantasy becomes involved. As Bette Gordon says,
"Pornographic films become extreme examples of mainstream
Hollywood cinema" (Gordon 194). And, "I insert
questions and discomfort into images, narratives, and
stories." By this point in the course, the students quickly
recognize and engage these questions, furthering the agenda
of Gordon and others studied.

144

Carson

Class reading: Bette Gordon, "Variety: The Pleasure in
Looking," in Pleasure and Danger: Exploring Female Sexuality
ed. Carol S. Vance. Boston: Routledge & Kegan Paul, 1984.

Unit Six: The Man Who Envied Women d. Yvonne Rainer 1985
125 minutes

The past two units have not been particularly difficult, but
this one makes up for the rest. The Man Who Envied Women is
a complex and innovative film that tells the fictional story
of Jack Deller, palyed by two actors. While Jack considers
himself sensitive to feminism. Using films from the 1940s
that represent how "real men" dealt with women, using
super-8 footage of policita demonstrations and
confrontations by New York artists, video footage, and
dialogue composed of collages lifted from modern American
thinkers and film theorists, Rainer weaves a film replete
with filmic and societal indictment by revealing the
superficial, stereotypical constructs that pass for romance,
thinking and reality. This film works beautifully at this
point in the semester. Students come prepared to interpret
the film theory as well as the film clips, to understand the
interactions between characters, and to enjoy the
confrontation of convention, especially the direct address
to the camera. While a difficult film, at this point in the
semester the students are excited by what they have learned
which has enabled them to deal constructively with this
film. Documentary and narrative footage are intercut,
academia, the art world, our film heritage--all are shown
revealing the usual sex, age, social status biases.

Class reading: Lucy J. Lippard, "Talking Pictures, Silent
Words: Yvonne Rainer's Recent Movies," Art in America,
May/June 1977, 86-90 and press packet with several reviews.

Unit Seven. Artists and Animators.

As part of this course, film beyond narrative mainstream
offerings and art other than film have been examined. To
further expand the horizon, the last week is both
application and celebration of any art exhibits in the area
and, during class screening time, of animated films which
reflect the same biases in the traditional offerings as
we've found elsewhere. Particularly useful here have been
films like "Interview" by Caroline Leaf and Veronika Soul
(13 1/2 minutes), which offers a cinematic elebration of the
two animators' friendship. Interview fits into the previous
theoretical discussions as a documentary using
non-documentary techniques, that is, the unique animation of
each artist, Leaf's and Soul's animated footage. Other

Carson

animators with numerous film from which to choose include
Emily and Faith Hubley, Carol Clement, Sally Cruikshank,
Joanna Priestly, and Kathy Rose, among many others. Perhaps
most appropriate here is Jessica Spohn's "Another Great Day"
which pokes fun at the absurdity of the American dream of a
nuclear family. Lampooned media images provide a nice
summary of previous discussions and a wonderful last laugh.

Readings on the above films and feminist film theory in
general:

Brunsdon, Charlotte, ed. Films for Women. London: BFI
    Publishing, 1986.

Cowie, Elizabeth. "Women, Representation and the Image,"
    Screen Education 23 (Summer 1977), 15-23.

De Lauretis, Teresa. Alice Doesn't: Feminism, Semiotics,
    Cinema. Bloomington: Indiana University Press, 1984.

Doane, Mary Ann. The Desire to Desire: The Woman's Film of
    the 1940s. Bloomington: Indiana University Press, 1987.

Doane, Mary Ann, Patricia Mellencamp and Linda Williams, ed.
    Re-Vision: Essays in Feminist Film Criticism. Los
    Angeles: University Publications of America, Inc. 1984.

Dubler, Linda. "Variety," Film Quarterly (Fall 1984), 24-28.

Erens, Patricia. Sexual Stratagems: The World of Women in
    Film. New York: Horizon Press, 1979.

Gledhill, Christine. "Recent Developments in Feminist
    Criticism," Quarterly Review of Film Studies (Fall
    1978), 457-493.

---- ed. Home Is Where the Heart Is: Studies in Melodrama
    and the Woman's Film. London: BFI Publishing, 1987.

Gordon, Bette. "Variety: The Pleasure in Looking," in
    Pleasure and Danger: Exploring Female Sexuality ed.
    Carol S. Vance. Boston: Routledge & Kegan Paul, 1984.

Heath, Stephen. The Sexual Fix. London: MacMillan Press,
    Ltd., 1982.

Kaplan, E.Ann. Women &Film: Both Sides of the Camera. New
    York: Methuen, 1983.

----- ed. Women in Film Noir. London: BFI Publishing, 1978.

146

Carson

Kuhn, Annette. Women's Pictures: Feminism and Cinema. London: Routledge & Kegan Paul, 1982.

----- The Power of the Image: Essays on Representation and Sexuality. London: Routledge & Kegan Paul, 1985.

Lippard, Lucy J. "Talking Pictures, Silent Words: Yvonne Rainer's Recent Movies," Art in America, (May/June 1977), 86-90.

Mellencamp, Patricia. "Images of Language and Indiscreet Dialogue-'The Man Who Envied Women,'" Screen, (Spring 1987) 87-101.

Mulvey, Laura. "Visual Pleasure and Narrative Cinema," Screen. (Autumn 1975) 6-18.

Porter, Carolyn. "Lumière," Film Quarterly (Spring 1977)53-57.

Williams, Linda and B. Ruby Rich. "The Right of Re-Vision: Michelle Citron's Daughter-Rite," Film Quarterly (Fall 1981), 17-22.

Woman's Image in Film

"Woman's Image in Film" is an advanced undergraduate Women's Studies course that counts towards the English Major and the Film Concentration of UMB's Communications Certificate. (Originally offered as a thriving sophomore course, "Woman's Image" was revised and upgraded as feminist criticism became more readily available in print.) Classes meet twice a week for a total of 4-5 hours. Most students enrolled in it have no background in film, but a few are experienced in this area and many have done some advanced work in the critical reading of texts. Occasional men do take the course, but most of its students are women. All are self-supporting commuters who come from diverse backgrounds and whose average age is twenty five. The course's goal is to help these students become critical feminist viewers of treatments of women by mainstream cinema, and to open discussion of alternatives to such practices. Given the diverse personal and political agendas students inevitably bring into such a course, the special challenge facing its instructor is the fostering of collaborative exchange in the classroom.

Starting off with an "images" formula which concerns films' treatments of an array of female archetypes, the syllabus moves to problematize that approach by building into the course attention to treatments of race, social class, and sexual orientation as shaped by particular historic and political considerations. That virtually all the films taught in "Women's Images" were directed by men and articulate a masculinist orientation towards gender, enables students to consider the ideological functioning of film within social and political structures. Issues of reception as well as production inform discussions throughout, and assigned readings aim to supplement this emphasis. These include both books and xeroxed articles of varying levels of difficulty. Some get discussed in class, but on the whole students understand these to be supplementary materials they are to read on their own as complements to the course's primary focus on films. To this end they keep journals and engage in frequent writing assignments.

Syllabus

Week 1: <u>The Wind</u> (Seastrom, 1928).

Readings: 1) Start Berger's <u>Ways of Seeing</u> (to be completed in two weeks).

2) Tyler, "The Horse: Totem Animal of Male Power--An Essay in the Straight-Camp Style" (Mast & Cohen).

3) Kolodny, "The Domestic Fantasy Goes West."

Recommended: Giannetti <u>Understanding Movies</u> (to be used as a Companion throughout the course).

Week 2: <u>Blonde Venus</u> (Von Sternberg, 1932).

Readings: 1) Nichols, <u>Blonde Venus</u>: Playing with Performance."

2) Walker, "Marlene Dietrich: At Heart a Gentleman" (Kay & Peary).

3) Baxter, "On the Naked Thighs of Miss Dietrich" (Nichols, <u>Movies & Methods</u>).

4) Kaplan, <u>Women and Film</u>, Chapter 3.

5) Mulvey, "Visual Pleasure and Narrative Cinema" (Kay & Peary).

6) Studlar, "Masochism and the Perverse Pleasure of Cinema" (Nichols, <u>Movies & Methods</u>).

Week 3: <u>I'm No Angel</u> (Ruggles, 1933).

Readings: 1) Johnston, "Myth of Women in Cinema" (Kay & Peary).

2) Williams, "Film Body: An Implantation of Perversions" (Rosen).

3) Herzog & Gaines, "Puffed Sleeves Before Teatime."

4) Silverman, "A Voice to Match: The Female Voice in Classic Cinema" (<u>Re-Vision</u>).

5) De Lauretis, <u>Alice Doesn't</u>, pp. 81-83.

Week 4: <u>Queen Christina</u> (Mamoulian, 1933).

Readings: 1) Kaplan, <u>Women and Film</u>, Chapters 1-5.

2) Tynan, "Garbo" (Mast & Cohen).

3) Barthes, "The Faces of Garbo" (Mast & Cohen).

Week 5:   Maedchen in Uniform (Sagan, 1931).

Readings: 1)   Rich, "From Repressive Tolerance to Erotic Liberation: Maedchen in Uniform" (Re-Vision).

Recommended: Russo, The Celluloid Closet.

Week 6:   Mildred Pierce (Curtiz, 1945).

Readings: 1)   "Introduction" (Kaplan Noir).

2)   Harvey, "Woman's Place: The Absent Family of the Film Noir (Kaplan Noir).

3)   Place "Women in Film Noir" (Kaplan Noir).

4)   Cook, "Duplicity in Mildred Pierce (Kaplan Noir).

5)   Nelson, "Mildred Pierce Reconsidered" (Nichols, Movies & Methods).

Week 7:   An Imitation of Life (Stahl 1934).

Readings: 1)   Kuhn, Women's Pictures: Feminism and Cinema, Chapters 1-6.

Bowser, "Sexual Imagery and the Black Woman in American Cinema" (Yearwood).

Recommended: Toni Morrison, The Bluest Eye (novel).

Week 8:   City Lovers (Simon, 1982).

Readings: 1)   Gordimer, "City Lovers" (short story).

2)   Kuhn, Women's Pictures, Chapter 7.

Week 9:   Ramparts of Clay (Bertocelli, 1971).

Readings: 1)   Kuhn, Women's Pictures, Chapters 8-9.

2)   MacDougall, "Beyond Observational Cinema" (Nichols, Movies & Methods).

Recommended: Kaplan, Women and Film, Chapters 6-11.

Week 10: A Brief Vacation (DeSica, 1974).

Readings: 1)   De Lauretis, "Introduction."

2)   De Lauretis, "Through the Looking Glass."

Week 11: <u>Klute</u> (Pakula, 1971).

        Readings: 1)   Gledhill,"<u>Klute</u> 1" (Kaplan <u>Noir</u>).

                2)   Gledhill, "Klute 2" (Kaplan <u>Noir</u>).

                3)   Giddis, "The Divided Woman: Bree Daniels in <u>Klute</u>" (Kay & Peary).

                4)   Welsh, "Bree Speaks on Tape and in Therapy: Women's Discourse in <u>Klute</u>" (manuscript).

Week 12: <u>Stage Door</u> (La Cava, 1937).

Week 13: Manuel Puig, <u>Kiss of the Spider Woman</u> (novel).

        Recommended: Williams, "<u>White Zombie</u>--Haitian Horror."

Week 14: <u>My Love Has Been Burning</u> (Mizoguchi, 1949).

        Recommended: De Lauretis, "Desire in Narrative."

Week 15: <u>Salt of the Earth</u> (Biberman, 1954).

        Readings: Wilson and Rosenfelt, <u>Salt of the Earth</u>.

        Recommended: Roffman and Purdy, <u>The Hollywood Social Problem Film</u>, pp. 252-256 & 262-295.

Works Cited

Berger, John. Ways of Seeing. New York: Penguin, 1972.

De Lauretis, Teresa. Alice Doesn't: Feminism, Semiotics, Cinema.
    Bloomington: Indiana UP, 1984.

Doane, Mary Ann, Patricia Mellencamp, and Linda Williams, eds. Re-Vision:
    Essays in Feminist Film Criticism. Frederick: American Film Institute,
    1984.

Giannetti, Louis. Understanding Movies. Englewood Cliffs: Prentice Hall,
    1987.

Herzog, Charlotte C. and Jane M. Gaines. "Puffed Sleeves Before Tea-Time':
    Joan Crawford, Adrian, and Women Audiences." Wide Angle 6, 4 (1985):
    24-33.

Kaplan, E. Ann. Women and Film: Both Sides of the Camera. New York:
    Metheun, 1983.

--- Ed. Women in Film Noir. London: British Film Institute, 1980.

Kay, Karyn and Gerald Peary, Eds. Women and the Cinema: A Critical
    Anthology. New York: Dutton, 1977.

Kolodny, Annette. The Land Before Her: Fantasy and the Experience of the
    American Frontiers, 1630-1860. Chapell Hill: North Carolina UP, 1984.

Kuhn, Annette. Women's Pictures: Feminism and Cinema. London: Routledge and
    Kegan Paul, 1982.

Mast, Gerald, and Marshall Cohen, Eds. Film Theory and Criticism:
    Introductory Readings. New York: Oxford UP, 1974.

Nichols, Bill. Ideology and the Image: Social Representation in the Cinema
    and Other Media. Bloomington: Indiana UP, 1981.

--- Ed. Movies and Methods, Vol. II. Berkeley: California UP, 1985.

Roffman, Peter, and Jim Purdy. The Hollywood Social Problem Film: Madness,
    Despair, and Politics from the Depression to the Fifties. Bloomington:
    Indiana UP, 1981.

Rosen, Philip, Ed. Narratives, Apparatus, Ideology: A Film Theory Reader.
    New York: Columbia UP, 1986.

Russo, Vito. The Celluloid Closet: Homosexuality in the Movies. New York:
    Harper and Row, 1981.

Williams, Tony. "The White Zombie--Haitian Horror." Jump Cut 28 (Spring
    1983).

Wilson, Michael and Deborah Silverton Rosenfelt. Salt of the Earth. Old
    Westbury: The Feminist Press, 1978.

Yearwood, Gladstone, Ed. <u>Black Cinema Aesthetics: Issues in Independent Black Filmmaking</u>. Athens: Ohio University Center for Afro American Studies, 1982.

Professor Linda Dittmar

Women Film Directors

"Women Film Directors" is an advanced companion course to "Woman's Image in Film," though the two are not required as a sequence. Like "Woman's Image," it is offered through UMB's Women's Studies Program, and it, too, attracts English Majors and Communications Concentrators as well as Women's Studies students. Most of its students do not have special training in film. Enrollment is somewhat smaller in this course, partly because it includes difficult non-narrative texts and partly because it takes a fairly sophisticated student to appreciate the ground-breaking potentials of this subject matter. (One student reported that her boyfriend dismissed the course with, "Women directors--You mean all TWO of them?") Students are mostly women, their average age is twenty five, and they are all commuting and self-supporting people who have had diversely interesting life experiences. Classes meet twice a week for a total of 4-5 hours.

While "Woman's Image" largely concerns mainstream practices, "Women Directors" counters that by affirming the scope of women's film-making and by examining such work closely. The syllabus surveys some eight decades of women's production, including documentary and avant-garde films as well as conventional narratives. Its organization is generic and thematic, but within this structure it acknowledges historicity and national origin partly through chronological sequencing within a given unit and partly through in-class discussion. The course assumes a feminist perspective, and it encourages attention to women's personal, political, and ideological investment in the thematic and formal preoccupations of the films they make. (In this it contrasts with "Woman's Image," which emphasizes men's investment

155

and women's reception.) Students find attention to the work of women directors very enabling, for it allows them to explore an array of active female interventions in a male-dominated medium, and it subjects women's work to a formal and political critique that presupposes women's equal power but also equal responsibility as directors. Thus, while students find the course a stimulating introduction to a body of work that affirms women's talents and strengths, they also find it empowering precisely because it subjects that work to serious analysis and assessment.

As last offered, the syllabus is crowded. Students find its intensive pacing exhilarating but also exhausting. Some thinning out and substitution may be advisable. (Maedchen in Uniform is important and got left out only because it is taught frequently at UMB. Lois Weber needs to be represented, as does Yvonne Rainer. Rosie the Riveter could be used well here, as could Julie Dash's Illusions or Sarah Maldoror's Sambizanga. On the other hand, Namibia and Amy did not work out well.) Clearly, each addition means a deletion, and such choices are difficult given the urgency rare, non-canonical works tend to inspire. Students benefit from discussing the selection of materials and the questions of canon, distribution, craft, and politics which go into the making of its syllabus.

Readings assigned in this course are gleaned from diverse sources and vary in difficulty. On any given week, some may glance forward to upcoming work. They are designated "secondary" and are given limited in-class attention. The emphasis is on films as primary texts, and students keep journals and do other frequent writing by way of recording their viewing experience and reflecting on that activity. Beyond studying the material and the assumptions latent in the syllabus, the course aims to make students aware of their own practices as viewers and critics. The syllabus includes the dates of both film releases and publications so as to guide students towards a historic reading of critical as well as filmic discourse.

Professor Linda Dittmar
Women Film Directors

Syllabus

Week 1:   **Matrimony Speed Limit** (Guy Blache, 1913).

          A House Divided (Guy Blache, 1923).

          Readings: 1)   Faure, "The Art of Cineplastics" (1923; Talbot).

                  2)   Tyler, "Hollywood's Surrealist Eye" (1944; Talbot).

                  3)   Norden, "Women in the Early Film Industry" (1984).

                  4)   Peary, "Alice Guy Blache: Czarina of the Silent Screen" (1972; Kay & Peary).

                  5)   Guy Blache, "Woman's Place in Photoplay Production" (1914; Kay & Peary).

                  6)   Rosen, "Epilogue" (1973).

          Recommended: Bordwell and Thompson, **Film Art** (for self-paced reading).

Week 2:   **Dance Girl, Dance** (Arzner, 1940).

          Readings: 1)   Kuhn, **Women's Pictures: Feminism and Cinema** (1982), Section I, II, and Chapter 5 of Section III, "Trouble in the Text."

                  2)   Houston, "Missing in Action: Notes on Dorothy Arzner" (1984).

                  3)   Kay and Peary, "Dorothy Arzner's **Dance Girl, Dance** (1973).

                  4)   Kay and Peary, "Interview with Dorothy Arzner" (1974).

Week 3:   **The Blue Light** (Riefenstahl, 1932).

          Readings: 1)   Kracauer, "National Epic" (1947).

                  2)   Sontag, "Fascinating Fascism" (1975).

                  3)   Gentile, **Film Feminists** (1985) "Introduction" and Chapters 1-4 (Chapter 2 optional).

Week 4:   **Marianne and Juliane** (Vot Trotta, 1981).

          Readings: 1)   Cavell, "The World as a Whole: Color" (1971).

                  2)   Seiter, "The Political is Personal: Margarethe Von Trotta's "'Marianne and Juliane'" (1985; Brunsdon).

3) Hansen, "frauen und Film" (1983; _Heresies_).

4) Kaplan, _Women and Film: Both Sides of the Camera_ (1983). Chapter 8, "Female Politics in the Symbolic Realm."

5) Gentile, _Film Feminists_, Chapter 6 (optional).

Week 5:   A Question of Silence (Gorris, 1981).

Readings: 1) Kaplan, _Women and Film_, "Introduction" and Chapter 1, "Is the Gaze Male?"

2) Gentile, _Film Feminists_, Chapter 8, "Feminist or Tendentious?"

3) Doane, "The Voice in Cinema: The Articulation of Body and Space" (1980; Nichols).

4) Silverman, "A Voice to Match" (1985; _Iris_).

5) Dittmar, "Dislocated Utterances" (1985; _Iris_).

6) Moi, _Sexual/Textual Politics_ (1985; optional).

Week 6:   Variety (Gordon, 1984).

Readings: 1) Kuhn, _The Power of the Image_ (1985), "Introduction" and Chapters 1-3.

2) Kuhn, _Women's Pictures_, Section III, 6: "The Body in the Machine."

3) Gordon, "_Variety_: The Pleasure in Looking" (1984).

4) Dubler's review of _Variety_ in _Film Quarterly_ (1984).

5) "Angry Arts" flyer on _Variety_ (1985).

6) Selection from Kappeler, _The Pornography of Representation_.

7) Silverman, "_History d'O_; The Construction of a Female Subject."

Week 7:   Jeanne Dielman, 23 Quai du Commerce, 1080 Bruxelles (Akerman, 1975).

Readings: 1) Brunsdon, "Introduction" to Part II.

2) Martin, "Chantal Akerman's Films: Notes on Issues raised for Feminism" (1979; Brunsdon).

159

3) Loader, "<u>Jeanne Dielman</u>: Death in Installments" (1977; Nichols).

4) Johnston, "Towards a Feminist Film Practice: Some Theses" (1976; Nichols).

Week 8:   <u>The Smiling Mme Beudet</u> (Dulac, 1922).

<u>Meshes of the Afternoon</u> (Deren, 1943).

Readings: 1)   Kuhn, <u>Women's Pictures</u>, Section III, 4, "Making Visible The Invisible."

2)   Van Wert, "Germaine Dulac: First Feminist Filmmaker" (1974; Kay and Peary).

3)   Deren, "A Letter to James Card" (1965; Kay and Peary).

4)   Kaplan, <u>Women and Film</u>, Chapter 6, "The Avant-Gardes in Europe and the USA."

Week 9:   <u>Namibia</u> (Choy, 1985).

<u>Las Madres de Plaza de Mayo</u> (Portillo, 1985).

Readings: 1)   Maldoror, "On Zambizanga" (1974; Kay and Peary).

2)   Brunsdon, "Introduction" to Part I.

3)   Lesage, "Political Aesthetic of the Feminist Documentary Film" (1978; Brunsdon).

4)   Springer, "Ethnocentric Circles: From Colonial Culture to Committed Cinema" (1984).

5)   Kaplan, <u>Women and Film</u>, Chapter 10, "The Realist Debates in the Feminist Film."

6)   Kuhn, "<u>Women's Pictures</u>", Section IV, "Introduction: Replacing Dominant Cinema," and Chapter 7, "Real Women."

7)   Agosta and Becker, "11,000 is not Enough" (1982; <u>Heresies</u>).

Week 10:   <u>One Way or Another</u> (Gomez, 1974).

Readings: 1)   Kaplan, <u>Women and Film</u>, Chapter 13, "The woman Director in the Third World: Sara Gomez's <u>One Way or Another</u>."

2)   Kuhn, <u>Women's Pictures</u>, Section IV, 8, "Textual Politics."

3)   Chanan, "One Way or Another" (1985).

Week 11:   <u>Daughter Rite</u> (Citron, 1979).

<u>The Ties that Bind</u> (Friedrich, 1984).

Readings: 1)   Friedrich,   "Gently   Down   the   Stream"   (1983; <u>Heresies</u>).

2)   Springer, "Representing History in <u>The Ties that Bind</u>" 1985; manuscript).

3)   Renov, "Re-Thinking Documentary: Towards a Taxonomy of Mediation" (1986; <u>Wide Angle</u>).

4)   Kaplan, <u>Women and Film</u>, Chapter 12, "Mothers and Daughters."

5)   Feuer, "'Daughter Rite'" Living with our Pain and Love" (1980; Brunsdon).

6)   Williams and Rich, "The Right of re-Vision: Michelle Citron's <u>Daughter Rite</u>" (1981; Nichols).

Week 12:   <u>Born in Flames</u> (Bordeon, 1983).

Readings: 1)   Earle, "Revolt Against Realism in the Films" (1968; Mast & Cohen).

2)   Fonoroff and Cartwright, "Narrative is Narrative: So What is New?" (1983; <u>Heresies</u>).

3)   De Lauretis, "Rethinking Women's Cinema Aesthetics and Theory" (1987).

4)   Borden, "Born in Flames" (1983; <u>Heresies</u>).

5)   Sayer and Jayamanne, "Burning an Illusion" (1983; Brunsdon).

6)   Minh-Ha, "Mechanical Eye, Electronic Ear, and the Lure of Authenticity" (1984; <u>Wide Angle</u>).

Week 13:   <u>Amy</u> (Mulvey and Wollen, 1979).

<u>Olympia</u> (Riefenstahl, 1938; The Diving Sequence).

<u>Bridges Go Round</u> (Clark, 1958).

<u>A Scary Time</u> (Clark, 1960).

<u>Four Women</u> (Dash, 1978).

Readings: 1) Kaplan, <u>Women and Film</u>, Chapter 11, "The Avante-Garde Theory Film."

2) De Hirsch and Clark, "A Conversation" (1967; Kay and Peary).

3) Campbell, "Reinventing Our Image. Eleven Black Filmmakers" (1983; <u>Heresies</u>).

Week 14: <u>Thriller</u> (Potter, 1979).

<u>For A Woman in El Salvador Speaking</u> (Halprin, 1985).

<u>Light Reading</u> (Rhodes, 1978).

Readings: 1) Kaplan, <u>Women and Film</u>, Chapter 9, "The American Experimental Women's Film."

2) Mayne, "The Woman at the Keyhole: Women's Cinema and Feminist Criticism" (1981).

3) Rhodes and Sparrow, "Her Image Fades as Her Voice Rises" (1983, <u>Heresies</u>).

4) Rhodes, "Light Reading" (1983, <u>Heresies</u>).

5) Agosta and Osborn, "If I Ever Stop Believing" (1983, <u>Heresies</u>).

Week 15: <u>Take Off</u> (Nelson, 1972).

<u>Hairpiece</u> (Chenzira, 1982).

<u>Asparagus</u> (Pitt, 1978).

Readings: 1) Kuhn, <u>Women's Pictures</u>, Section IV, 9, "The Production of Meaning and the Meaning of Production."

2) Kaplan, <u>Women and Film</u>, Chapter 14, "The Future of the Independent Feminist Film," and Chapter 15, "Conclusion: Motherhood and Patriarchal Discourse."

162

Works Cited

Bordwell, David and Kristin Thompson. Film Art: An Introduction. New York: Knopf, 1986.

Brunsdon, Charlotte, Ed. Films for Women. London: British Film Institute, 1986.

Cavell, Stanley. The World Viewed: Reflections on the Ontology of Film. New York: Viking, 1971.

Chanan, Michael. The Cuban Image. Bloomington: Indiana UP, 1985; London: British Film Institute, 1985.

De Lauretis, Teresa. Technologies of Gender: Essays on Theory, Film, and Fiction. Bloomington: Indiana UP, 1987.

Dubler, Linda. "Review [of Variety]." Film Quarterly 38,1 (Fall 1984): 24-28.

Gentile, Mary. Film Feminists: Theory and Practice. Westport: Greenwood, 1985.

Gordon, Bette. "Variety: The Pleasure in Looking." Pleasure and Danger: Exploring Female Sexuality. Carol S. Vance, Ed. Boston: Routledge and Kegan Paul, 1984.

Heresies: A Feminist Publication on Art and Politics. #16 (1983).

Houston, Beverle. "Missing in Action: Notes on Dorothy Arzner." Wide Angle: A Film Quarterly of Theory, Criticism, and Practice 6, 3 (1984): 24-31.

Iris: A Journal of Theory on Image and Sound 3, 1 (1985) [France].

Kaplan, E. Ann. Women and Film: Both Sides of the Camera. New York: Methuen, 1983.

Kappeler, Susanne. The Pornography of Representation. Minneapolis: Minnesota UP, 1986.

Kay, Karyn and Gerald Peary, Eds. Women and the Cinema: A Critical Anthology. New York: Dutton, 1977.

Kracauer, Siegfried. From Caligari to Hitler; A Psychological History of the German Film. Princeton: Princeton UP, 1947.

Kuhn, Annette. Women's Pictures: Feminism and Cinema. London: Routledge and Kegan Paul, 1982.

---. The Power of the Image: Essays on Representation and Sexuality. London: Routledge and Kegan Paul, 1985.

Mast, Gerald and Marshall Cohen, Eds. Film Theory and Criticism: Introductory Readings. New York: Oxford UP, 1974.

Mayne, Judith. "The Woman at the Keyhole: Women's Cinema and Feminist Criticism." <u>New German Critique</u> 23 (Spring/Summer, 1981).

Minh, Ha, Trinh. "Mechanical Eye, Electronic Ear, and the Lure of Authenticity." <u>Wide Angle: A Film Quarterly of Theory, Criticism, and Practice</u> 6, 2 (1984): 58-63.

Moi, Toril. <u>Sexual/Textual Politics: Feminist Literary Theory</u>. New York: Metheun, 1985.

Nichols, Bill, Ed. <u>Movies and Methods</u>, Vol. II. Berkeley: California UP, 1985.

Norden, Martin F. "Women in the Early Film Industry." <u>Wide Angle: A Film Quarterly of Theory, Criticism, and Practice</u> 6,3 (1984): 58-67.

Renov, Michael. "Re-Thinking Documentary: Towards a Taxonomy of Mediation." <u>Wide Angle: A Film Quarterly of Theory, Criticism, and Practice</u> 8, 3 & 4 (1986): 71-77.

Rosen, Marjorie. <u>Popcorn Venus: Women, Movies, and the American Dream</u>. New York: Coward McCann and Geoghan, 1973.

Silverman, Kaja. "<u>Histoire d'O</u>: The Construction of a Female Subject." <u>Pleasure and Danger: Exploring Female Sexuality</u>. Carole S. Vance, Ed. Boston: Routledge and Kegan Paul, 1984. 320-49.

Sontag, Susan. "Fascinating Fascism." <u>The New York Review of Books</u> (February 6, 1975).

Springer, Claudia. "Ethnocentric Circles: From Colonial Culture to Committed Cinema." <u>The Independent</u> 7, 11 (December 1984): 13-18.

---. Representing History in The Ties That Bind." Manuscript (1985).

Talbot, Daniel, Ed. <u>Film: An Anthology</u>. Berkeley: California UP, 1966.

Yearwood, Gladstone L., Ed. <u>Black Cinema Aesthetics: Issues in Independent Black Filmmaking</u>. Athens: Ohio University Center for Afro American Studies, 1982.

E. Ann Kaplan
Fall Semester
Women's Studies

Women and Film

This course aims first to show the evolution of both the Woman's
Film and the Woman's Melodrama in Hollywood from the 1920's to the
present, and second to look at films made independently (i.e.
outside of Hollywood) by women in America and Europe during the
same period. Since many cinematic strategies in the films made by
independent women filmmakers take their shape from a critique of
the commercial Hollywood film, we will begin by looking at several
examples of women's films, exploring the distinctions that lead to
the two main types. We will discuss what "melodrama" means, how it
arose and why it has become a dominant female form, and then go on
to talk about the more "resisting" film form addressed to women.
        Using structuralism and psychoanalysis, we will analyze the
ways in which the films construct a particular position for the
male and female spectators, vis a vis the image of women. But we
will also consider sociological issues having to do with the female
image as these are appropriate and relevant to any specific films.
Indeed, a central and on-going aspect of the course will be attention
to (and evaluation of) the various critical methods we are using
ourselves and that we find in the assigned readings. The theoretical debates will come sharply into focus towards the end of the
course when we deal with different conceptions of what a feminist
cinema should be.

Course Hours: 4:10 to 6:00, 304 Barnard;
Required Film Showings: 7:00 to 9:00,
(Attendance at films is essential; please do not sign up for the
course if you cannot come regularly to the showings.)

Required Texts: 1. E. Ann Kaplan, Women and Film: Both Sides of
                     the Camera (Methuen, 1983) (WIF)
                 2. John Berger, Ways of Seeing (Penguin, 1972) (WS)
                 3. Doane, Mellencamp, Williams, eds. Revision:
                     Essays in Feminist Criticism (American Film
                     Institute, 1984) (REVISION)
                 4. Sigmund Freud, Dora: A Case History (1905) (Dora)
                 5. Reserve Readings (listed in syllabus) (R)

Recommended (especially if this is your first film course): David
            Bordwell and K. Thompson, Film Art (Addison Wesley, 1981)

SYLLABUS

9/09   Introduction: The Development of Feminist Film Criticism
        Film: George Cukor Camille U.S.A. 1936 (Greta Garbo)
               (Credits in Kaplan, WIF)

9/16   The Male Gaze and Female Sexuality in the Hollywood Film
        Readings: Kaplan, WIF, Introduction, Chapters 1 & 2, pp.
                   1-49. Doane, Mellencamp, Williams, "Feminist
                   Film Criticism: An Introduction," REVISION, 1-17
                   Berger, WS, Ch. 1 & 2
        Film: Sam Wood Madame X U.S.A. (1937) (Gladys Young)

9/23   Constructions of the Mother in the Woman's Melodrama
        Readings: Glossary of Film Terms
                   Christian Viviani "Who Is Without Sin?" (Reserve)
                   Claire Johnston, "Myths of Women in the Cinema" (R)
        Films: Lois Weber The Blot U.S.A. 1921 (Claire Windsor)
                Von Sternberg Blonde Venus U.S.A. 1932 (Dietrich)

9/30   Constructions of the Mother in the Woman's Film
        Readings: Kaplan, WIF, Ch. 3; Kaplan, "Theories of
                   Melodrama;" (R)
                   L. Rudman, "Lois Weber" (R)
        Film: Dorothy Arzner Christopher Strong U.S.A. 1932
               (Katharine Hepburn)

10/07   Female Desire and Subjectivity in Patriarchy, I (Sexuality)
        Readings: J. Suter, "Feminine Discourse in Christopher Strong"
                   Berger, Ch. 3 & 4
        Film: Dorothy Arzner Craig's Wife U.S.A. 1936 (Rosalind
               Russell)

10/14   Female Desire and Subjectivity in Patriarchy, II (Mothering)
        Readings: Cook & Johnston on Arzner as "progressive"
                   director (R)
                   Laura Mulvey, "Visual Pleasure" (R)
        Film: Orson Welles The Lady from Shanghai U.S.A. 1946
               (Rita Hayworth)
        Mid-Semester in-class exam (one hour)

10/21   Film Noir: Struggle for Control of Female Sexuality
        Readings: Kaplan, WIF, Ch. 4
                   Karen Horney, "The Dread of Woman" (R)
                   Mary Ann Doane, "The Woman's Film: Possession
                   and Address", In REVISION, pp. 67-82.
        Film: Douglas Sirk All That Heaven Allows U.S.A. 1956
               (Jane Wyman)

10/28   50's Maternal Melodrama: Exposing Melodramatic Modes?
        Readings: Laura Mulvey, "Notes on Sirk and Melodrama" (R)
                   John Ellis, "Star/Industry/Image" (R)
        Film: Richard Brooks Lipstick U.S.A. 1976 (Margo Hemingway)

166

11/04   Contemporary Melodrama: Representations of Rape in the
         Commercial Film
         Readings: Kaplan, WIF, Ch. 5
                  Rosalind Coward, "Sexual Violence and Sexuality" (R)
                  Linda Williams, "When The Woman Looks", REVISION
                  83-99.
         Films: The Smiling Madame Beudet France 1922
               Maya Deren Meshes in the Afternoon U.S.A. 1943
               At Land U.S.A. 1944

11/11   PART II; DISCOVERING THE FEMALE VOICE: EXPERIMENTAL,
      AVANT-GARDE AND FOREIGN FILMS BY WOMEN DIRECTORS

         Feminine Discourse and Cinematic Innovation in Avant-Garde
         Women's Films
         Readings: Kaplan, WIF, Ch. 6
                  Peter Wollen, "The Two Avant-Gardes" (R); &
                  "Counter-Cinema: Ven D'EST" (R)
                  Maya Deren, "Cinema As An Art Form" and "Letter
                  to James Card."
         Film: Marguerite Duras Nathalie Granger France 1972
         (Credits WIF)

11/18   The Politics of Silence in Films by Women
         Readings: Kaplan, WIF, Ch. 7; Domna Stanton, "Language &
                  Revolution"
                  Silverman, "Disembodying the Female Voice,"
                  REVISION, pp. 131-149.
         Film: Margareta Von Trotta, Marianne and Juliane Germany
               1980 (Jutta Lampe, Barbara Sukowa) (Credits WIF)

11/25   Feminine Discourse and the Politics of Terrorism
         Readings: Kaplan, WIF, Ch. 8; A. Tindall & A. McCall,
                  "Political Discourse" (R)
                  Judith Mayne, "The Woman at the Keyhole: Women's
                  Cinema and Feminist Criticism," REVISION, pp:
         Film: Yvonne Rainer, Lives of Performers U.S.A. 1972

     PART III; THE AVANT-GARDE THEORY FILM AND THE DEBATE ABOUT
            REALISM AND A FEMINIST CINEMA

12/02   The American Experimental Woman's Film
         Readings: Kaplan, WIF, Ch. 9
                  Christine Gledhill, "Developments in Feminist
                  Film Criticism," REVISION, pp, 18-48.
         Films: Sara Gomez One Way or Another Cuba 1974
               Mulvey/Wollen, Amy! (short) (Credits, WIF)

12/09   Theories of Realism and Third World Film
         (a) Readings: Kaplan, WIF, Ch. 10 & 13;
         (b) Final Session on Avant-Garde Theory Films:
         Sigmund Freud's Dora & Thriller

         Readings: Kaplan, WIF, Ch. 11; Freud, Dora
                  Scripts for Dora, Thriller, Amy!

12/13-20 FINAL EXAM (to be announced)

VI. INTERDISCIPLINARY AND CULTURAL APPROACHES TO FILM

Professor Linda Dittmar

America on Screen

"America on Screen" is a sophomore-level Core Distribution Elective offered through American Studies. Students enrolled in it are mature (25 years old, on the average) self-supporting commuters. There are no prerequisites to this course beyond completion of the University's writing requirement. Some students enroll in it because they expect it to be a fun way to fulfill a general education requirement; some are English Majors or American Studies Concentrators for whom it can serve as a lower-division elective; some enroll because they are Communications Concentrators with special interest in film, and among them a few have a strong background in film studies. The course, then, must pursue several agendas at once. It has to help beginning students become "literate" and actively critical concerning film technique and rhetoric, but it must also challenge experienced English and Communications students, and it has to do all that with an eye to the interdisciplinary orientation posited by American Studies. That "American on Screen" is taught as an American Studies course means an emphasis on history and film criticism as interrelated. In-class discussion of films situates each within its particular historic and cultural context. As the course progresses, students move beyond reading films as records of reality towards an analytic reading which sees films as ideological insriptions shaped for specific audiences at particular points in history.

The diversity of the student body enrolled in this course requires careful balancing of elementary and advanced work. The course manages this by relying on an introductory text(Giannetti), by incorporating into class discussion ongoing attention to specific cinematorgrapic practices, and by written "dialogue" where student's frequent writing exercises receive close reading and detailed response. In-class discussions highlight formal and thematic analysis in ways that even experienced students find freshly illuminating. The historical perspective is new to all, especially as it is coupled in this course with special attention to social and political history. In addition, focus on the ways films function ideologically involves students in challenging discoveries that belie the expectations some have, to begin with, that the course will merely be entertainment haven.

The course rests on a thematic outline that clusters its diverse materials into units which protect it from seeming too dispersed and inclusive. The Wind, My Darling Clementine, and The Public Enemy introduce archtypal treatments of frontiers, individualism, and gender as these occur filmically at specific points in time. The Birth of A Nation, An Imitation of Life, and Nothing but a Man focus on treatments of race at specific points in time and are informed by the groundwork laid by the preceding unit. The Grapes of Wrath and Air Force extend the preceding unit's focus on racial conflict in the midst of social change to questions of social class and mass mobilization during the Depression and World War II. On the Waterfront and Salt of the Earth (both released in 1954) offer two contrasting treatments of individual and collective responses to social and economic disenfranchisement, while The Hustler picks up on On the Waterfront's special interest in the alienated and solitary male's development and integration into society. Finally, Inherit the Wind and The Footlight Parade help summarize and review questions that recurred throughout the semester--the former through its critique of social blindness, prejudice, and facile beliefs, and the latter through its use of entertainment to combine virtuoso performance and ideological manipulation.

The following syllabus is amenable to substitutions. One can replace a given Western or Gangster or War film with another; one can introduce a film noir or screwball comedy fruitfully; one can reduce the current emphasis on labor or bring the semester to a different closure than currently inscribed in the syllabus. Such changes will affect the discussion of particular themes, genres, or periods, but not the principle on which the course rests-- namely, its highlighting of a historical and ideological perspective as it affects reception. Assigned readings in this course reflect this principle. Coming from diverse sources, they include history, biography, culture studies, journalism, and magazines published by special interest groups, as well as film criticism. Such selections, too, can be changed to reflect changes in the syllabus and scholarly developments.

Professor Linda Dittmar
America on Screen

Syllabus

Week 1: <u>The Wind</u> (Seastrom 1928).

    Reading: Giannetti: Chapter 1, "Photography."
             Turner: "The Significance of the Frontier."
                     "The West and American Ideals."
             Nash: "The Wilderness Cult."
             Kolodny" "The Domestic Ghost Goes West" and "Epilogue."
             Bascomb: "Painting the Legend: Frederick Remington and
                     the Western."

Week 2: <u>My Darling Clementine</u> (Ford 1946).

    Reading: Giannetti: Chapter 2, "Mis-en-scene."
             Frantz: "The Frontier Tradition: An Invitation to
                     Violence."
             Tompkins: "West of Everything."
             Bisking: "The Local Hero."
             Cawelti: "The Western: A Look at the Evolution of a
                     Formula."
             Warshow: "Movie Chronicle: The Westerner."
             McMurtry: "Cowboys, Movies, Myths, and Cadillacs."

Week 3: <u>The Public Enemy</u> (Wellman 1931).

    Reading: Giannetti: Chapter 3, "Movement."
             Lupsha: "American Values and Organized Crime."
             Cawelti: "The Mythology of Crime."
             Warshow: "The Gangster as Tragic Hero."
             Baxter: "The Gangster Film."

Week 4: <u>The Birth of a Nation</u> (Griffith 1915).

    Reading: Giannetti: Chapter 4, "Editing."
             Selections from <u>Crisis</u> Magazine June, December 1915).
             Rogin: "The Sword Became a Flashing Vision."
             Neal: "The Same Old Story."
             Turner et al: "The Ku Klux Klan: A History of Racism and
                     Violence."
             Woodward: "The Man on the Cliff."
             Cawelti: "The Best-Selling Social Melodrama."
             Jacobs: "D.W. Griffith: I. New Discoveries. II. <u>The</u>
                     <u>Birth of a Nation</u> and <u>Intolerance</u>."

Week 5: <u>An Imitation of Life</u> (Stahl 1934).

    Reading:Giannetti: Chapter 5, "Sound," and Chapter 6, "Player."
             Bowser: "Sexual Imagery and the Black Woman in Cinema."
             Roffman and Purdy: "The Minorities."
             Bogle: "Imitation of Life: Mother Knows Best."
             Heung: "'What's the Matter with Sara Jane?':
                     Daughters and Mothers in Douglas Sirk's
                     <u>Imitation of Life</u>."

    Recommended reading:
                     Nella Larsen, <u>Quicksand</u>.

Week 6:   <u>Nothing But a Man</u> (Roemer 1964).

          Reading: Giannetti: Chapter 8, "Literature."
                    Cripps: "Nothing But a Man."
                    Harris: "The Legacy of Slavery."
                               "Black Workers During the Depression and War."

Week 7:   Review:
          Mid-Term Exam.

Week 8:   <u>The Grapes of Wrath</u> (Ford 1940).

          Reading: John Steinbeck: <u>The Grapes of Wrath</u>.
                    Pells: "Novels of Protest."
                    Bluestone: "The Grapes of Wrath."

Week 9:   <u>Air Force</u> (Hawkes 1943).

          Reading: Giannetti: Chapter   7,   "Drama,"   and   Chapter   8,
                               "Documentary."
                    Suid: "Introduction: Mythmaking for the War Effort."

Week 10: <u>On the Waterfront</u> (Kazan 1954).

          Reading: Kael: "The Glamor of Delinquency."
                    Anderson: "The Last Sequence of On the Waterfront."
                    Hughes: "<u>On the Waterfront</u>: A Defence and Some
                               Letters."
                    Biskind: "Friendly Persuasion" and "<u>On the Waterfront</u>."
                    Hey: "Ambivalence as a Theme in <u>On the Waterfront</u>."

Week 11: <u>Salt of the Earth</u> (Biberman 1954).

          Reading: "Screenplay," "Commentary," "Contemporary Accounts," and
                    "Documenting the Opposition," in Wilson's <u>Salt of the
                    Earth</u>.

Week 12: <u>The Hustler</u> (Rossen 1961).

          Reading: Polsky: "The Hustler."

Week 13: Review.

Week 14: <u>Inherit the Wind</u> (Kramer 1960).

          Reading: Weinberg: "The Robin Hood of the Courtroom."
                              "Tennessee <u>Versus</u> Scopes."
                    Hofstader: "William Jennings Bryan."
                    Leuchtenberg: "Political Fundamentalism."
                    Selections from <u>Passport</u> Magazine: "Humanism in our
                              Public Schools."

Week 15:   <u>The Footlight Parade</u> (Bacon 1933; dance by Busby Berkeley).

      Reading: Pells: "The Radical Stage."
                 Bergman: "The Gangsters" and other selections.
                 Cawelti: "Pornography, Catastrophe, and Vengeance."

Works Cited

Anderson, Lindsay. "The Last Sequence of <u>On the Waterfront</u>." <u>Sight and Sound</u> (January-March 1955): 127-130.

Bascombe, Edward. "Painting the Legend: Frederick Remington and the Western." <u>Cinema Journal</u> 23,4 (Summer 1984): 12-27.

Baxter, John. "The Gangster Film." <u>Crossroads to the Cinema</u>. Ed. Douglas Brode. Boston: Holbrook Press, 1975. 292-309.

Bergman, Andrew. <u>We're in the Money: Depression on America and Its films</u>. New York: Harper, 1971.

Biskind, Peter. <u>Seeing is Believing: How Hollywood Taught us to Stop Worrying and Love the Fifties</u>. New York: Pantheon, 1983.

Bluestone, George. <u>Novels into Films</u>. Berkeley: California UP, 1966.

Bogle, Donald. <u>Toms, Coons, Mulattoes, Mammies, and Bucks</u>. New York: Viking, 1973.

Bowser, Pearl. "Sexual Imagery and the Black Woman in Cinema." <u>Black Cinema Aesthetics: Issues in Independent Black Filmmaking</u>. Ed. Gladstone L. Yearwood. Athens: Ohio University Center for Afro-American Studies, 1982. 42-51.

Cawelti, John G. <u>Adventure, Mystery and Romances: Formula Stories as Art and Popular Culture</u>. Chicago: Chicago UP, 1976.

---. "Pornography, Catastrophe, and Vengeance; Shifting Narrative Structures in a Changing American Culture." <u>The American Self; Myth, Ideology and Popular Culture</u>. Ed. Sam B. Girgus. Albuquerque: New Mexico UP, 1981. 182-192.

Cripps, Thomas C. <u>Black Film as Genre</u>. Bloomington: Indiana UP, 1978.

Frantz, Joe B. "The Frontier Tradition: An Invitation to Violence." <u>Violence in America: Historical and Comparative Perspectives</u>. Eds. Hugh Davis Graham and Ted Robert Gurr. New York: Bantam, 1969. 127-154.

Giannetti, Louis. <u>Understanding Movies</u>. Englewood Cliffs: Prentice Hall, 1987.

Heung, Marina. "What's the Matter with Sara Jane?": Daughters and Mothers in Douglas Sirk's <u>Imitation of Life</u>." <u>Cinema Journal</u> 26, 3 (Winter 1987): 21-43.

Hey, Kenneth R. "Ambivalence as a Theme in <u>On the Waterfront</u> (1954): An Interdisciplinary Approach to Film Study." <u>Hollywood as Historian: American Film in a Cultural Context</u>. Ed. Peter C. Rollins. Lexington: Kentucky UP, 1983. 159-189.

Hofstadter, Richard. *The American Political Tradition and the Men Who Made It.* New York: Vintage, 1948.

Hughes, Robert et al. "On The Waterfront: A Defence and Some Letters," *Sight and Sound* (Spring 1955): 214-216.

Jacobs, Lewis. *The Rise of the American Film.* New York: Harcourt, Brace & Co., 1939.

Kael, Pauline. *I Lost it at the Movies* New York: Bantam, 1965.

Kolodny, Annette. *The Land Before Her: Fantasy and Experience of the American Frontiers, 1630-1860.* Chapell Hill: North Carolina UP, 1984.

Larsen, Nella. *Quicksand* and *Passing.* New Brunswick: Rutgers UP, 1986.

Leuchtenberg, William. *The Perils of Prosperity, 1914-1832.* Chicago: Chicago UP, 1958.

Lupsha, Peter A. "American Values and Organized Crime: Suckers and Wiseguys." *The American Self: Myth, Ideology, and Popular Culture.* Ed. Sam B. Girgus. Albuquerque: New Mexico UP, 1981. 144-154.

McMurtry, Larry. "Cowboys, Movies, Myths, and Cadillacs: Realism in the Western." *Man and the Movies.* Ed. W.R. Robinson. Baltimore: Penguine, 1969.

Nash, Roderick. *Wilderness and the American Mind.* New Haven: Yale UP, 1967.

Neal, Steve. "The Same Old Story: Stereotypes and Difference." *Screen Education* (Autumn/Winter 1979/1980. *History, Ideology, Suture* Special): 32-37.

Passport Magazine. Calvary Chapel of West Covina (June-July 1986. *Humanism in our Public Schools* Special).

Pells, Richard H. *Radical Visions and American Dreams: Culture and Social Thought in the Depression Years.* New York: Harper, 1977.

Polsky, Ned. *Hustlers, Beats, and Others.* Chicago: Aldine, 1967.

Roffman, Peter & Jim Purdy. *The Hollywood Social Problem Film: Madness, Despair and Politics from the Depression to the Fifties.* Bloomington: Indiana UP, 1981.

Rogin, Michael. "'The Sword Became a Flashing Vision': D.W. Griffith's *The Birth of A Nation.*" *Representations* 9 (Winter 1985): 151-195.

Steinbeck, John. *The Grapes of Wrath.* New York: Viking, 1939.

Suid, Howard Lawrence, Ed. *Air Force.* Madison: Wisconsin UP, 1983.

Tompkins, Jane. "West of Everything." *South Atlantic Quarterly* 86, 4 (1987): 357-377.

Turner, Frederick Jackson. <u>The Frontier in American History</u>. New York: Holt Rinehart, 1962.

Turner, John et al. <u>The Ku Klux Klan: A History of Racism and Violence</u>. Montgomery: The Southern Poverty Law Center, 1986.

Warshow, Robert. <u>The Immediate Experience: Movies, Comics, Theater, and Other Aspects of Popular Culture</u>. New York: Doubleday, 1962.

Weinberg, Arthur and Lila. <u>Clarence Darrow: A Sentimental Rebel</u>. New York: Putnam, 1980.

Wilson, Michael, and Deborah Silverton Rosenfelt. <u>Salt of the Earth</u>. Old Westbury: The Feminist Press, 1978.

Woodward, C. Vann. <u>The Strange Career of Jim Crow</u>. New York: Oxford, 1966.

Leslie Fishbein   Spring, 1986
American Studies Department   Monday, Thursday 2nd: 9:50-11:10
F.A.S., Rutgers University   in Food Science Auditorium
                                         Wednesday: 7:00-9:00 P.M. in
                                         Hickman Hall 138

AMERICAN STUDIES 01:050:262: AMERICAN FILM AND AMERICAN MYTH

BOOKS REQUIRED FOR PURCHASE:

1. David Bordwell and Kristin Thompson, Film Art: An Introduction, second
   edition. New York: Alfred A. Knopf, Inc., 1986. $20.00.

2. Lillian Hellman, Scoundrel Time, with an introduction by Garry Wills.
   1976; reprinted New York: Bantam Books, Inc., 1977. $3.50 new. ordered
   used at $2.60 (out of print).

3. Gerald Mast, ed., The Movies in Our Midst: Documents in the Cultural
   History of Film in America. Chicago: University of Chicago Press, 1982.
   $13.50.

4. Robert Sklar, Movie-Made America: A Cultural History of American Movies.
   1975; reprinted New York: Vintage Books, Random House, 1976. $8.95.

5. John Steinbeck, The Grapes of Wrath. 1939; reprinted Harmondsworth,
   Middlesex, England: Penguin Books, 1985. $3.95.

6. Nathanael West, The Day of the Locust, with an introduction by Alfred
   Kazin. 1939; reprinted New York: New American Library, 1983. $2.95.

COURSE REQUIREMENTS:

Monday, February 10th: Quiz

Thursday, March 6th: Midterm exam

One 3-5 page critical paper due according to topic chosen. The paper is
   to be typed, double-spaced, on white, unlined paper on one of the
   assigned topics only. Research is not required, but, if you do rely
   on assigned readings or outside sources for facts or opinions, such
   sources must be acknowledged in footnotes and bibliography. You will
   be required to sign up for the topics in advance on a first-come
   basis. If you need help in preparing the paper, I would be happy to
   meet with you. NO LATE PAPERS WILL BE ACCEPTED.

Thursday, May 8th, 8:30 A.M. - 11:30 A.M.: Final examination.

NOTE: Films will be shown on Wednesday evenings beginning at 7:00 P.M.
   in Hickman Hall 138. Films are shown once and only once; there will
   be no makeup screenings whatsoever. In accordance with University
   Fire Department regulations and Government Association recommendations
   there is to be NO SMOKING at any time during the films or during the
   classes. Normally the Wednesday screenings will be completed by 9:00
   P.M., but you should be prepared to stay longer at times, particularly
   in the case of The Birth of a Nation on January 29th and The Godfather
   on April 30th. Attendance at all classes and screenings is required.
   Examinations will be given ONLY on the dates listed except in the
   case of a documentable medical emergency, hospitalization, or death
   in the family. THERE WILL BE NO EXCEPTIONS.

Leslie Fishbein
American Studies Department
F.A.S., Rutgers University

Spring, 1986
Monday, Thursday, 2nd: 9:50-11:10
in Food Science Auditorium
Wednesday: 7:00-9:00 P.M. in
Hickman Hall 138

AMERICAN STUDIES 01:050:262: AMERICAN FILM AND AMERICAN MYTH

CRITICAL PAPER TOPICS:

1. Compare and contrast the attitudes toward women on Shanghai Express (1932) and Gold Diggers of 1933 (1933). How clearly do these films distinguish between respectable women and their fallen sisters? How do such women react respectively in crisis situations? Shanghai Express had a European director transplanted to Hollywood, Josef von Sternberg, Gold Diggers of 1933 an American one, Mervyn LeRoy. Do you discern any cultural differences in their portrayals of women? DUE ONLY ON MONDAY, FEBRUARY 17TH.

2. Compare and contrast the racial attitudes of The Birth of a Nation (1915) and King Kong (1933). How do these films distinguish white and black culture? Which aspects of black culture do they celebrate? Which do they denigrate? Do you see any substantial alteration in racial attitudes by the time of King Kong? DUE ONLY ON MONDAY, FEBRUARY 24TH.

3. Compare and contrast the social values in two films directed by John Ford, Stagecoach (1939) and The Grapes of Wrath (1940). How do these films treat such issues as the relationship between society and the individual, criminality, the social function of women within a community, the role of the West, and economic opportunity? Are these films pessimistic or optimistic or neither regarding American society? DUE ONLY ON MONDAY, APRIL 7TH.

4. Compare and contrast the treatments of the success theme in Citizen Kane (1941) and Mildred Pierce (1945). Citizen Kane deals with a successful businessman and Mildred Pierce with a successful business-woman. How do these films treat such issues as ethics in business, family life, romance, and ambition? Do the foci and attitudes in these films differ substantially on account of the differing gender of their respective protagonists? Do these films posit any substantial difference in the way in which the American Gospel of Success affects men and women? DUE ONLY ON MONDAY, APRIL 14TH.

OFFICE: Language Arts 024C

OFFICE HOURS: Monday: 1:30-2:30
Wednesday: 12:30-2:30
and by appointment

OFFICE TELEPHONE: 932-9179

Leslie Fishbein
American Studies Department
F.A.S., Rutgers University

Spring, 1986
Monday, Thursday, 2nd: 9:50-11:10
in Food Science Auditorium
Wednesday: 7:00-9:00 P.M. in
Hickman Hall 138

AMERICAN STUDIES 01: 050:262: AMERICAN FILM AND AMERICAN MYTH

ASSIGNMENTS:

No.	Week of:	Readings and Films:
I.	January 20th	January 20th: Film Firsts (1963) January 22nd: Basic Film Terms: A Visual Dictionary (1970); CITIZEN KANE (1941) January 23rd: The Life of an American Fireman (1903); The Great Train Robbery (1904) Bordwell and Thompson, Chapter 1, pp. 3-20 Chapter 4, pp. 82-116; pp. 277-284, 345 353. Sklar, Chapter 1, pp. 3-17; Chapter 2, pp. 18-32, Ch. 3, pp. 33-47.
II.	January 27th	January 27th: The Musketeers of Pig Alley (1912) January 29th: THE BIRTH OF A NATION (1915) (175 minutes) Bordwell and Thompson, Chapter 2, pp. 23-43 Sklar, Chapter 4, pp. 48-64. Mast, pp. 41-135.
III.	February 3rd	February 3rd: LITTLE CAESAR (1930) February 5th: Basic Principles of Film Editing SHANGHAI EXPRESS (1932) Bordwell and Thompson, Chapter 3, pp. 44-81 pp. 364-367. Sklar, Chapter 5, pp. 67-85; Chapter 6, pp 86-103. Mast, pp. 239-308, 379-383.
IV.	February 10th MONDAY, FEBRUARY 10TH: QUIZ	February 12th: Film: The Art of the Impossible (1972) GOLD DIGGERS OF 1933 (1933) Bordwell and Thompson, Chapter 5, pp. 119-150. Sklar, Chapter 8, pp. 122-140; Chapter 9, pp. 141-157; Chapter 10, pp. 161-174. Mast, pp. 315-365.

Leslie Fishbein
American Studies Department
F.A.S., Rutgers University

Spring, 1986
Monday, Thursday 2nd: 9:50-11:10
in Food Science Auditorium
Wednesday: 7:00-9:00 P.M. in
Hickman Hall 138

AMERICAN STUDIES 01:050:262: AMERICAN FILM AND AMERICAN MYTH

ASSIGNMENTS:

No.	Week of:	Readings and Films:
V.	February 17th MONDAY, FEBRUARY 17TH: FIRST CRITI-CAL PAPER DUE	February 17th: The Three Little Pigs (1933) February 19th: KING KONG (1933) Bordwell and Thompson, Chapter 6, pp. 151-198. Sklar, Chapter 11, pp. 175-194; Chapter 12, pp. 195-214. Mast, pp. 315-365.
VI.	February 24th MONDAY, FEBRUARY 24TH: SECOND CRITI-CAL PAPER DUE	February 26th: I AM A FUGITIVE FROM A CHAIN GANG (1932) Bordwell and Thompson, Chapter 7, pp. 199-231. Sklar, Chapter 13, pp. 215-227. Mast, pp. 201-204.
VII.	March 3rd THURSDAY, MARCH 6TH: MIDSEMESTER EXAM	March 3rd: Easy Street (1917) March 5th: MODERN TIMES (1936) Bordwell and Thompson, Chapter 8, pp. 232-260. Sklar, Chapter 7, pp. 104-121. Mast, pp. 155-157.
VIII.	March 10th	March 10th: The Battle at Elderbush Gulch (1913) March 12th: Gunsmoke Editing STAGECOACH (1939) Bordwell and Thompson, pp. 296-300. Sklar, Chapter 14, pp. 228-246. Mast, pp. 383-403, 419-438.
IX.	March 17th	MIDSEMESTER BREAK
X.	March 24th	March 26th: REBECCA (1940) Sklar, Chapter 16, pp. 269-285. Mast, pp. 441-496, 620-639.

Leslie Fishbein
American Studies Department
F.A.S., Rutgers University

Spring, 1986
Monday, Thursday 2nd: 9:50-11:10
in Food Science Auditorium
Wednesday: 7:00-9:00 P.M. in
Hickman Hall 138

AMERICAN STUDIES 01:050:262: AMERICAN FILM AND AMERICAN MYTH

ASSIGNMENTS:

No.	Week of:	Readings and Films:
XI.	March 31st	March 31st: The Plow That Broke the Plains (1936) April 2nd: GRAPES OF WRATH (1940) John Steinbeck, The Grapes of Wrath pp. 1-502.
XII.	April 7th MONDAY, APRIL 7TH: THIRD CRITICAL PAPER DUE	April 9th: MILDRED PIERCE (1945) Nathanael West, The Day of the Locust, Biographical Note on Nathanael West; Introduction by Alfred Kazin, v-xvii; pp. 21-202. Mast, pp. 403-419.
XIII.	April 14th MONDAY, APRIL 14TH: FOURTH CRITICAL PAPER DUE	April 16th: THE SNAKE PIT (1948) Sklar, Chapter 15, pp. 249-265. Mast, pp. 496-594.
XIV.	April 21st	April 23rd: SALT OF THE EARTH (1954) Lillian Hellman, Scoundrel Time, Introduction by Garry Wills, pp. 1-31; pp. 35-150; About the Author, p. 151.
XV.	April 28th	April 30th: THE GODFATHER (1972) (171 minutes) Sklar, Chapter 17, pp. 286-304; Chapter 18, pp. 305-317. Mast, pp. 655-749.

THURSDAY, MAY 8TH, 8:30 A.M. - 11:30 A.M.:
FINAL EXAMINATION

184

HISTORY AND CRITICISM OF FILM: THE CONCEPT OF SPECTATORSHIP (352:527)
Miriam Hansen / Spring 1988
Office Hours: T 1:00-2:00, Th 11:30-12:30, 43 Mine St., Tel. 932-7355

Meetings: T 9:50am-12:30pm, 43 Mine St.
Screenings: M 7:40pm, Media Dept., Kilmer Library (or by arrangement)
Readings: Philip Rosen, ed. Narrative, Apparatus, Ideology (=R)
               + books and xeroxes on reserve at Alexander Library (=x)

Requirements: One short paper (5-7pp.), due Feb. 23, and one longer paper
               (15-20pp.), draft due March 29, final version due April 26.

Jan. 26:   THE CINEMATIC TEXT: HETEROGENEITY, UNQUOTABILITY, DÉFILEMENT

               Metz, excerpts from Film Language (R + x)
               Bellour, "The Unattainable Text" (x)
               Kuntzel, "A Note Upon the Filmic Apparatus," "Le Défilement" (x)

               Stagecoach (1/26, 7:40pm, 211 Van Dyck; opt.)

Febr. 2:   THE CINEMATIC APPARATUS: PERCEPTUAL TECHNOLOGY/IDEOLOGY

2/1:   Uncle Josh at the Moving Picture Show (Porter/Edison, 1902)
               Sherlock Jr. (Keaton, 1924)

               Plato, Parable of the Cave (x)
               Barthes, "Upon Leaving the Movie Theater" (x)
               Baudry, "Ideological Effects of the Basic Cinematographic
                    Apparatus" and "The Apparatus" (R, opt.)
               Metz, excerpts from The Imaginary Signifier (R), "The Fiction
                    Film and Its Spectator" (x, opt.)
               Doane, "Ideology and the Practice of Sound Editing and Mixing"
                    (x) and "The Voice in the Cinema" (R)

Febr. 9:   THE ECONOMY OF CLASSICAL NARRATIVE

2/8:   The Big Sleep (Hawks, 1946)

               Bordwell, "Classical Hollywood Cinema" (R)
               Heath, "Narrative Space" (R)
               Mulvey, "Visual Pleasure and Narrative Cinema" (R)
               Bellour, "The Obvious and the Code" (R)
               Kuhn, "The Big Sleep: Censorship, Film Text and Sexuality" (x)
               de Lauretis, Alice Doesn't, ch. 5, "Desire in Narrative" (opt.)

Febr. 16:   VISION, ENUNCIATION, IDENTIFICATION

2/15:   Marnie (Hitchcock, 1964) (6:10pm, D/C, Art History 200)

               Flitterman, "Woman, Desire, and the Look" (x)
               Bellour, "Hitchcock: The Enunciator" (x)
               Silverman, "Suture" (R, opt.)
               Branigan, "Formal Permutations of the Point-of-View Shot" (x)
               Browne, "The Spectator-in-the-Text: The Rhetoric of Stagecoach"

Febr. 23:   THE HISTORICAL CONSTRUCTION OF SPECTATORSHIP

2/22:   Correction Please (Burch, 1979)
              The Cheat (DeMille, 1915)

              In class: The "Teddy" Bears (Porter, 1907) + POV films

              Burch, "Primitivism and the Avant-Gardes" (R), "Porter, or
                  Ambivalence" (x), "How We Got into Pictures" (x) and
                  "Narrative/Diegesis—Limits, Thresholds" (x)
              Brewster, "A Scene at the 'Movies'" (x)
              Musser, "The Nickelodeon Era Begins" (x)
              Selected texts by Munsterberg and Woods (x)

              Stella Dallas (Vidor, 1937) (2/23, 7:40pm, VD 211)

March 1:   EXHIBITION, DISTRACTION, CONSUMERISM

2/29:   The Crowd (Vidor, 1929)

              Gunning, "The Cinema of Attractions," "An Unseen Energy..." (x)
              Kracauer, "Cult of Distraction" (x)
              Merritt, "Nickelodeon Theaters 1905-1914" (x)
              Allen, "Motion Picture Exhibition in Manhattan 1906-1912" (x)
              Peiss, Cheap Amusements: Working Women and Leisure in Turn-of-
                  the Century New York, ch. 6

March 8:   STAR SYSTEM; FEMALE SPECTATORSHIP

3/7:   The Son of the Sheik (Valentino, 1926)

              Dyer, Stars, part III, excerpts
              Doane, "Film and the Masquerade: Theorising the Female Spectator"
              Mayne, "Feminist Film Theory and Women at the Movies" (x)
              Hansen, "Pleasure, Ambivalence, Identification: Valentino and
                  Female Spectatorship" (x) + response by deCordova (x)

March 15:   GENRE AND IDENTIFICATION: MELODRAMA AND MASOCHISTIC MOBILITY

3/14:   Christopher Strong (Arzner, 1933)
              Stella Dallas (VHS tape)

              Kaplan, "The Case of the Missing Mother" (x)
              Williams, "'Something Else Besides a Mother" + Kaplan's response (x)
              Suter, "Feminine Discourse in Christopher Strong" (x)

March 29:   SPECTACLE AND NARRATIVE: PLEASURES OF PERFORMANCE

3/28:   Gilda (Charles Vidor, 1946) (VHS)
              or The Blue Angel (Sternberg/Dietrich, 1930)
              (Blonde Venus and Scarlet Empress, VHS tapes)

              Jacobs/deCordova, "Spectacle and Narrative Theory" (x)
              Studlar, "Masochism and the Perverse Pleasures of the Cinema" (x)
              Dyer, "Resistance through Charisma," "Entertainment and Utopia" (x)

April 5:   ASSAULTS ON VISUAL PLEASURE

4/4:   Un Chien Andalou (Bunuel/Dali, 1928)
             Weekend (Godard, 1967)

             Barthes, "Diderot, Brecht, Eisenstein" (R)
             Wollen, "Godard and Counter-Cinema: Vent d'Est" (R)
             Henderson, "Toward a Non-Bourgeois Camera Style" (x)
             Heath, "Lessons from Brecht" (x)

April 12:   ALTERNATIVE VISIONS

4/11:   Jeanne Dielman (Akerman, 1975) (6:10pm, D/C)

             Mulvey/MacCabe, "Images of Woman, Images of Sexuality"
             Bergstrom, Interview with Chantal Akerman (x)

April 19:   SPECTATORSHIP AND NATIONAL HISTORY/IDENTITY: GERMANY (I)

4/18:   Triumph of the Will (Riefenstahl, 1936)
             (tentatively: The Crimes of Dr. Mabuse)

             Neale, "Triumph of the Will: Documentary and Spectacle" (x)
             Kracauer, "The Mass Ornament" (x)
             Benjamin, "The Work of Art in the Age of Mechanical Reproduction" (x)

April 26:   SPECTATORSHIP AND NATIONAL HISTORY/IDENTITY: GERMANY (II)

4/25:   Lili Marleen (Fassbinder, 1980)--VHS

             Elsaesser, "Primary Identification and the Historical Subject:
                 Fassbinder and Germany" (R) and "Lili Marleen: Fascism and
                 the Film Industry" (x)

             Imitation of Life (4/26, 7:40pm, VD 211)

May 3:   AESTHETICISM, SELF-REFLEXIVITY, CULT; SPECTATORSHIP AND
             POSTMODERNISM

5/2:   Prizzi's Honor (Huston, 1985)--VHS
             (tentatively: Eraserhead or Choose Me--VHS)

             Polan, "Towards a Politics of Self-Reflexive Film" (x)
             Corrigan, "Film and the Culture of Cult" (x)

Professor Neil Isaacs
Professor Joe Miller

ENG 479: INDIVIDUAL INITIATIVE
AND THE LAW IN AMERICAN CINEMA

This course will probe the tradition of individual initiative ("enterprise") in American society as it relates to the flexible and inflexible parameters of the Law. Films grouped roughly within several distinct dramatic contexts will reveal what kind of "myth" law and order has been to the American consciousness. Structures of law missing, ignored, fought and transcended will be discussed after screenings of fourteen films from the years 1932 to 1971.

FRONTIER LAW: ORIGINS AND REVISIONS
Jan. 16th.   Welcome to Hard Times (Burt Kennedy, 1967)
Jan. 23rd.   Shane (George Stevens, 1953)
Jan. 30th.   McCabe and Mrs. Miller (Robert Altman, 1971)

DOMESTIC LAW
Feb 6th.   Rebel Without a Cause (Nicholas Ray, 1955)
Feb 13th.   The Grapes of Wrath (John Ford, 1940)
Feb 20th.   Night of the Hunter (Charles Laughton, 1955)

LAW FOUGHT OR IGNORED
Feb 27th.   Fury (Fritz Lang, 1935)
Mar 6th.   Bonnie and Clyde (Arthur Penn, 1967)
Mar 20th.   Lonely are the Brave (David Miller, 1962)

LAW TRANSCENDED
Mar 27th.   Cool Hand Luke (Stuart Rosenberg, 1967)
Apr 3rd.   Trouble in Paradise (Ernst Lubitsch, 1932)
Apr 10th.   They Shoot Horses, Don't They? (Sidney Pollack, 1969)

LAW AT THE TOP
Apr 17th.   Dr. Strangelove (Stanley Kubrick, 1963)
Apr 24th.   Topaz (Alfred Hitchcock, 1969)

Course Requirements: Attendance at Wednesday screenings and Friday discussions; one critical essay or research paper (typewritten, about ten pages) examining some aspect of the course's topic -- due April 17th; a final exam in class on May 1st.

COURSE REVIEW

A THEME IN AMERICAN CINEMA

My Life, Liberty and the Pursuit of Happiness = a Declaration
of Independence; or,

How are individual initiative and communal responsibility reconciled?

"I rebel, therefore we exist." -- Albert Camus

INDIVIDUAL AUTONOMY   Trouble in Paradise (?)

                             Cool Hand Luke

                             Lonely are the Brave

                             Bonnie and Clyde

                             Rebel Without a Cause

COMMUNAL RESPONSIBILITY   Welcome to Hard Times

                             Shane

                             The Grapes of Wrath

                             Fury

                             McCabe and Mrs. Miller

DISSOLUTION OF INDIVIDUAL   They Shoot Horses, Don't They?
AUTONOMY AND COMMUNAL
RESPONSIBILITY   Topaz

                             Dr. Strangelove

"Authority" ---Traditional, Patriarchal, Legal.
             ---Charismatic; autonomous, anarchic.

"Community"---Desireable? (Hard Times, Shane, Grapes of Wrath, etc.)
           ---Ambivalent? (Cool Hand Luke, Trouble in Paradise, Topaz, etc.)
           ---Impossible? (Rebel Without a Cause, Lonely are the Brave, They Shoot
                            Horses, Strangelove, etc.)

"Individuality"
             ---solitary? alienated? Indifferent? competitive, aggressive, exclusive?

189

Dr. E. Ann Kaplan
Office: 43 Mine St.
Hours: 2-0-3-0, and
        by appointment
Phone: #7355 or 8209

Syllabus: Popular Culture 350:367

The overall aim of this course is to understand the meanings and functions
of popular culture in the modern period. We will achieve this aim through analysis
of select theories of popular culture, from 1869 to 1986, and select examples of
different kinds of popular texts.

The course has four main parts after the Introduction: in Part I, we
examine how the concept of a "popular" as against a "high" culture evolved;
certain questions that will provide the framework for the rest of the course,
and that we hope to answer there, will be raised; for example, what does the
term "popular culture" mean? How is "popular" different from "folk" culture?
Why did popular culture come to be viewed as a largely "feminine" terrain?
What defenses emerged to counter this feminine identification? Is popular
culture necessarily reactionary/conservative, or progressive/liberal? Is its
main function entertainment, wish-fulfillment, a conveyor for ideologies,
subversion of the status quo? If none of these, what needs does it satisfy?
Why has the popular/high culture dichotomy recently become more difficult to
sustain? How do theories of postmodernism help explain the changed cultural
consciousness in the '80's?

In Part II, we examine some main women's genres in popular culture.
The literary origins of the popular woman's novel will be traced briefly
from Richardson's Clarissa to the Harlequin Romance. We will then study
selections from a popular 1930's woman's novel, Fannie Hurst's Imitation of
Life, analyzing its particular literary devices. We will look at the 1934
film version of Hurst's novel as an example of one popular Hollywood film
genre, the Woman's Film.

Study of the television Soap Opera, as a recent genre that takes off
from the popular woman's novel and Woman's Film will be studied next. The
study will however be prefaced by analysis of the impact of television on
the family, and of the various discourses that surrounded its invention and
proliferation as a kind of apparatus very different from the filmic one.
We will look at how ads function on television, studying the relationship
between ads and women's TV dramas. A session on Dallas, as a popular genre
appealing to both men and women, will conclude this unit of the course.

Part III will begin after the mid-semester exam on February 23rd.
This unit will study popular male genres, such as the crime story, film
noir, 50' television crime series. These arguably emerged to parade
masculinity in defense against the proliferation of female popular genres.
The development of the crime story from such so-called "high culture" texts
like Poe's and Hemingway's fiction will precede examination of one main male
popular Hollywood film genre, film noir. We will compare and contrast
Hemingway's "high culture" short story "The Killers" with two Hollywood film
versions, and then look at a 50's crime series with noir overtones, The
Untouchables. We will end this unit with examining a recent crime show,
Miami Vice, that betrays postmodernist characteristics.

It is to the development of a supremely postmodernist TV genre, the rock video, that we turn in the last section of the course; here we will study various theories of postmodernism: we will try to account for the causes of the new cultural developments and study their implications for the future.

Required Texts: Please buy at once the following texts:

Roland Barthes Mythologies (Barthes)

E. Ann Kaplan, ed. Regarding Television: Critical Approaches--An Anthology (RT)

Hal Foster, ed. The Anti-Aesthetic: Essays in Postmodern Culture (AA)

Book of Readings, available for purchase at Kinko's (BR)

Course Requirements:

1. Class attendance required: many sessions involve visual materials which cannot be repeated and on which you will be examined.

2. Class participation encouraged, although this is a large class.

3. You must come to class prepared to discuss readings; there will be occasional quizzes on readings and students may be asked verbal questions about them; responses will count toward the grade.

4. Two in-class exams (a mid-semester and a final exam.).

5. One paper in second half of the course.

Class Materials and Assignments

1/19   Introduction
       Readings: BR M. Arnold, From Culture and Anarchy (1869)
                  BR D. MacDonald, "Mass Cult, Parts I & II" (1960)

1/22   Lecture: What does "Popular Culture" mean?
       Definitions of "high" versus "low" culture
       Visual Examples, to make the concepts clear
       Readings: BR Ortega Y Gasset, From The Dehumanization of Art (1922)
                  Barthes, on Wrestling, pp. 15-25; and pp. 56-64; pp. 103-105
                  BR E. A. Kaplan, "Is the Gaze Male?"

1/26   Lecture: Popular Culture, the Everyday and the Place of Women in the Development of Mass Culture.
       Slides re the "male" gaze as it constructs women
       Readings: BR Excerpts from Fannie Hurst novel, Imitation of Life
                  BR: Richard Dyer, "Entertainment or Utopia"

1/29   Unit I: Women's Genres in Popular Culture
       (a)   The Woman's Popular Novel
       Lecture: The Literary Origins of the Woman's Popular Novel: Problems of Mass Culture, the feminine and race (Issues raised here to be taken up in March 10 lecture by Jane Gaines)
                  Barthes, "Myth Today," pp. 109-159
                  McCluhan, Understanding Media (Excerpts)

2/02 (b) The "Woman's Film":
      Film Showing (entire period): John Stahl's Imitation of Life
      Reading: Fannie Hurst's Imitation of Life (Excerpts)

2/05 Lecture: The Hollywood Woman's Film, Imitation of Life:
                Myth, Realism and the "classical" style
                Show video clips from the film
      Reading: BR L. Mulvey, "Notes on Melodrama"

2/09 Lecture: Melodrama, the family and Soap Opera: the 1940's
                From Radio Soaps to TV Soaps
                The Impact of World War II on Women's mass culture
                (Possible) Extract from Film Rosie the Riveter
      Readings: RT" Feuer on Live TV, pp. 12-22; and J. Allen on Social Matrix
                of TV, pp. 109-119

2/12 Lecture: TV Reception in the '50's
                Clip from The Honeymooners re TV discourses about TV
      Readings: RT Modleski and Brunsdon on TV Soaps, pp. 67-83
                R. Allen, "On Reading Soaps," pp. 84-108

2/16 Lecture: TV Soaps as Female Mass Culture Form
      (c) TV Soaps: General Hospital as example
      Readings: RT, Flitterman, pp. 84-95
                Barthes, pp. 36-38; 41-42

2/19 Lecture: TV, Soaps and Advertising: Ideology and Mass Culture
                Show/discuss ads in General Hospital episode
      Readings: BR Poe and Hemingway Stories
                BR: Kaplan, "Introduction to Women in Film Noir"
                BR: Place/Peterson, "Some Visual Motifs in Film Noir"
                BR Schrader, "Notes on Film Noir"

2/23 In-Class Mid-Term Exam: Whole Period

2/26 Unit III: Popular Male Genres
      (a) The Crime Story: 1920's-30's
      Lecture: Male Genres as Defense Against Feminization of Popular Culture
      (b) Film Noir: Impact of World War II on Male Mass Culture
      Readings: BR: R. Warshow, "The Gangster as Tragic Hero"

3/02 Film Showing: Siodmak's The Killers (1946) (Whole period)

3/05 Guest Lecture: Prof. William Walling, Rutgers University
      "Masculinity and Film Noir in The Killers"
      Reading: Hemingway's "The Killers"; select tales by Poe

3/09 Guest Lecture: Prof. Jane Gaines, Duke University
      Lecture: "Black Beauty Culture in the South"
      Slide Show
      (With ref. to issues raised in unit on Imitation of Life)
      Reading: Jane Gaines essay in Culture Critique (1986)

3/12 (c) TV Crime Genre: Case of The Untouchables
         Lecture: TV Appropriation of the Crime Story & Film Noir: Changing
                   Images of the Investigator and Criminal
         Show Clips from The Untouchables
         Readings: BR: Barthes, "The Death of the Author"
                   AA: Jameson, "Postmodernism and Consumer Society"
                   AA: Baudrillard, "The Ecstasy of Communication"

3/16 & 3/19: Vacation

3/23 Film Showing: 1974 version of The Killers (Lee Marvin) (Whole period)
         Short paper by students on differences between the film versions, with
         reference to Hemingway's original
         Readings: AA: Introduction, pp. ix-xvi
                   AA: E. Said, "Opponents, Audiences . . .", pp. 135-159

3/26 Unit IV: Postmodernism in Recent Mass Culture-
         (a) The Postmodernist Crime Genre: Miami Vice
         Lecture: Postmodernism and Contemporary Culture in Miami Vice
                   Excerpts of the show for analysis
         Readings: RT: R. Stam, "Television News" pp. 23-40; Morse, on TV
                   Sport, pp. 44-67;
                   AA: Owens on "Feminists and Postmodernism," pp. 57-82

3/30 (b) The Televisual Apparatus as "postmodernist"
         Lecture: Women, Television and Postmodernism
         Clips from the News, Sports
         Readings: BR: Ien Ang, "Dallas and The Ideology of Mass Culture"
                   Barthes, "Striptease," pp. 84-87

4/02 Lecture: Women and TV: The Case of Dallas
         Show clips from the show
         Readings: BR: Kaplan, "A Postmodern Play of the Signifier?"

4/06 (c) Postmodernism and Television: The Case of The Rock Video
         Lecture: Self-Relexivity and Music Television: An Avant-garde Popular
                   Aesthetic? The end of high/low concepts?
         Intro to the Five Types of Video
         Reading:

4/09 Lecture: Production and Exhibition of Rock Videos
                   Advertising, Pastiche and Schizophrenia
         Clips re similarities ads and videos; the 24 hour flow
         Reading: BR: White and Stallybrass: From The Politics and Poetics
                   of Transgression

4/13 Lecture: Sexual Difference in Videos on MTV: I
                   Clips from and analysis of videos with male stars

4/16 Lecture: Sexual Difference in Videos on MTV: II
                   Clips from and analysis of videos with female stars
         Reading: BR: Baudrillard, "The Precession of Simulacra"

4/20 Lecture: Simulation and the "Socially Conscious" Video
                Clips from and analysis of Socially Conscious Videos

4/23 Lecture: The Postmodernist Video: Subversion/regression and signs of
                the future.
                Clips from and analysis of select postmodernist and avant-garde
                videos

4/27 Showing of tape of recent movie, _Videodrome_ (tentative) (Whole period)

4/30 Postmodernism, Consumer Culture and the Televisual Apparatus: The new
      cultural Consciousness
      Discussion of _Videodrome_; review of the course

Dr. E. Ann Kaplan

Informal and Anonymous Survey of
Students' Consumption of Popular Culture

Part I: Hours Spent on Activities:

1. How many hours a week do you watch TV?
    (a) at home _____
    (b) at college _____

2. How many times a week do you go to the cinema?
    (a) at home _____
    (b) at college _____

3. How many hours do you listen to popular music on the radio?
    (a) at home _____
    (b) at college _____

4. How many hours do you spend listening to the radio for programs other than
    music?
    (a) at home _____
    (b) at college _____

5. How many hours do you spend reading popular novels and magazines?
    (a) at home _____
    (b) at college _____

6. How many hours do you spend doing other kinds of popular culture activities?
    activity _____ (a) at home _____
    _____ (b) at college _____
    _____
    _____

Part II: Kinds of Materials Consumed:

1. Which TV Programs to you watch regularly? Give Brief Reasons:
    _____
    _____

2. Which TV Programs do you watch occasionally? Give Brief Reasons:
    _____
    _____

3. Which TV Programs do you avoid? Give Brief Reasons:
    _____
    _____

4. Which kinds of films do you enjoy? Give Brief Reasons:
    _____
    _____

5. Which kinds of popular music do you listen to? Give Reasons:

_____

_____

6. What other radio programs do you enjoy? Give Reasons:

_____

_____

7. What do you get out of the popular culture activities you listed in Part I, question 6? Briefly explain:

_____

_____

Part III: Ideas about Popular Culture:

Put a check ( ) where you agree, a cross ( ) where you disagree:

Popular Culture...:

(a) is sheer entertainment _____
(b) is loaded with ideology _____
(c) is a release from tension _____
(d) satisfies certain of my needs _____
(e) is boring _____
(f) is interesting _____
(g) is junk _____
(h) has artistic merit _____
(i) is often sexist _____
(j) is never racist _____

Put a check ( ) where you agree, a cross ( ) where you disagree:

The TV set...:

(a) is something I control _____
(b) is something I have no control over _____
(c) tempts me to keep switching channels _____
(d) is an intrusion in my room _____
(e) is comforting in my room _____
(f) hypnotises me _____
(g) is fun to watch with friends _____
(h) is a distraction from my work _____
(i) enables me to concentrate on my work _____
(j) helps me forget I'm lonely _____
(k) causes conflict with friends/family _____
(l) ensures no fights take place _____
(m) irritates me _____

I consider myself above popular culture _____
I consider myself a popular culture addict _____
I never thought one way or another about my relation to popular culture _____

AL 310

AMERICAN FILM: ECONOMICS

PROFESSOR CECIL MACKEY

This course uses feature films and selected readings as a
basis for exploring major issues of economics and public policy.
It begins with an examination of the impact of technology and the
competitive position of the US in the world economy, then deals
with specific contemporary economic problems.   These include:
the role and status of women in the   economy; the history and
current status of the American labor movement; minorities and the
economy, focusing particularly on the rural south and the urban
north; depression, recession and unemployment, together with
problems of the migrant worker; immigration policy and the U. S.-
Latin American economic relations; the role of the modern
corporation in society; international finance, foreign debt, and
oil in the world economy.

The class will be discussion, analysis, and question-and-
answer format, calling on the students to interpret the issues in
the context of the films and the assigned readings, and to
formulate their ideas as to possible solutions or proposed
methods of dealing with problems, as well as legislative and
public policy implications.   Tests will be essay type, asking
students to apply their knowledge and analysis to new, complex
fact situations.   The laboratory hours are for film screening.

AL 310

AMERICAN FILM: ECONOMICS

FILMS USED

1. MODERN TIMES

2. HEARTLAND

3. THE MOLLY McGUIRES

4. NORMA RAE

5. SOUNDER

6. RAISIN IN THE SUN

7. GRAPES OF WRATH

8. EL NORTE

9. EXECUTIVE SUITE

10. ROLLOVER

AL 310 - AMERICAN FILM: ECONOMICS

Assigned Readings for Individual Films

1. **Modern Times**

    Automation
    - Report "America's Competitive Challenge: The Need for a National Response," submitted by the Business Higher Education Forum to the President of the U.S. in May, 1983.

    FDR Speech
    - Campaign Address, Sept. 23, 1932. (Handout)

2. **Heartland**

    "The Problem That Has No Name"
    - Feminine Mystique by Betty Friedan.

    Two sections from Women and the West
    - A Short Social History by William Forrest Sprague. (Handout)

    The Status of Women: A Chronology
    - Handout

3. **The Molly McGuires**

    "Anthracite"
    - American Labor Struggles 1877-1934, by Samuel Yellen.

    Songs of Labor:

    "My Sweetheart is a Mule"
    "Talking Union"
    "Joe Hill"
    "Solidarity Forever"
    "The Avondale Mine Disaster"
    - Songs of Work and Protest, collected by Edith Fowke and Joe Glazer, N.Y., Dover Publications, Inc. 1973.

    Labor: A Chronology
    - Handout

4. Norma Rae

Songs of Labor	- Same as for The Molly McGuires
"The Southern Textile Strikes and Gastonia"	- American Labor Struggles 1877-1934, by Samuel Yellen.

5. Sounder

"Stepping Across the Line"	- MS Magazine, November 1984.
"Fifth Avenue Uptown: A Letter from Harlem"	- Nobody Knows My Name, James Baldwin, N. Y., Dell Publication
Rights in the U. S.: A Chronology	- Handout
"We Shall Overcome"	- Songbook, by Joan Baez.
Article: "Carma"	- Cane, by Jean Toomer, New York: Liveright, 1975.

6. Raisin in the Sun

    Same as Sounder

7. Grapes of Wrath

Agriculture in the U. S.: A Chronology	- Handout
Migrant Labor in the U. S.: A Chronology	- Handout
"Migrant Farm Workers Still Face a Harsh Life"	- U. S. News & World Report, Aug. 9, 1982, Vol. 93.
"The Migrants Stoop, the Growers Conquer"	- The Progressive, March, 1982, Vol. 46.

8. **El Norte**

    U. S. Immigration   - Handout
    Policy: A Chronology

    "Mexican   Illegal   - A History of the Mexican-
    Aliens"   American People, Julian Samora
                                    and   Patricia   V.   Simon,
                                    University   of   Notre   Dame
                                    Press, 1977.

    "Who is La Raza"   - Makers of America -- Emergent
                                 Minorities,   1955-1970,   Vol.
                                 10.   Encyclopedia   Britannica
                                 Educational Corporation, 1971.

    "Congress   and   Mexican   - In   Their   Place: White
    Immigration   America Defines Her
    Restriction"   Minorities. 1850-1950,   Lewis
                                    H.   Carlson   and   George   A.
                                    Colburn,   Editors,   New   York:
                                    John Wiley & Sons, Inc., 1972.

    "Immigration Reform   - Congressional Quarterly, Vol.
    Snagged on Issue of   42, No. 39, Sept. 29, 1984.
    Discrimination"

9. **Executive Suite**

    "The Big Corporation"   - The Age of Uncertainty, John
                                 Kenneth   Galbraith,   Houghton
                                 Mifflin Co., Boston, 1977.

    "The Business of   - Harpers, December 1976
    Buying Friends"

    "The   Lockheed   Scandal"   -   Americana   Annual   1977
                                 (Yearbook   of   Encyclopedia
                                 Americana.)

10. <u>Rollover</u>

"Global Recovery and   - An Address by Walter B.
World Debt"   Wriston,   Chairman,
                            Citibank/Citicorp,   June   4,
                            1984.

"Latin American Debt   - Addresses by William R.
Update"   Rhodes, Senior Vice President,
                            Citibank/Citicorp,   April,
                            1984.

"OPEC's Crude New   - <u>Newsweek</u>, Nov. 12, 1984.
Strategy"

"For OPEC, Worst   - <u>U. S. News & World Report</u>,
is Yet to Come"   Nov. 5, 1984.

"Making Oil a Scarcer   - <u>Time</u>, Nov. 12, 1984.
Commodity"

202

PROFESSOR CECIL MACKEY
AL 310
AMERICAN FILM: LAW

Spring 1988

This course, using major American feature films and selected readings, is intended to provide an introduction to the American legal system, its role and functions. It begins with material dealing with the English history and background of common law concepts, introduces principal legal philosophies, and then deals specifically with several current legal issues of major public policy impact. These include: the Supreme Court, the nature of its internal operations and its role in American life; First Amendment issues, with particular attention to the role of the press in society today; constitutional issues of the free exercise of religion and the relationship of religion to the school curriculum; criminal law and procedure, especially the trends in judicial treatment of the rights of the accused; the jury system, its history and origins, as well as an assessment of its effectiveness and suitability today and for the future; the penal system, its underlying philosophy and objectives, together with an assessment of its performance and needs; trends in the law of torts, particularly in the area of medical malpractice, and legislative implications; family law and the impact on the law of rapidly changing social and cultural norms, particularly the abused family member (spouse, parent, or child); the treatment of U.S. citizens by other nations' legal systems.

The class will be discussion, analysis, and question-and-answer format, calling on the students to interpret the issues in the context of the films and the assigned readings, and to formulate their ideas as to possible solutions or proposed methods of dealing with problems, as well as legislative and public policy implications. Tests will be essay type, asking students to apply their knowledge and analysis to new, complex fact situations. The laboratory hours are for film screening.

The use of a number of judicial decisions in the reading assignments is intended to provide insight into the process of judicial reasoning, as well as an understanding of the importance of the use of precedent in the Anglo-American legal system.

A typical university student, indeed, the average citizen, knows little of the nature and workings of the nation's legal system, has infrequent personal contact with the system, and rarely understands the importance of the legal system in determining political, economic and social policy and decisions. This course is designed to bring the student into direct contact with each of these areas. It utilizes several excellent, award winning films as a principal vehicle for examining some of the most important personal and institutional relationships that exist as a part of our legal system.

AL 310 AMERICAN FILM: LAW

Films Used

1. A MAN FOR ALL SEASONS

2. THE FIRST MONDAY IN OCTOBER

3. ABSENCE OF MALICE

4. INHERIT THE WIND

5. THE STAR CHAMBER

6. TWELVE ANGRY MEN

7. BRUBAKER

8. THE VERDICT

9. THE BURNING BED

10. MIDNIGHT EXPRESS

AL 310 - American Film: Law

Assigned Readings for Individual Films

A Man for All Seasons

A History of American Law
Lawrence M. Friedman, Simon and Schuster, 1973
Prologue, pp, 13 - 25

The First Monday in October

The Brethren: Inside the Supreme Court
Bob Woodward and Scott Anderson
Simon and Schuster, 1979
Prologue, pp. 9 - 26

Court at the Crossroads
TIME, October 8, 1984
pp. 28 - 33

Marbury v. Madison
1 Cranch 137, 2 L., ED. 60 (1803)

Harvard Law School Bulletin
The Greying of the Court: Constitutional
  History's Halley's Comet
Laurence H. Tribe

Even A Lower-Court Nominee Gets Microscopic
  Treatment
Howard Jenkins, Jr.
INSIGHT, February 1, 1988
pp. 16 - 17

Absence of Malice

The Press: Journalism Under Fire
TIME, December 12, 1983
pp. 76 - 93

New York Time Company v. Sullivan
376 U.S. 254 (1964)

Gertz v. Robert Welch, Inc.
418 U.S. 323 (1974)

Inherit the Wind

The Constitution, That Delicate Balance
Fred W. Friendly and Martha J. H. Elliott
Random House, 1985
God in the Classroom - The Exercise of
Religion v. Establishment of Religion
(Chapter 7), pp., 109 - 129

Epperson v. Arkansas
393 U.S. 97 (1968)

The Star Chamber

The Constitution, That Delicate Balance
Fred W. Friendly and Martha J.H. Elliott
Random House, 1985
A Knock at the Door, How the Supreme Court
Created a Rule to Enforce the Fourth Amendment
(Chapter 8), pp. 129 - 142

Crime in America
Ramsey Clark
Simon and Schuster, 1970
Nature and Causes of Crime
pp. 20 - 51

Miranda v. Arizona
384 U.S. 436 (1966)

Gordon V. Wainwright
316 U.W. 455, pp. 336-345 (1963)

Twelve Angry Men

Law and Modern Society
P.S. Atiyah
Oxford University Press, 1983
Juries, pp. 20 - 24

The American Legal System
David E. Brody
C. C. Heath & Co., 1979
The Jury System, Role of the Judge and
Rules of Evidence
pp., 103 - 112

Duncan v. Louisiana
391 U.S. 145 (1968)

Williams v. Florida; Apodaca v. Florida
399 U.S. 78 (1970)   406 U.S. 404 (1972)

206

Brubaker

Crime in American
Ramsey Clark
Simon and Schuster, 1970

Prisons, Factories of Crime
(Chapter 13), pp. 192 - 218

The Verdict

A History of American Law
Lawrence M. Friedman
Simon and Schuster, 1973
Torts, (Chapter VI), pp., 409 - 427

Slater v. Baker and Stapleton
95 Eng. Rep. 860 (KB 1776)

The Burning Bed

Criminals and Victims
Lois G. Forer
W. W. Norton, 1980
Family Crimes
(Chapter XII), pp. 175 - 193

Criminals and Victims
Lois G. Forer
W. W. Norton, 1980
The Child and the Law
(Chapter XVI) pp. 248 - 265

A History of American Law
Lawrence M. Friedman
Simon and Schuster, 1973
The Law of Personal Status: Wives, Paupers
   and Slaves
(Chapter IV)
Marriage and Divorce
pp. 179 - 184

Family Property
pp. 184 - 186

Midnight Express

The Law of Nations
J. L. Brierly
6th Edition, Edited by Sir Humphrey Waldock
Oxford at the Clarendon Press, 1963

The Jurisdiction of States - (Chapter VI)
    Section 5, The Limitation Upon a State's
    Treatment of Aliens, pp. 275 - 291

    Section 6, Limits Upon a State's
    Treatment of Its Own Nationals,
    pp. 291 - 299

    Section 7, The Limits Upon a State's
    Criminal Jurisdiction, pp. 299 - 304

Laura M. B. James Claim
(United States v. Mexico)
United States and Mexico General Claims
  Commission (1926)
    1927 Opinions of Commissioners 108
    4 U. N. Report of International Arbitral
    Awards 82

B. E. Chattin Claim
(United States v. Mexico)
United States and Mexico General Claims
  Commission (1926)
    1917 Opinions of Commissioners 422
    4 U.N. Report of International Arbitral
    Awards 282

The Charter of the United Nations
Articles 55 and 56

Professor Charles J. Maland, University of Tennessee

FILM AND AMERICAN CULTURE

This course is cross-listed with the American Studies
Program and concentrates, as the course title suggests, on the
relationship between American narrative feature films and the
culture in which they were made. Sometimes the course has a greater
emphasis on film history than it does on the syllabus below. When
film history plays a larger role, Robert Sklar's <u>Movie-Made
America</u> is one of the required texts. Three broad approaches are
emphasized in this version of the course: formalist, genre, and
cultural/ideological. But students are also encouraged to draw
on these or other approaches--like feminist or <u>auteur</u>--when they
prepare their research papers.

Film and American Culture
English 3445

MW 10-10:50 (lec/disc)
T 3-5:15 (screening)

Film and American Culture is based on the assumption that there is
a close and complex relationship between feature films and the
society in which they are made. It also assumes that movies, if
examined carefully and thoughtfully, are much richer sources for
cultural analysis than we normally assume. Proceeding from these
two assumptions, we will consider films both as art works and as
social documents. By the end of the course you should be able to
do several things:

1. To trace the evolution of American movies in the sound
    era, and to discuss the historical context of the films we
    see during the term.
2. To carry out convincing analysis of individual film narratives,
    showing how character interaction and development of conflict
    lead to affirmation or criticism of particular cultural values,
    attitudes, and ways of living.
3. To understand and recognize narrative and stylistic conventions
    of the "Classical Hollywood Cinema."
4. To discuss with some sophistication the ways in which American
    society and American movies relate, drawing especially from the
    formalist, ideological, and genre approaches to films. (Are
    films more closely related to the material world or the world
    of ideas? Do movies reflect, shape, criticize, affirm, or
    distort culture and society?)

To reach these objectives, eveyone will need to participate actively
by reading assignments before class time of the day they're assigned,
watching films (most in class, some outside of the class), discussing and writing about the readings and films. Above all, each
student will need to think about movies more actively and penetrat-
ingly than we may be used to doing.

REQUIRED BOOKS:

Robert Ray, <u>A Certain Tendency in the Hollywood Cinema, 1930-1980</u>
Thomas Schatz, <u>Hollywood Genres</u>

PAPERS:

Each student will write one brief (600 words or less) essay and
one longer (2500 words) research essay; both should be typewritten.
The first, which will be graded pass/no credit, should focus on
what cultural values are endorsed and criticized through the central
character conflicts of <u>Mr. Smith Goes to Washington</u>. Do your own
analysis without research on paper one. The longer paper should
analyze one or several films to develop a thesis or an argument about
the cultural/ideological significance of popular American films.
For this paper, you have more leeway in developing your topic, including the use of recent popular films (for example, you might
explore how some of the heroes of popular films in recent years--
like <u>An Officer and a Gentleman</u> or <u>Top Gun</u>--relate to the heroic types
described in Ray's book). However, I'd like you to talk to me about
your topic as you begin thinking about it. You ought to do research for the second paper (including drawing from our assigned
readings if you wish). Be sure to use proper citation form.
(See me if you have questions about that.)

                    Due Dates:
        October 16   (600 words)--essay one
        November 25 (2500-3000 words)--research essay

Essays will be evaluated according to three criteria: 1) quality
and clarity of the main idea; 2) quality and clarity of the presentation of that main idea; and 3) general correctness and effectiveness
of mechanics, grammar, and style. Make the writing your most effective. Though the first essay is pass/fail, a failed essay must
be rewritten until acceptable if you wish to pass the class.

RESERVE READING:

I have placed on reserve in Hodges Library a considerable number
of texts generally related to the course and some specifically
related to the films we are seeing this term. Periodically through
the term I will suggest outside reading from these works. You also
may wish to look them over as you think about and plan your research
essay.

Allen, Robert, and Douglas Gomery. Film History: Theory and Practice
Basinger, Jeanine, ed., The "It's a Wonderful Life" Book
Bergman, Andrew. We're in the Money
Bordman, Thompson, and Staiger. The Classical Hollywood Cinema
Capra, Frank. Name Above the Title
Carringer, Robert. The Making of "Citizen Kane"
Cawelti, John. The Six-Gun Mystique
Gallagher, Tag. John Ford
Giannetti, Louis, Masters of the American Cinema
Grant, Barry, ed., Douglas Sirk
Halliday, Jon. Sirk on Sirk
Haskell, Molly. From Reverence to Rape
Jowett, Garth. Film: The Democratic Art
Kolker, Robert. A Cinema of Loneliness
McBride, Joseph. Orson Welles
Maland, Charles. Frank Capra
Mellen, Joan. Big Bad Wolves
Naremore, James. Orson Welles
Rosen, Marge. Popcorn Venus
Sarris, Andrew. The American Cinema
Sklar, Robert. Movie-Made America
Wood, Robin. Hollywood from Vietnam to Reagan

EXAMS:

All students will take a mid-term and a final exam.

GRADING:
  Short papers, any quizzes or library projects, and class
    participation: 20%
  Midterm Exam: 20%
  Longer Paper: 30%
  Final Exam: 30%

READING AND VIEWING SCHEDULE

     (Unless otherwise indicated, the films will be shown in
Art and Architecture 111. Attendence is, of course, required.
You will note that several of our showings will be at Non-Print,
which is located in the second floor of Hodges Library. If you
can not make an extra group showing, you should see the film on
your own before the next scheduled class period. Simply take your
ID to Hodges Non-Print and ask to see the film."
                    R = Ray, A Certain Tendency
                    S = Schatz, Hollywood Genres

   I. CLASSICAL HOLLYWOOD CINEMA AND FILM FORM

SEPTEMBER
28: Introduction to the course--the language of movies
29: <u>Tootsie</u> (1984)--R, 25-55
30: <u>Narratives</u> and Cultural Values--R, 55-69, S, 29-34

OCTOBER
 5: The Classical Hollywood Cinema and Variations
 6: <u>Citizen Kane</u> (1941)--S, ch. 5
 7: Discuss Narrative, Style, and Cultural Values in <u>Kane</u>
 8: SPECIAL SCREENING: <u>Mr. Smith Goes to Washington</u> (1939),
    3:10-5:10 in Hodges 251 (Alternative screening: Saturday,
    Oct. 10, 9:30-11:30 in Hodges 251)

II. FILM GENRES AND AMERICAN CULTURE

12: The Screwball Comedy--S, chs. 1, 2, and 6; PAPER ONE DUE
13: <u>Adam's Rib</u> (1954)
14: Discuss <u>Adam's Rib</u> and Romantic Comedy

19: The Western: America's "Foundation Myth"--R, ch. 2 and 215-43
    SPECIAL SCREENING: <u>The Man Who Shot Liberty Valance</u> (1962)
    3:30-5:30 in Hodges 252 (Alternate screening Oct. 20, 7-9
    in Hodges 211)
20: <u>Stagecoach</u> (1939)--S, ch. 3
21: Discuss <u>Stagecoach</u>, <u>Liberty Valance</u> and the Western

26: The Family Melodrama--S. ch. 8 and Epilogue
27: <u>All That Heaven Allows</u> (1955)
28: Discuss Family Melodrama and American Cultural Values

III. MYTH, HISTORY, AND AMERICAN FILM

NOVEMBER
 2: Movies, WWII, and American Myths--Ray, chs. 3-4
 3: <u>Casablanca</u> (1943)
 4: Discuss <u>Casablanca</u>--Official Heroes vs. Outlaw Heroes

 9: Challenges to American Optimism in the Postwar Years--Ray,
    pp. 129-37
10: <u>It's a Wonderful Life</u> (1946)--Ray, 175-215
11: Discuss <u>Wonderful Life</u>

16: Social Problem Films and America in the 1950s--R, 137-52 and
    ch. 6
17: <u>On the Waterfront</u> (1954)
18: Discuss <u>On the Waterfront</u>
20: SPECIAL FRIDAY MEETING: Contemporary American Cinema,
    the Right and the Left--Ray, chs. 8-9, Schatz, ch. 4

```
23:  NO CLASS
24:  The Graduate (1967)
25:  Discuss The Graduate and American Film in the 1960s--R, ch. 10

DECEMBER
 1:  El Norte (1983)
 2:  Discussion of El Norte

 7:  Final exam--10-11:40 a.m.
```

Art History 177   Nan Rosenthal, Fall 1984
Surrealism and the Visual Arts   Tu Th 10:45-12:45 D144 Porter
Theater Arts 171   Vivian Sobchack, Fall 1984
Film Genres: Surrealist Cinema   Th 7:30 pm Thimann Lecture 3

                    "Taboos are made to be violated."
                     Marcel Mauss (c. 1925)

Taboos, perhaps. But not bureaucracy. Please read the following carefully . . .

CLASS REQUIREMENTS: Whether you are taking the course for Art History or Theater
Arts credit, you will be required to attend both the Tuesday and Thursday class
meetings and the Tuesday evening Film Series. (Although some films will be
shown in class on Thursdays, they will not duplicate the series in most
instances; thus, Tuesday evenings will be your only opportunity to see the week's
films.) You will also be required to pay a $15.00 special fee to help support
the film rentals. Upon receipt of your name, current address and student ID#,
you will receive a ticket which will admit you to the evening screenings.
(You will be billed by mail for the fee and will not be considered registered
for the course until it is paid.) There may be optional screenings which will
be announced during the course of the quarter.

PAPERS AND EXAMS: The course work required (in addition to attendance and
readings) will be one creative project produced by groups (the "Exquisite
Corpse" assignment) and turned in by October 9: an in-class midterm quiz
(slides and short essay questions on readings and films) on Tuesday, October
30; a 6-8 page paper on a focused topic pertinent to course concerns due in
class on Tuesday, November 6, and a take-home final (with choices of questions
on Art History and Film) due no later than Thursday, November 29. These
requirements will be repeated on the class by class schedule below. Late work
is not acceptable!

READINGS: The following books and reader are required. (Assignments will be
made during the progress of the course.) They can be purchased at either
the Bay Tree bookstore or Bookshop Santa Cruz. The reader will be available
at KINKO'S on Front Street.

    Breton, Andre. Nadja. Trans. Richard Howard. New York: Grove
      Press, 1960.
    Freud, Sigmund. Five Lectures on Psycho-Analysis. Trans. James
      Strachey, New York: W.W. Norton, 1977.
    Hammond, Paul, ed. The Shadow and its Shadow: Surrealist Writings on
      Cinema. London: British Film Institute, 1978. THIS IS THE READER
      WHICH CAN BE BOUGHT ONLY AT KINKO'S. (It also includes some additional
      material from other sources which we have added).
    Rubin, William S. Dada, Surrealism and their Heritage. New York:
      The Museum of Modern Art, 1968.
    Waldberg, Patrick. Surrealism. New York: Oxford University Press,
      1965.

The following books and articles have been placed on reserve in McHenry Library.
Readings will be recommended during the quarter and the various books will be
helpful as resource materials for your projects and papers.

Aranda, Francisco.	Luis Bunuel: A Critical Biography.
Artforum (September 1966).	The entire issue is devoted to Surrealism.
Balakin, Anna.	Andre Breton.
------------	Surrealism: The Road to the Absolute.
Breton, Andre.	Nadja.
------------	What is Surrealism?
------------	Manifestoes of Surrealism.
------------	Surrealism and Painting.
Bauche, Freddy.	The Cinema of Luis Bunuel.
Bunuel, Luis.	My Last Sigh. (Bunuel's autobiography)
Camfield, William.	Francis Picabia.
Clifford, James.	"On Ethnographic Surrealism."
Descharnes, Robert.	The World of Salvador Dali.
Ducasse, Isadore	(a.k.a. de Lautremont) Maldoror.
Durgnat, Raymond.	Luis Bunuel.
Foucault, Michel.	This is Not a Pipe.
Freud, Sigmund.	Five Lectures on Psycho-Analysis.
------------	"The Uncanny."
Hammond, Paul, ed.	The Shadow and its Shadow: Surrealist Writings on Cinema.
Jean, Marcel.	The Autobiography of Surrealism.
------------	The History of Surrealist Painting.
Krauss, Rosalind.	Joan Miro: Magnetic Fields.
Kyrou, Ado.	Luis Bunuel.
Lebel, Robert.	Marcel Duchamp.
Lippard, Lucy.	Surrealists on Art.
Man Ray.	Self Portrait.
Martin, Katrina.	"Marcel Duchamp's Anemic Cinema.
Matthews, J.H.	Surrealism and Film.
Mellen, Joan, ed.	The World of Luis Bunuel: Essays in Criticism.
Michelson, Annette.	"Breton's Aesthetics."
Motherwell, Robert.	Dada Painters and Poets.
Museum of Modern Art.	Giorgio de Chirico.
-----------------	Rene Magritte.
-----------------	Alberto Giacometti.
-----------------	Pablo Picasso.
Nadeau, Maurice.	The History of Surrealism.
Raymond, Marcel.	From Baudelaire to Surrealism.
Rubin, William.	Dada, Surrealism and their Heritage.
-----------------	Dada and Surrealist Art.
Russell, John.	Max Ernst.
Schwarz, Arturo.	Complete Works of Marcel Duchamp.
Shattuck, Roger.	The Banquet Years.
Sitney, P. Adams.	Visionary Film.
Vogel, Amos.	Film as a Subversive Art.
Waldberg, Patrick.	Surrealism.

Art History 177   Fall 1984

CLASS SCHEDULE:

Th 9/20   Introductory Remarks.
               Films: Program Melies (1903, 10 min.): The
               Monster, The Terrible Turkish Executioner, and
               The Magic Lantern. The Cabinet of Dr. Caligari
               (1919, Robert Wiene, c. 50 min.)

Tu 9/25 Art-- Marcel Duchamp's Bride Stripped Bare by her Bachelors,
               Even, an erotic frustration; Andre Breton's Lighthouse
               of the Bride.

               Evening Screening (7:30 p.m., Thimann 3)
                    Le Retour a la Raison (1923, Man Ray, 3 min.)
                    Entre'Acte (1924, Rene Clair, 14 min.)
                    Ballet Mechanique (1925, Fernand Leger, 15 min.)
                    Anemic Cinema (1926, Marcel Duchamp, 7 min.)
                    The Seashell and the Clergyman (1926 Germaine
                      Dulac, 39 min.)
                    Emak Bakia (1927, Man Ray, 18 min.)
                    L'Etoile de Mer (1928, Man Ray, 15 min.)
                    Ghosts Before Breakfast (1928, Hans Richter, 9 min.)
                    Un Chien Andalou (1929, Luis Bunuel and
                      Salvador Dali, 16 min.)

Th 9/27   Film as a Surrealist Medium: The Maniac Juggler (1907,
               6 min.) and Magic Memories (9 min.) which includes:
               Montmarte Magic (1904), Naughty Lulu (1903),
               Englishman Swallows Photographer (1901), Magic Dice
               (1902), Dream Lover (1914), The Lost World (1925),
               a Hal Roach comedy (1923).
               Impressionism versus Surrealism: The Smiling Madame
               Beudet (Germaine Dulac, 1922, 40 min.)

Tu 10/2 Art-- "He is as handsome . . . as the fortuitous encounter on a
               dissecting table of a sewing machine and an umbrella": origins
               of Surrealism in World War I, Freud's writings, Giorgio de
               Chirico, and Dada.

               Evening Screening
                    Charlie Chaplin Cavalcade (Films from 1916, 80 min.)
                    Includes One A.M., The Pawnshop: The Floorwalker;
                    and The Rink. Sherlock, Jr. (1924, Buster Keaton,
                    75 min.)

Th 10/4   Surrealism and Silent Comedy
               Film: Tillie's Punctured Romance (1914, Mack Sennet with
               Chaplin, 52 min.)

Tu 10/9 Art-- From Cubist collage to Surrealist Juxtaposition, chance,
               biomorphism: the art of Ernst, Arp, Miro.
               *****Exquisite Corpses due today!!!*****

                 Evening Screening
                      L'Age d'Or (1930, Luis Bunuel, 60 min.)
                      The Blood of a Poet (1930, Jean Cocteau, 51 min.)

Th 10/11   Surrealism versus Symbolism: Bunuel and Cocteau. Portions
                 of L'Age d'Or will be screened on video. Un Chien
                 Andalou (1929, Bunuel and Dali, 16 min.) will also be shown.

Tu 10/16 Art-- Dream worlds, memories, and foiled illusions; the art of
                 Magritte, Tanguy, Dali.

                 Evening Screening
                      Entre'Acte (1924, Rene Clair, 14 min.)
                      Animal Crackers (1930, Marx Brothers, 97 min.)

Th 10/18   Hollywood Dada and Surrealism: The Marx Brothers and Busby
                 Berkeley. Portions of Duck Soup (1933, Marx Bros.)
                 will be screened on video as will be a number of Hollywood
                 "dance" numbers, primarily staged by Busby Berekeley.

Tu 10/23 Art-- Surrealism and photography: illustrating journals,
                 distorting bodies, juxtaposing the unlikely, eroticizing
                 the banal; the special case of Breton's novel Nadja and
                 the world of the city.

                 Evening Screening
                      King Kong (1933, Ernest Schoedsack and Merriam C.
                      Cooper, 115 min.)

Th 10/15   Hollywood "L'amour fou": the jungle and the city. The
                 "Hot Voodoo" dance number from von Sternberg's Blonde
                 Venus with Marlene Dietrich will be shown and discussed in
                 relation to excerpts from King Kong. (on video)

Tu 10/30 Art-- MIDTERM QUIZ (slides and short essay questions on readings
                 and films).

                 Evening Screening
                      Meshes of the Afternoon (1943, Maya Deren,
                      16 min.)
                      Dreams that Money Can Buy (1944, Hans Richter,
                      80 min.)
                      Fireworks (1947, Kenneth Anger, 15 min.)

Th 11/1   Film Dreams: Deren and Anger. Deren's Choreography for
                 the Camera (1945) and Ritual in Transfigured Time (1945-46)
                 will be shown on video--as well, a film screening of Kenneth
                 Anger's Scorpio Rising (1963, 29 min.)

Tu 11/6 Art-- The Surrealist Object: Giacometti, Man Ray, Bellmer,
                 Oppenheim and friends; the attraction of tribal art.
                 *****6-8 pp. Paper due*****

Art History 177   Fall 1984

Evening Screening
          A Trip to the Moon (1902, Georges Melies, 10 min.)
          The Incredible Shrinking Man (1957, Jack Arnold,
          94 min.)

Th 11/8   The Surrealist Object: a screening of Two Men and a
            Wardrobe (1957, Roman Polanski, 15 min.) and discussion of
            transformations in The Incredible Shrinking Man:
            Science Fiction and Surrealism: screening of Stranger
            than Science Fiction (27 min.) which has numerous excerpts
            from 50s SF films.

Tu 11/13 Art-- Picasso as "surrealist"; Surrealist politics

Evening Screening
          Un Chien Andalou (Bunuel and Dali, 1929, 15 min.)
          The Phantom of Liberty (1974, Luis Bunuel, 104 min.)

Th 11/15   Bunuel and Surrealism with attention to "ethnographic
            surrealism." Land Without Bread (1932, Bunuel, 30 min.)
            will be screened.

Tu 11/20   Surrealism Exiled to New York in World War II: Masson, Gorky
            and the movement's relation to Abstract Expressionsim

Evening Screening
          Color Cartoon Festival (Fleisher cartoons including
          Duck Amok 20 min.)
          Fist Fight (1964, Robert Breer, 9 min.)
          Hold Me While I'm Naked (1966, George Kuchar,
          15 min.)
          Unsere Afrikareise (1961-66, Peter Kubelka,
          12 min.)
          Our Lady of the Spheres (1969, Larry Jordan,
          1969, 10 min.)
          Guacamole (1976, Chick Strand, 10 min.)
          Strong Willed Women Subdue and Subjagate
          Reptiles (1982, C. Larry Roberts, 10 min.)

Th 11/22   HOLIDAY

Tu 11/27 Art-- Surrealism's gifts to art since 1955: acausality, license to
            shock, eroticizing everyday life, flirting with Utopias.

Evening Screening
          Impostors (1980, Mark Rappaport, 110 min.)

Th 11/29   Screenings of Bruce Conner's A Movie (1958, 12 min.) and
            Strong Willed Women Subdue and Subjagate Reptiles (1982,
            C. Larry Roberts, 10 min.)
            Wrap-up
            *****Take-Home Final due*****

Department of Cinema Studies   Spring Term, 1987
Tisch School of the Arts   Mon., 6-9 p.m.
New York University

H72.1701   POLITICS AND FILM

Professor Robert Sklar

Schedule of Lectures, Screenings, and Reading Assignments

February 9   Screening: POINT OF ORDER (Emile de Antonio, 97 min., 1964)

                No Reading Assignment

February 16   Washington's Birthday Holiday; No Class

February 23   Screening: ADVISE AND CONSENT (Otto Preminger, Col., 139 min., 1962)

                1.George E. Mowry and Blaine A. Brownell, The Urban Nation, 188-210
                2.C. Wright Mills, The Power Elite, 225-297
                3.Robin Wood, "Attitudes in ADVISE AND CONSENT," Movie, #4 (1962), 14-17

March 2   Screening: EYES ON THE PRIZE (Henry Hampton, 1986, 60 min. segment)
                           another short film will be screened

                1.David J. Garrow, Bearing the Cross: Martin Luther King, Jr.,
                   and the SCLC, 231-286, 668-677
                2.Allen J. Matusow, "From Civil Rights to Black Power: The Case of SNCC, 1960-
                   1966," Twentieth Century America, ed. Bernstein and Matusow, 531-557
                3.Richard Dyer MacCann, The People's Films, 173-200

March 9   Screening: DR. STRANGELOVE (Stanley Kubrick, Col., 93 min., 1964)

                1.Charles Maland, "DR. STRANGELOVE (1964): Nightmare Comedy and the Ideology of
                   Liberal Consensus," Hollywood as Historian, ed. Peter C. Rollins, 190-210
                2.Thomas Allen Nelson, Kubrick: Inside a Film Artist's Maze, 79-98
                3.Mowry and Brownell, The Urban Nation, 237-255

March 16   Screening: THE BATTLE OF ALGIERS (Gillo Pontecorvo, Italy, 123 min., 1966)

                1.Robert Stam & Louise Spence, "Colonialism, Racism and Representation: An
                   Introduction," Movies and Methods II, ed. Bill Nichols, 632-649
                2.PierNico Solinas, ed., Gillo Pontecorvo's THE BATTLE OF ALGIERS, 161-201
                3.John J. Michalczyk, The Italian Political Filmmakers, 182-199, 280

March 30   Screening: BONNIE AND CLYDE (Arthur Penn, WB, 111 min., 1967)
                           REPORT (Bruce Connor, 13 min., 1963-67)

                1.Lawrence L. Murray, "Hollywood, Nihilism, and the Youth Culture of the Sixties:
                   BONNIE AND CLYDE (1967)," American History/American Film, ed. O'Connor and
                   Jackson, 237-256
                2.Richard Schickel and John Simon, eds., Film 67/68, 25-58
                3."Bruce Connor," Film Comment, 5:4 (1969), 16-25

April 6   Screening: THE GREEN BERETS (John Wayne/Ray Kellogg, WB, 141 min., 1968)

1. Alasdair Spark, "The Soldier at the Heart of the War: the Myth of the Green Beret in the Popular Culture of the Vietnam Era," Journal of American Studies, 18:1 (1984), 29-48
2. Lawrence Suid, Guts and Glory, 221-235
3. Gilbert Adair, Vietnam on Film, 33-52

April 13   Screening: HANOI: TUESDAY THE 13TH (Santiago Alvarez, Cuba, 40 min., 1967)
                        A DAY OF PLANE HUNTING (North Vietnam, 20 min., 1968)
                        STRUGGLE FOR LIFE (NLF, South Vietnam, 20 min., 1968)

1. John Hess, "Santiago Alvarez: Cine-Agitator for the Cuban Revolution and the Third World," "Show Us Life", ed. Thomas Waugh, 384-402
2. David James, Presence of Discourse/Discourse of Presence: Representing Vietnam," Wide Angle, 7:4 (1985), 41-51
3. David Chanoff and Doan Van Toai, Portrait of the Enemy, 84-134, 158-173

April 20   Screening: PARIS IN THE MONTH OF MAY (Chris Marker, France, 40 min., 1968)
                        COLUMBIA REVOLT (Newsreel, 50 min., 1968)

1. Sylvia Harvey, May '68 and Film Culture, 3-43
2. Bill Nichols, "Newsreel, 1967-72: Film and Revolution," in "Show Us Life", ed. Waugh, 135-153
3. Noam Chomsky, "The Function of the University in a Time of Crisis," For Reasons of State, 298-317

April 27   Screening: DAVID HOLZMAN'S DIARY (Jim McBride, 78 min., 1968)
                        BLACK POWER (Leonard Henny, 15 min., 1968)

1. L.M. Kit Carson, "A Voice-Over," Film Library Quarterly, 2:3 (1969), 20-22
2. Mowry and Brownell, The Urban Nation, 211-236
3. Cornel West, "The Paradox of the Afro-American Rebellion," The 60s without Apology, ed. Sayres et al, 44-58

May 4   Screening: THE EDGE (Robert Kramer, Newsreel, 105 min., 1968)

1. Peter Clecak, Radical Paradoxes: Dilemmas of the American Left, 233-272
2. Thomas Powers, Diana: The Making of a Terrorist, 193-225
3. Jane Alpert, Growing Up Underground, 194-227

May 11   Screening: GREETINGS (Brian De Palma, 88 min., 1969)
                        WINTER SOLDIER (Newsreel, 20. min, 1971)

1. Michael Bliss, Brian Di Palma, pages to come
2. Mark Baker, Nam, 187-257
3. Mowry and Brownell, The Urban Nation, 256-279

May 18   Screening: MEDIUM COOL (Haskell Wexler, Par., 110 min., 1969)

1. Barbara Zheutlin and David Talbot, Creative Differences, 105-128
2. Ellen Willis, "The Lessons of Chicago," New American Review #6 (1969), 100-112
3. Fredric Jameson, "Periodizing the 60s," The 60s without Apology, 178-209

ENG 572
Summer 1987
M-F 10:20-12:30

American Movies in the Age of Reagan

Prof. G. Waller
1259 Patterson
257-1292

Office Hours: 9:00-10:00 MWF and by appointment

In this course we will study in detail a series of commercially
successful and/or critically acclaimed films produced and
released since 1983. We will pay particular attention to the
cinematic techniques and narrative strategies these films employ,
the type(s) of pleasure they offer the viewer, and the ways they
speak of and to contemporary American culture. Along the way we
will consider the organization of the motion-picture industry in
the 1980s, certain trends in recent film criticism, and the
central role of genre, topicality, and ideology in popular
culture.

Requirements: Attendance and participation in class discussion
is required. Written work will include short exercises, two
essays (one on an assigned topic), and a final exam covering the
films, readings, lectures, and discussions. If class size
permits, a brief in-class presentation will also be required.

Text: The Movie Business Book, ed. Jason E. Squire (NY: Simon &
      Schuster)

Library Reserve

Caughie, J. "Popular culture: notes and revisions" in High
      Theory/Low Culture ed. Colin MacCabe, pp. 156-171
Forsyth, Scott. "Fathers, Feminism and Domination" (xerox)
Forsyth, Scott. "Capital at Play: Form in Popular Film" (xerox)
Jameson, Fredric. "Reification and Utopia in Mass Culture"
      (xerox)
Wood, Robin. "80s Hollywood: Dominant Tendencies" (xerox)

Reading Schedule:

June 15 (M) Squires, 13-61, 207-239
     17 (W) Squires, 95-156, 175-188
     19 (F) Wood, Jameson articles
     22 (M) Squires, 243-300, 314-337
     26 (F) Forsyth articles
     29 (M) Squires, 86-92, 354-384
July 2 (R) Caughie article
      6 (M) Squires, 387-403

221

Screening Schedule: You are required to see each film at least
once and preferably twice (even if you saw the film on video or
in a theater last week, last month, or last year). Films will be
screened in CB 340.

Date		Film	Time
June 11	(R)	BEVERLY HILLS COP (1984)	1:00
12	(F)	BEVERLY HILLS COP	8:30
15	(M)	SIXTEEN CANDLES (1984)	10:20
15	(M)	SIXTEEN CANDLES	1:00
16	(T)	A NIGHTMARE ON ELM STREET (1984)	1:00
17	(W)	A NIGHTMARE ON ELM STREET	8:30
17	(W)	OUT OF AFRICA (1985)	1:00
18	(R)	OUT OF AFRICA	1:00
22	(M)	DESPARATELY SEEKING SUSAN (1985)	10:20
22	(M)	DESPARATELY SEEKING SUSAN	1:00
23	(W)	STRANGER THAN PARADISE (1984)	1:00
24	(R)	STRANGER THAN PARADISE	8:30
29	(M)	WARGAMES (1983)	10:20
29	(M)	WARGAMES	1:00
30	(T)	RAMBO: FIRST BLOOD PART II (1985)	1:00
July 1	(W)	RAMBO: FIRST BLOOD PART II	8:30
1	(W)	THE TERMINATOR (1984)	1:00
2	(R)	THE TERMINATOR	8:30
6	(M)	TOP GUN (1986)	10:20
6	(M)	TOP GUN	1:00
7	(T)	SALVADOR (1985)	1:00
8	(R)	SALVADOR	8:30

Please arrive on time for the screenings. No smoking or eating in the
screening room.

Professor Andrea Walsh
Clark University
Dept. of Sociology
Screen Studies

SOC/SCRN 251: SOCIOLOGY OF MASS COMMUNICATIONS
SPRING 1987
Tues. 3:30-6:00 ;Thurs.3:30-4:45 (Note:Mandatory extra
screening time on Tues.)
3rd Floor Atwood Classroom
Prof. Andrea Walsh; Office:AC 409;Phone:793-7230; 793-
7243(main office)
Office Hours: Tues and Thurs. 9:30-11:30, 1-2, and by appt.

****

"When the world crashes in, into my living room
 Television made me what I am
 People like to put the television down
 But we are just good friends
 (I´m a) television man"
                    Talking Heads, "Television Man",
                    CREATURES OF LOVE(1985)

"NEWSWEEK is there every week;
 Exploring the world
 Defining the world"
                    TV ad for NEWSWEEK

"Movies of the past are like samples-
 swatches of cloth-of the period in which
 they were made"
                    Pauline Kael, REELING(1972)

****
                        --

REQUIRED READINGS

CAPTAINS OF CONSCIOUSNESS- Stuart Ewen

MILESTONES IN MASS COMMUNICATIONS RESEARCH - Shearon Lowery
and Melvin Defleur

HOW TO READ A FILM(2nd Ed.) - James Monaco

MOVIE-MADE AMERICA- Robert Sklar

                        223

TV:THE CRITICAL VIEW (3rd ed.)- Horace Newcomb(ed.)

DECIDING WHAT´S NEWS - Herbert J. Gans

WOMEN´S FILM AND FEMALE EXPERIENCE- Andrea Walsh

NOTE: The first six books have been assigned in this course
or other Screen courses previously. They may be available
for purchase second-hand.
****

COURSE DESCRIPTION

     SOC/SCRN 251 analyzes the history and development of
the modern media of mass communications (especially film and
television) and explores key issues in the sociology of
popular culture. In advanced industrial societies, mass
media --their imagery, sound and technology--are central to
our everyday lives. Americans, for example, wake up to the
morning radio, blare car music en route to work,school, or
errands, read newspapers and magazines at lunch and on
breaks, and relax after work/school in front of TV and movie
screens. With the development of new video and
communications technology, mass media could potentially
consume the majority of our waking hours. Some media
analysts claim that the international diffusion of American
cultural symbols has strengthened U.S. world domination as
well as creating a "global village" mentality.
     This course analyzes the role of mass media in shaping
our perceptions of ourselves, our families, workplaces,
communities, as well as key social issues and problems.
SOC/SCRN 251 presents a range of competing theoretical and
methodological approaches to socio-cultural analysis.
Through intensive in-class analysis of film and television
as cultural documents, students learn to interpret the
language of visual media and analyze the relationship
between form and content in the production of cultural
meaning. This courses focuses primarily on American film
and television, and emphasizes the ways in which media both
influence and are influenced by the historical context(s) in
which they are produced and received.
     Course issues include: What is the relationship between
pre-industrial popular culture and modern mass-produced
popular culture ? How can one assess the effects- short and
long-term- of mass media on individuals,social groups and
institutions and society as a whole ? What are the
differences in media influence upon adults as compared to
children ? What roles have women, people of color, gays and
lesbians, older and disabled persons played in the history

of mass communications ? What historical role(s) have the media played in creating or reinforcing societal stereotypes of these groups ? Can modern mass media be characterized as institutions of social control, reinforcing dominant social values or institutions of social change, transforming society in more liberal, radical or conservative directions ? What does the future hold for mass media, especially given new developments in cable and video ?

SOC/SCRN 251 is designed for students with a major or concentration/minor in Sociology, Screen Studies or Communications, as well as those with a more general interest in mass culture. The course is run on a lecture/discussion basis, with mandatory, in-class screenings during the Tuesday session from 3:30-6:00. There will be no opportunity for make-up screenings.

Students can fulfill course requirements through:

MEDIA AUTOBIOGRAPHY	
3 SHORT PAPERS	45%
MEDIA JOURNAL	20
TAKE-HOME ESSAY	
FINAL	25
ATTENDANCE/	
PARTICIPATION	10

100%

NOTE: Students can earn extra credit for oral and/or written reports on various topics in the sociology of mass media. See me if you are interested in this option.

SOC/SCRN 251: TERM SYLLABUS

WEEK 1: SOCIOLOGY OF MASS COMMUNICATIONS: AN OVERVIEW AND
SAMPLING OF COURSE ISSUES

Tues 1/13 -Thurs. 1/15

Tues. 1/13- Screening- KING OF COMEDY

READ   In Lowery and De Fleur, MILESTONES IN MASS
       COMMUNICATIONS RESEARCH

       Ch. 1, "Developing Frameworks for Studying
         Mass Communications", pp. 1-30

     BEGIN Ewen, CAPTAINS OF CONSCIOUSNESS,up to p. 102

     In Newcomb(ed.), TV: THE CRITICAL VIEW

     Paul M. Hirsch, "The Role of Television and Popular
Culture in Contemporary American Society, pp. 280-310.

     Peter H. Wood, "Television As Dream", pp. 510-528.

ASSIGNMENT #1: Media Autobiography Distributed

****
WEEK 2: LOOKING BACKWARD: THE HISTORY OF POPULAR AND MASS
CULTURE
 Tues 1/20 -Thurs 1/22

NOTE: No film screening on Tues, 1/20.

READ: In Lowery and DeFleur, MILESTONES...

     Ch.3, "The Invasion From Mars...", pp.58-84.

     Ch.4, "The People's Choice...",pp.85-112.

     Finish Ewen, CAPTAINS OF CONSCIOUSNESS

Thurs., 1/22 -Media Autobiography due.
     ,   1st paper assignment distributed (on Ewen)

****

WEEK 3 CONCEPTUALIZING MASS MEDIA:ASSESSING EFFECTS; ROLES
OF MEDIA IN ADVANCED CAPITALIST SOCIETIES

Tues. 1/27 -Thurs. 1/29

Tues. 1/27 -Screening -On Advertising

READ   In Newcomb, TV:THE CRITICAL VIEW

        Todd Gitlin, "Prime Time Ideology", pp.426-454

        Douglas Kellner, "TV, Ideology...", pp.386-425
        In Lowery and DeFleur, MILESTONES...

        Ch. 6, "Communication and Persuasion...", pp.148-175.

        Ch. 7, "Personal Influence...", pp.176-203.

****
WEEK 4 THE HISTORY OF AMERICAN POPULAR FILM :A CASE STUDY IN
THE SOCIOLOGICAL ANALYSIS OF POPULAR CULTURE

Tues.2/3 -Thurs 2/5

Tues. 2/3- Screening -CHAPLIN SHORTS; Videotape: THE UNKNOWN
        CHAPLIN

READ
        BEGIN Sklar, MOVIE MADE AMERICA

        Selections - Monaco, HOW TO READ A FILM

        In Lowery and DeFleur, MILESTONES...

        Ch. 2,"Payne Fund Studies:The Effects of Movies on
Children",pp.31-57.

NOTE:Thurs., 2/5- 2nd Assignment-Paper on Ewen due.

****

WEEK 5: THE GOLDEN AGE OF HOLLYWOOD: THE 1930s

Tues.2/10-Thurs.2/12

Tues. 2/10-Screening:HIS GIRL FRIDAY (1939)

READ
        CONTINUE Sklar, MOVIE MADE AMERICA

        Selections, Monaco, HOW TO READ A FILM

Begin Walsh, WOMEN'S F-ILM AND FEMALE
EXPERIENCE,1940-1950

****

WEEK 6: THE GOLDEN AGE OF HOLLYWOOD: the 1940s

Tues.2/17-Thurs.2/19

NOTE: Tues 2/17: Screening: THE GRAPES OF WRATH

READ
    CONTINUE Sklar, MOVIE MADE AMERICA

            Walsh, WOMEN'S FILM...

****

WEEK 7: HOLLYWOOD IN THE 40s:A CASE STUDY OF FEMALE IMAGES

Tues.2/24 -Thurs. 2/26

Tues. 2/24: Screening: MILDRED PIERCE(1945)

READ
    CONTINUE Sklar, MOVIE MADE AMERICA

    Selections, Monaco, HOW TO READ A FILM

    Finish Walsh, WOMEN'S FILM...

****
WEEK 8: POSTWAR FILM IN AMERICA:SOCIAL ISSUES AND RACIAL
STEREOTYPES; THE RED SCARE

Tues.3/3-Thurs.3/5

Tues. 3/3: Screening: PINKY(1949)

READ
    FINISH Sklar, MOVIE MADE AMERICA

    Begin Gans, DECIDING WHAT'S NEWS

****
WEEK OF 3/9- SPRING BREAK

****

WEEK 9 CONSENSUS AND CONFLICT IN POSTWAR MASS CULTURE;THE
BIRTH OF TV

Tues.3/17-Thurs.3/19

NOTE: Tues 3/17: Screening: THE MEN (1951)

READ

In Lowery and DeFleur, MILESTONES...

Ch. 8, "Project Revere", pp.205-232

Ch. 9, "Seduction of the Innocent...",pp.233-266

In Newcomb, TV:THE CRITICAL VIEW

Michael Kerbel, "The Golden Age", pp.47-63

David Antin, "Video...",pp.455-477.

Horace Newcomb, "Toward a TV Aesthetic",pp.478-494.

John Fiske,et al, "Bardic TV",pp.495-509.

NOTE: Ist film paper due on PINKY -Tues 3/17

****

WEEK 10: REASSESSING THE ´50s: FILM AND TV AS SOCIAL MIRRORS
Tues. 3/24 -Thurs.3/26

Tues. 3/24 -Screening: Classic Television

READ

In Newcomb, TV:THE CRITICAL VIEW

David Thorburn, "Television Melodrama", pp.529-

Muriel Cantor, "Audience Control", pp.311-334

Michael Novak,"Television Shapes the Soul",pp.335-350.

Michael Arlen, "Prufrock...",pp.367-372.

Roger Rosenblatt,"Growing Up On TV",pp.373-385.

David Sohn interviews Jerzy Kosinski, pp.351-366.

Continue Gans, DECIDING WHAT´S NEWS

****

WEEK 11 TV IN THE GOLDEN AGE: FAMILY IDEALS AND NIGHTMARES

Tues.3/31- Thurs. 4/2

Tues. 3/31- THE BAD SEED(1956)

READ
    In Newcomb, TV:THE CRITICAL VIEW

    Robert S. Alley, "Television Drama", pp. 89-121

    Dennis Porter, "Soap Time...",pp.122-131.
    Bernard Timberg, "The Rhetoric of the Camera...",pp.132-146.

    Michael Real, "The Super Bowl...",p.206-239.

    Martin Esslin,"Aristotle and the Advertisers",pp.260-276.

    In Lowery and DeFleur, MILESTONES..

    Ch. 10, "TV In the Lives of Our Children",pp.267-295.

****

WEEK 12 MASS MEDIA IN THE 60s AND 70s

Tues. 4/7 -Thurs. 4/9

Tues. 4/7- Screening :COOL HAND LUKE (1967)

READ
    In Lowery and De Fleur, MILESTONES...
    Ch. 11, "Violence and the Media",pp. 296-323

    Ch. 12, "TV and Social Behavior", pp.324-357.

    In Newcomb, TV:THE CRITICAL VIEW

    Robert Sklar, "The Fonz...",pp.77-88

    Richard Corliss, "Happy Days", pp.64-76.

    Karin Blair, "The Garden...",pp.181-197.

Roger Hofelt,"Cultural Bias...",pp.158-166

Anne Roiphe,"Ma and Pa and John Boy...",pp.198-205

CONTINUE Gans, DECIDING WHAT´S NEWS

NOTE : Third short paper due Thurs. 4/9 on THE BAD SEED

****
WEEK 13 AMERICAN MEDIA IN TRANSITION;THE POLITICS OF THE NEWS

Tues. 4/14-Thurs.4/16

Tues. 4/14 -TV Screening

READ
    FINISH Gans, DECIDING WHAT´S NEWS

    In Newcomb, TV:THE CRITICAL VIEW

    Jonathan Black, "The Stung,"pp.247-259.

    Daniel Menaker, "Art and Artifice in Network News",pp.240-246.

    James Chesebro, "Communications...",pp.8-46.

    Robert Craft, "Elegy...",pp.148-157.

    Newcomb, "Texas...",pp.167-174

    Michael Schudson, "The Politics of Lou Grant",pp.175-180

    Ella Taylor and Andrea Walsh, "The Rise and Fall of the Social Problem TV Movie" (on reserve)

****
WEEK 14   FUTURE VISIONS IN FILM AND TV PRODUCTION AND RESEARCH

Tues.4/21- Thurs. 4/23

Tues. 4/21 -TV Screening

READ

    In Lowery and De Fleur, MILESTONES...

    Ch. 13, ''Pathways...'', pp. 358-387

****
****

VII. THE FILM SCHOLAR AND THE ACADEMY

Commentary on Questionnaires Returned by

Kevin Brownlow, Judith Crist, Leslie Halliwell, and John McCabe

Erik S. Lunde and Douglas A. Noverr

As part of our solicitation of course materials for publication in this volume we invited submissions from twenty-five individuals who were not permanently connected with educational institutions but who might be involved in university film studies programs in various ways and who might be teaching courses. We wrote to film reviewers and historians, filmmakers, and individuals who have published significant books on film. In addition to seeking their course materials, if any were available, we sent them a brief, one-page questionnaire in order to determine the extent and nature of their contacts with and involvement in academic film studies instruction. Admittedly, our sample was selective and focused on well-known national reviewers as well as on individuals who have published significant books on film.

While our hope for a high level of return on the questionnaires was not realized, we did receive four responses that are instructive in their information and contrasts. We thank these individuals for their time and for their cooperation in this project.

Two of our respondents are English film scholars: Kevin Brownlow and Leslie Halliwell. Kevin Brownlow, of course, is well known for The Parade's Gone By (1968), The War, the West, and the Wilderness (1979) and Napoleon - Abel Gance's Classic Film (1983) as well as the producer of documentary films such as Unknown Chaplin (1983) and Buster Keaton (1987). Brownlow has directed numerous documentaries and television series on film history. His contributions to our knowledge of the silent film have been monumental and have enriched our appreciation of the silent film's technical and artistic qualities and its vision. He has recovered much of what otherwise would have been lost or neglected, and film history is richer and more complete because of his efforts. Leslie Halliwell has published some of the most reliable, richly detailed, and assiduously researched reference books on film, including The Filmgoer's Companion (8th edition, 1984) and Halliwell's Film Guide (1979), as well as other specialized studies of film genres and studio history. His Halliwell's Movie Quiz (1978) and The Filmgoers Book of Quotes (1974) are rich sources of information about film.

Their responses to our questionnaire indicated that neither had any formal affiliation with an English university, had not offered a film course or participated as a guest lecturer in a course, and had never considered offering a course on film. Leslie Halliwell indicated that he had "infrequently" given campus presentations, and Kevin Brownlow informed us that in the early to mid 1970s he had served as a consultant to student filmmakers at the National Film School.

In many ways, the information they provided is not surprising. Both men have established careers separate from any possible university affiliation: Kevin Brownlow with Thames Television and his writing and filmmaking, and Leslie Halliwell as a professional film writer, dramatist, and fiction writer. Halliwell works for Granada Television as a film buyer. Their careers are time consuming, absorbing, and rewarding without additional responsibilities and commitments. However, clearly these individuals would be more regularly sought out by American university film programs if they worked in the United States since they possess knowledge and expertise that are considerable and since they are each authors of several established books in the field. Part of the reason their contacts with English universities has apparently been limited can be explained by the more traditional curriculums of British universities and colleges and the relative lack of a tradition and practice of bringing in individuals from other sectors of society. American institutions of higher education have historically utilized and benefited from the teaching and research of individuals who have established themselves as authorities without benefit of the doctorate. These individuals have even gained the status of tenured professors and found their place in the academy.

Judith Crist has held an appointment as associate lecturer and adjunct professor of critical writing and journalism at Columbia University's Graduate School of Journalism since 1958. She regularly gives courses in critical writing, primarily about film, and of course is known as one of the country's most prominent film reviewers. Her reviews appear in TV Guide, Playgirl, Saturday Review, and New York, and from 1963-1973 she appeared regularly on the "Today Show" as film commentator. Her three film books include The Private Eye, The Cowboy and the Very Naked Girl: Movies from Cleo to Clyde (1968); Judith Crist's TV Guide to the Movies (1974); Take 22: Moviemakers on Moviemaking, edited with Shirley Sealy (1984). She regularly presents guest lectures on film writing in other professors' courses and formal presentations "several times a year" on a variety of campuses. She has also organized Judith Crist Film Weekends in Tarrytown, New York, bringing together actors, producers, directors, writers, and film professionals to share viewpoints with film fans and scholars in an open forum.

John McCabe's career began in the theatre and in the study of English literature. He holds the doctor of philosophy degree from The Shakespeare Institute, Stratford-upon-Avon, England, and he has been a professional actor, writer, and director. He was a professor of dramatic art at New York University, where he began teaching film history and began his work as one of the foremost show business biographers. His books include Mr. Laurel and Mr. Hardy (1961), George M. Cohan: The Man Who Owned Broadway (1973), The Comic World of Stan Laurel (1975), Laurel and Hardy (1975), and Charlie Chaplin (1978). He also served as James Cagney's consultant in the writing of the autobiography of Cagney by Cagney (1976). He has been an author-in-residence and regularly gives presentations on campuses all across the country. Professor McCabe's career is an interesting and diverse one, as he came to his writing about film stars through his study of drama, his career as an actor and director, and his teaching of dramatic arts. He has been writer-in-residence at Lake Superior State University since 1970, after serving as professor and chairman of the theatre department there. He has written Grand Hotel, a history of the most famous building on Mackinac Island, where Professor McCabe has been a long-time resident.

The information from Judith Crist and John McCabe illustrates several important things. First, they have had long and distinguished affiliations with universities that have valued them as writers and prominent contributors to film study and history. They illustrate that those who can do, can also teach and that American institutions of higher education consider qualifications other than degrees, although of course it should be noted that John McCabe has had the Ph.D. as part of his credentials. Second, both are

236

willing to give of their time and expertise and are actively involved in the discussion of film history and studies in a variety of forums within the university. This active involvement characterizes many individuals who write about, discuss, and research film. They are not just valuable resource people for university teachers of film; they are central to the activities involved in the enterprise of film and to its development and advancement. Their expertise comes from the marketplace and from the "inside" of areas that enrich our culture's response to film: journalism, the media, professional publishing, independent research. Film studies programs must involve these individuals, seek out their expertise and knowledge, listen to their often different perspectives, appreciate their understandings, and acknowledge them as a valuable ally to specialized film scholarship and a sphere of its own standing.

Our observations on this topic here are, of necessity, limited and speculative. In the future we hope to carry out this survey in a more complete and comprehensive manner. We do believe that a biographical dictionary or directory of individuals outside and inside the institutions of higher education -- individuals who have not had primarily an academic career -- would be helpful and useful to teachers of film and film scholars. The study of film brings together a rich and diverse collection of talents, and the varying perspectives on film provide a rich discourse when brought together. The university has provided and continues to provide such an intersection, as do film societies and public film programs. Film is best understood and appreciated when a rich variety of perspectives are made available and when the dialogue is informed by the widest possible variety of experiences with film.

VIII. RESOURCES FOR TEACHING AND RESEARCH

THE MAGNIFICENT AMBERSONS Under license from RKO

The Magnificent Ambersons is the ninth title in The Criterion Collection, a continuing series of classics and important contemporary films. This edition of *The Magnificent Ambersons* has been made from the best available 35mm negative. Every effort has been taken to make this videodisc as close to the original film as possible.

If events had turned out differently, *The Magnificent Ambersons*, Orson Welles' second film, might well be widely regarded as "the greatest film of all time" rather than *Citizen Kane*. But in Welles' absence, RKO Studios recut the original version of the film mercilessly -- Welles said it looked like it had been "edited with a lawn mower" -- reducing its running time from 131 to the present 88 minutes. Nevertheless, what survives is still one of the most strikingly beautiful and technically innovative films ever to come out of Hollywood. It also tells a good story -- about the decline of a once powerful and wealthy turn-of-the-century midwestern family -- with a conviction and maturity that are rare for the old Hollywood system.

It was a well-kept secret then that *Citizen Kane* left Welles so emotionally and creatively exhausted that he was sent away on doctor's orders to undergo a rest cure. The only surprise in this is that he had managed to hold out for so long. *Citizen Kane* was the culmination of almost a decade of frenetic energy that included early fame on Broadway and in radio, a short-lived but widely felt revolution in the American theatre, the international scandal of the "War of the Worlds' broadcast, and a Hollywood contract that virtually gave him carte blanche. In *Kane*, at age 25, he had taken on one of the most powerful figures in American public life, publisher William Randolph Hearst, and after the film was made, had had to resist crushing pressures from all sides to get it released.

When he turned to his second film, Welles was in a quieter, more reflective mood. Critics have puzzled over his choice of *The Magnificent Ambersons*. Perhaps we should see it as an episode of personal stock-taking after a prolonged interval of intense stress. With its strongly autobiographical elements -- its setting at the time and place of Welles' own youth, its brash and arrogant and supremely self-confident young hero, and its obsessive Oedipal concerns -- clearly Tarkington's novel is serving at one level as a means for Welles to delve into his own roots and search out the meaning of his own personal past.

In an earlier, simpler time, how many millions of American boys read *Penrod*, Booth Tarkington's modern version of Huckleberry Finn? Welles did, and many other Tarkington works. Tarkington was a regular staple for Welles' Mercury Theatre radio show, and on the Mercury Theatre broadcast of the novel he called *The Magnificent Ambersons* "the truest, cruelest picture of the growth of the Middle West." At 240 pounds and well over six feet, Welles was wrong for George, Tarkington's college-boy hero, in the film. In a move that surprised everyone, he selected RKO contract player Tim Holt for the role. (Usually thought of as just a cowboy actor, Holt turned in several notable dramatic performances in his career, most especially in *The Magnificent Ambersons* and in John Huston's *The Treasure of the Sierra Madre*.) For the mother, Welles brought silent star Dolores Costello, one of the great beauties of the 1920s and the former Mrs. John Barrymore, out of retirement. For George's sweetheart, he selected an unknown, starlet Anne Baxter -- another inspired choice, as her subsequent career, especially in *All About Eve*, amply shows. The roster was filled out with Mercury Theatre players who had also been in *Citizen Kane* -- most notably Joseph Cotten, at his most insinuatingly charming, and, unforgettably, Agnes Moorehead, who won the New York Film Critics' Award for her performance. Although Welles did not appear onscreen himself, he was present in the role he perhaps coveted most -- that of the voice-over narrator, intoning Tarkington's elegant, old-fashioned prose. On the technical side, Bernard Herrmann, another holdover from *Citizen Kane*, composed one of his subtlest scores; Stanley Cortez, a relative unknown, as cinematographer was responsible for the astonishingly beautiful lighting of the interior scenes; and veteran art director Mark-Lee Kirk was borrowed from 20th Century Fox to oversee the design and construction of the Amberson mansion, one of the costliest and most complex sets ever built on a Hollywood sound stage.

241

Midway through the shooting of *The Magnificent Ambersons*, Welles was recruited by the U.S. State Department Committee on Inter-American Affairs to make a film in South America as a gesture to promote hemispheric relations in wartime. He rushed *Ambersons* to completion, entrusting the final editing (according to his close instructions) to Robert Wise, another holdover from *Citizen Kane*, and departed for South America. When the Welles version elicited disastrous results in sneak previews, the RKO regime ordered Wise to recut *The Magnificent Ambersons* into "releasable" shape. More than 50 minutes of Welles' footage were removed, and several scenes were rewritten and reshot by others. This radically shortened version was put into release, and the studio ordered all surviving footage from the original version destroyed. Welles was terminated from RKO, and never again in his career was he entrusted with the direction of a major studio feature.

Inevitably, the film we are left with conveys a strong sense of disconnectedness. It is not so insistent at first; in fact, the first 30 minutes of *The Magnificent Ambersons* are a match on any grounds, technical, dramatic, or aesthetic, for any 30 minutes of footage from *Citizen Kane*. But after that, *The Magnificent Ambersons* increasingly loses dramatic cohesion, and the final third of the film seems scarcely more than a series of fragments. The narration on Audio Track 2 attempts to restore some of the cohesion by pointing out where major cuts occurred and what they consisted of and by isolating the footage that was shot by others during the re-editing. In this way, we are able to arrive at a much better sense of what Welles' original plan would have been like. On Audio Track 2 there are also close "readings" of all the film's major scenes, giving special attention to the performances, Welles' bravura visual style, Stanley Cortez's cinematography, and the truly extraordinary set for the *Ambersons'* mansion. Even in its truncated form, the brilliance of *The Magnificent Ambersons* is evident. This was demonstrated most strikingly in 1982, when leading international film critics voted it one of the ten greatest films ever made.

--Robert Carringer

AN 80-MINUTE ESSAY by film historian Robert Carringer analyzing the film in depth is included on the second audio track and can be listened to separately while watching the film.

Full Feature Format (CAV) All laserdisc functions are available including freeze-frame, slow and fast motion and random access.

Supplementary materials:
● **SIDE FOUR** contains an extensive collection of Supplementary Materials, including the complete and original shooting script of *The Magnificent Ambersons*, a Visual Essay by Robert Carringer, the Mercury Theatre radio version and excerpts from *Pampered Youth*, the lost 1925 silent film version.

CAST AND CREDITS

Eugene Morgan	Joseph Cotten
Isabel Amberson Minafer	Dolores Costello
George Amberson Minafer	Tim Holt
Lucy Morgan	Anne Baxter
Aunt Fanny Minafer	Agnes Moorehead
Uncle Jack Amberson	Ray Collins
Major Amberson	Richard Bennett
Wilbur Minafer	Don Dillaway
Production	A Mercury Theatre Production for RKO Radio Pictures

Direction	Orson Welles
Screenplay	Orson Welles
Writing Assistant	Amalia Kent
Source	*The Magnificent Ambersons* (1918), novel by Booth Tarkington
Cinematography	Stanley Cortez, A.S.C.
Second Unit	Harry Wild, A.S.C.
Art Direction	Mark-Lee Kirk
Storyboards and Sketches	Joe St. Amon
Sound	Bailey Fesler and James G. Stewart
Costumes	Edward Stevenson
Score (Uncredited)	Bernard Herrmann
Additional music	Roy Webb
Editing	Robert Wise

Shot at the RKO-Pathe Studios, Culver City, CA

VIDEODISC PRODUCTION CREDITS

Produced by Robert Stein and Robert Carringer

Side Four Material, Selection and Arrangement by Robert Carringer

Audio Essay Recording and Editing by
Nijole Kuzmickas

Production Assistants
Aaron Mendelsohn, Kim Worthy

Film-Negative to Tape Transfer Supervised by
Robert Carringer

Post-Production on Side Four,
Crawford Communications, Atlanta, Georgia

Still-Frame Sequence Recording by
Mark Brems, Sam Nicholson
Pampered Youth Fragment restored and preserved by
David Bradley and Kevin Brownlow

Manufactured by 3M, St. Paul, Minnesota 55144

Cover Produced by Maya Gingery

243

Robert Carringer is the author of numerous books and articles on American films and literature, including the highly acclaimed The Making of **Citizen Kane** (1985). *He is presently at work on a reconstruction of the plan for Welles' original, uncut* **The Magnificent Ambersons** *under a grant from the National Eudowment for the Humanities. He is Professor of English and Film at the University of Illinois.*

SIDE 1
CHAPTER 1: Prologue narrated by Welles
CHAPTER 2: The Ambersons' Ball
CHAPTER 3: George and Fanny after the ball
CHAPTER 4: Snow ride

SIDE 2
CHAPTER 5: Wilbur Minafer's death
CHAPTER 6: George and Fanny in the kitchen
CHAPTER 7: The Morgan automobile factory
CHAPTER 8: Eugene and Isabel in the arbor
CHAPTER 9: George and Lucy's ride
CHAPTER 10: The dinner for Eugene Morgan
CHAPTER 11: George turns Eugene away
CHAPTER 12: Eugene's letter to Isabel

SIDE 3
CHAPTER 13: George and Lucy's walk
CHAPTER 14: Uncle Jack visits the Morgans
CHAPTER 15: Isabel's homecoming
CHAPTER 16: "She loved you!"
CHAPTER 17: Major's "sun" meditation
CHAPTER 18: Uncle Jack's leavetaking
CHAPTER 19: Eugene & Lucy in their garden
CHAPTER 20: Fanny's financial plight
CHAPTER 21: George's "comeuppance"
CHAPTER 22: Eugene and Fanny at the hospital
CHAPTER 23: Credits narrated by Welles

SIDE 4
SUPPLEMENTARY MATERIALS
Part One: The Unmaking of a Film Classic

CHAPTER 24: A brief history of the film's production

CHAPTER 25: The Re-editing
CHAPTER 26: Welles on the impact of *The Magnificent Ambersons* on his career (video clip)

Part Two: The Lost Ambersons

Part Three: The Other *Ambersons*

Audio Track 1 – Movie Soundtrack
Audio Track 2 – Audio Essay by Robert Carringer

88 Minutes, shortened from 131 minutes
Black and White, 1942
Full-Feature Format (CAV), 2 Discs

The Criterion Collection
a joint venture of Janus Films and Voyager Press

2139 Manning Avenue   First Printing, 1986
Los Angeles, CA 90025   Catalog No. CC1109L
(213) 474-0032   ISBN 0-931393-30-2

Magnificent ruins
'Ambersons' questions answered on laserdisc

By Dave Kehr
Movie critic

On Dec. 10, 1942, Charles Koerner, the head of RKO Radio studios, ordered the destruction of all of the unused footage from Orson Welles' production "The Magnificent Ambersons." There have been few darker days in the history of movies.

"The Magnificent Ambersons" was to be Welles' follow-up to "Citizen Kane." Based on Booth Tarkington's novel of the decline of an aristocratic family in the turn-of-the century American midwest, it was, as Welles planned and shot it, to run 131 minutes. But a disastrous sneak preview in Pomona, Calif. -- punctuated by whistles, boos, and walk-outs -- convinced RKO that the film was unreleasable in Welles' cut.

While Welles was away in Brazil, working on the documentary "It's All True," "The Magnificent Ambersons" was unmade. Some 50 minutes of Welles' footage was removed, scenes were taken out of context and shuffled around, and new footage -- including a grotesque "happy ending" -- was shot by studio assistants and inserted.

The 88-minute "Magnificent Ambersons" that survives today is a ruin, but it is a magnificent ruin. Even in its shattered form, the film remains a work of immense beauty and power, blending an epic social vision with an acute and intimate personal tragedy. "Ambersons" is a film of great warmth, humor, and nostalgia; at the same time, it is absolutely terrifying in its vision of human spitefulness, isolation, and waste.

Charles Koerner's decision to scrap the footage deleted from the release version of the film means that, barring a miracle, we will never see "The Magnificent Ambersons" as Welles intended it to be seen.

But now, thanks to a California publishing company, "The Magnificent Ambersons" can be seen at its best. Criterion Video, a joint venture of the Voyager Press of Los Angeles and Janus Films, has released a laserdisc version of "Ambersons" that, by combining superb image and sound reproduction with a rich selection of supplementary materials, makes it possible to imagine the "Ambersons" that might have been while enjoying the "Ambersons" that is as never before.

Unless, that is, you were lucky enough to see the film on its first release in 1942 [when RKO finally issued it, it was as half of a double bill with Lupe Valez "Mexican Spitfire" comedy]. The co-producers of the Criterion version, Bob Stein and Welles scholar Robert Carringer have returned to the original nitrate negative, remastering the image track shot by shot to bring out the full range of tones in Stanley Cortez's burnished black-and-white cinematography. Although it's impossible, today, to recapture the exact quality of the nitrate original [highly inflammable, nitrate stock was replaced in 1950 by more stable though less supple acetate film], the Criterion version comes closer to the unique, silvery glow of nitrate than any 35-mm. print currently on the revival circuit.

Backed by the high resolution of the laserdisc format [which yields a depth and sharpness far superior to that of videotape], the meticulous work of Stein and Carringer unveils a number of details that most prints in circulation leave in the dark.

The visual plan that Welles and Cortez devised for "Ambersons" relies on a mottled, chiaroscuro lighting that isolates pools of brightness within oceans of textured shadow -- exactly the kind of effect that is most vulnerable to indifferent printing [and which, on television, comes across as sheer mud].

In one of "Ambersons's" most devastating moments, Isabel [Dolores Costello] has just received a letter from her lover that threatens to bring their relationship to an end. Welles begins his shot with Isabel moving toward a large window in a darkened room, her figure reduced to an inky black silhouette by the sunlight that streams in behind her. Isabel turns from the window and walks toward the camera, into the deep shadows of the room. But as she moves into the darkness, Cortez brings up an oblique, half-light that dimly illuminates her features -- she becomes a shadow with a human face. In the last frames of the shot, Isabel looks up, and the pupils of her eyes suddenly capture two bright, white pinpoints of light, reflected from an unknown source.

If movies are the art of light and shadow, this is one of the most pure moments the movies have achieved: Shades of light are translated, through the most natural and unobtrusive of metaphors, into the shades of the soul.

To give this moment back to "The Magnificent Ambersons" -- and the others on the same order that the film contains -- is the noblest achievement of the Criterion edition.

But co-producers Stein and Carringer have also taken advantage of the laserdisc's unique storage capacities, which include a still frame feature sharp enough for text and frame-by-frame indexing, to evoke the spectre of "Ambersons'" original stature.

The fourth side of the two-disc set is devoted to 11,000 still exposures that contain Welles' complete original shooting script, the full set of storyboard sketches made for the production, and photographs from the excised scenes.

There are also video clips from a BBC interview with Welles, in which he discusses "Ambersons" and its destruction, plus 20 minutes of footage from "Pampered Youth," the 1925 silent film based on Tarkington's novel.

With the video switched off, the audio track reproduces, complete, Welles' 1939 Mercury Theater radio production of the Tarkington novel, featuring Walter Huston as the genteel industrialist Eugene Morgan and Welles himself as the arrogant scion of the Ambersons, George [the role is taken in the film by Tim Holt].

Finally, there is the running commentary by Carringer that accompanies "Ambersons" itself on the second audio track [that is, the unused right hand stereo channel -- a touch of a button turns it on or off].

Taken together, this added material provides a road map through the often rocky terrain that is the surviving version of "The Magnificent Ambersons," supplying narrative continuity where the existing prints fall apart into fragments and logic to actions that once appeared arbitrary.

Carringer suggests that, in cutting "Ambersons," the studio had three main objectives: To make the character of George more sympathetic to audiences [a consummately self-centered snob, he is also directly responsible for his mother's death], to accelerate the action by eliminating the scenes that dealt with the Amberson's financial decline [in the surviving version, they are suddenly and all but inexplicably reduced to poverty], and to soften the edges of Agnes Moorehead's performance as George's spinster Aunt Fanny [what must have seemed like hysterical excess to audiences of 1942 now suggests the unbridled intensity of a classic method performance].

With these elements restored to Welles' intentions -- in the imagination, at least -- "The Magnificent Ambersons" acquired a much greater emotional depth and delicacy, as well as a much more satisfying and complete epic sweep.

Welles' juxtaposition of psychological and historical forces suddenly seems strikingly contemporary: This is the territory that would be explored in the '70s by such filmmakers as Bernardo Bertolucci, Rainer Werner Fassbinder, and Jean-Luc Godard.

Armed with the hindsight of 1987, it would be easy to condemn the executives of RKO Radio Pictures for what they did to Orson Welles 45 years ago.

Confronted with the evidence contained on this laser-disc, no one could maintain that "The Magnificent Ambersons" is anything less than one of the greatest films ever made -- certainly as great, in its own, very different way, as "Citizen Kane."

But we would do well to remember that, in order for RKO to have unmade "The Magnificent Ambersons," it was necessary, first, to have made it. Would any of today's Hollywood studios have done as much?

Wm. H. Phillips / Cal. State U., Stanislaus

HELPING STUDENTS WRITE MORE EFFECTIVELY

adapted from the Instructor's Manual for <u>Analyzing</u> <u>Films</u> (1985)

by William H. Phillips

Early in the course tell your students that <u>how</u> they write is inseparable from <u>what</u> they write. (How can their information and ideas be effective if carelessly expressed?) And tell them that you will be reading their writings carefully, though you will not (normally) be correcting them. (It's enormously time-consuming and tedious to correct their errors; it's also very discouraging for them and largely ineffective.)

My strong conviction is that regardless of the class size, students should write often in a film analysis course. You may not grade all they write; you may not even collect all that they write. But you want to convey the message that writing helps them figure out what they know and don't know and that it's unlikely they will be able to analyze any film in depth without writing. Writing, I tell students, is thinking.

Though you cannot bring about radical improvement in their writing in a mere semester, you can help your students write more effectively if you require them to write, make it clear that how carefully they write is important, and react to what they write. In my classes I assign a few short writing exercises in the early weeks, then a short essay (500-1,000 words) on one aspect of one film seen twice in the course.

Besides conveying to your students the importance of writing, you can help them by reacting to what they have written.

249

To do so need not be terribly time-consuming. Do not--as I urged above--correct their errors: marking their every misspelling/mistyping, for example, only intimidates and depresses them. You can merely note at the end of the essay or writing exercise something to the effect that the many misspellings are distracting and that the writer should use a dictionary more often while checking the final draft.

Your comments, I think, should be brief and infrequent. But you want to communicate to the student that the ideas and information are or are not clear and persuasive. When they are not, you need merely note briefly what aspect(s) distract from the desired effect.

Some guidelines for the notations you put on student essays:

1. Keep comments brief and occasional.

2. Form many of your responses as brief questions.

3. For each paper try to give some positive comments. (Probably the biggest mistake beginning writing teachers make is to give too little encouragement.)

4. If you make corrections, avoid conventional correction symbols, e.g., D, sp, frag, agr. Many students will not read them.

5. Direct your comments to the writing, not the writer, particularly if the comments are negative.

Some comments/questions are appropriate for the margins, some for the end of the writing. Below are sample comments/questions suitable for the margins:

Wm. H. Phillips / Cal. State U., Stanislaus

-Define what you mean by this term (or, this term
 is unclear to me)--and underline the term.
-I have trouble understanding the point of this
 sentence (or paragraph).
-How does this paragraph fit into the essay?
-The many spelling errors (or punctuation errors) make
it difficult to follow this paragraph.
-I don't see what you mean because this paragraph
 has so few examples.
-Write more like you talk (for students who are
 trying to impress you with their shaky command of
 advanced vocabulary).
-I have trouble understanding this--and underline
 the phrase or sentence fragment or ungrammatical
 sentence. Or, you may just want to put a
 question mark in the margin and underline the
 unclear part.
-What evidence did you have in mind for this?
-This point is important; give it more space.
-Effective word choice--and underline the word.
-Well put--and underline the phrase or sentence
 that is especially well phrased.
-Is this the word you mean?--and underline the
 word.
-Helpful transition.
-Helpful example(s)--underline.

Wm. H. Phillips / Cal. State U., Stanislaus

-Good use of the semicolon/colon. (Students have
 so much trouble with these two punctuation marks,
 they need all the encouragement they can get in
 their usage.)
Some sample concluding comments:
-What is the essay's thesis or main point?
-The ideas of this essay are sometimes unclear
 because so few examples are given.
-The many spelling errors (or some other aspect) are
 distracting. Please check a dictionary more often for
 words you use infrequently.
-Next time, please check a handbook for the
 punctuation of each sentence.
-Clear, well-organized, and persuasive essay.
 Clearly you worked hard on it.
-This essay seems to have some interesting/useful
 ideas, but they are not always expressed clearly.
-(At the end of what seems to be a rush job) Did
 you begin the assignment early and write several
 drafts during the last two (or whatever) weeks?
-Did you read the assignment carefully and
 repeatedly as you were working on your essay?
-You should be going to the Writing Center (or
 whatever it is called on your campus) for
 practice in sentence/paragraph construction (or
 whatever remedial work is necessary).

Wm. H. Phillips / Cal. State U., Stanislaus

Remember that poor student writers are unlikely to show much improvement in <u>one</u> semester no matter what you say or do, but your attitude, assignments, and comments/questions can contribute to the long-term process of improving student writing and thinking.

Wm. H. Phillips / Cal. State U., Stanislaus

NANOOK OF THE NORTH: HUMAN BEHAVIOR/HUMAN NATURE
(selections from student responses after seeing the film)
October 8, 1985

1. The Eskimos are presented as resourceful, busy, and good-
natured people. In the film they are shown to be working, almost
always working at some survival skill.
2. In a frozen wasteland, where . . . a °civilized' person . . .
could [not] survive, Nanook manages to feed, cloth, and shelter
himself and his family using only his own strength, ingenuity,
and knowledge of himself and his world.

    Nanook, I believe, represents the best in all men. Instead
of contemplating ideals and meanings of life, as many of us
civilized people often do (and bitterly at that), Nanook finds
happiness and contentment in his life of constant struggle. This
can readily be seen as he struggles for food, on the edge of
starvation, and emerges laughing and happy when victory is
finally won. Nanook seems to have everything he could want from
life, where others with an infinite amount more would say he has
nothing.
3. This film makes one proud to be human rather than be ashamed
of our inheritance from primitive peoples. . . . Out of
necessity these people were strong and determined, yet gentle,
loyal, and lovable even by our standards.

    After becoming charmed by their childlike simplicity and
warmth, we are jarred by their primitive ways of eating; yet we
are able to assimilate this and broaden our own outlook beyond
what is now culturally acceptable.

254

4. Nanook of the North is a spellbinding documentary film even to the modern viewer. The warmth of the human spirit is displayed in this film. . . . Through this film comes the message that a modern viewer doesn't very often come across--that human beings possess . . . the gift of adaptability. We see through Nanook of the North just how well human beings can survive under the harshest of circumstances and yet maintain a light-hearted, gentle, and warm nature. Even under inhuman conditions, the human can prevail.

5. I believe that the theme of this film is how resourceful and incredibly self-sufficient the Eskimo people are. . . I think Flaherty made this movie to show the rest of civilization how admirable the Eskimo people are. Perhaps he also made it to show how humans can adapt to almost any lifestyle and still enjoy life and its challenges.

6. The film shows that Eskimos are no different from other people. They have a hard life but they make the best of it.

Perhaps this is because they are isolated and they don't know that other people have a much easier life. . . .

They worry about the important thing: survival. They have full lives, and since they aren't searching for happiness, they have it.

7. Nanook is a depiction of man versus nature. Flaherty does a remarkable job of showing man at his best while nature is handing out her worst. . . .

The clearest [theme] in this documentary is that human behavior can (and must) adapt to any environment and not only survive, but thrive. . . .

Wm. H. Phillips / Cal. State U., Stanislaus

APOCALYPSE NOW (1979)

(apocalypse = both prophetic disclosure and Revelation, the last book of the New Testament, which describes in part the violent end of time)

Film begins with Capt. Willard in Saigon waiting for a mission and getting weak and unstable in his hotel room, while "Charlie" (VC) gets stronger squatting in a bush. Right away, the film suggests the strong will of Viet Cong to win.

Willard gets a secret mission: to find and "terminate with extreme prejudice" Col. Kurtz. He gets under way. His diverse boat crew not poor soldiers but drugs and morale a problem. Lance water-skis behind boat. Another, Clean, is lost in his loud recorded music. Chef is high-strung. Boat capt. (Phillips) dislikes Capt. Willard.

Willard sees Col. Kilgore (Robert Duvall) abruptly abandon one of his wounded soldiers to whom he was about to give water from his own canteen to go talk with Lance about surfing. Next a.m.: they attack village; then Lance surfs even though the area is still very "hot." Under way in boat again: in voice-over Willard says if this is the way the war is being waged, Kurtz may not be so wrong.

A nighttime USO show for the GIs is open, loud, raunchy, and large. As noisy GIs watch it, behind wire fences Vietnamese watch passively. The show nearly results in a riot as the GIs storm the stage to get at the sexy Playboy bunnies. In his voice-over commentary Willard contrasts this show with the VC's R & R: cold rice and a little rat meat.

Wm. H. Phillips / Cal. State U., Stanislaus

In a meeting with a sampan, a nervous Clean opens fire when a woman moves toward a container. All but the woman are killed in the panic. Chef discovers in the container a puppy. When they see the woman is still alive, Willard finishes her off with a shot (rather than allow Phillips to take her somewhere and delay the mission) and orders him to move on.

At the bridge outpost before they cross into Cambodia, no one is in charge, and men are spaced out on drugs. One man there calls it the "asshole of the world." The psychedelic smoke and colors and loud music reflect their states of mind. Many men there seem to want to desert: they call out to those on the boat to take them home.

Under way again, a rocket kills Clean; later Phillips is speared; then before he dies he tries to kill Willard. During the trip, Willard studies the papers and photos of Kurtz (in one photo we see only a darkened head) and to grow increasingly fascinated with him and to grow more and more concerned about how he will react to Kurtz. (A man sent earlier to assassinate Kurtz joined him instead.) Willard learns that Kurtz had a brilliant military record and a promising future until after his first tour of duty in Vietnam. Then Kurtz requested and finally got transferred to airborne special forces (and took a big demotion and major setback in his career).

Arriving in Kurtz country, Willard soon sees for himself that Kurtz has indeed gone mad. He rules his own world, and evidence of atrocities, such as mutilated bodies and severed heads, are everywhere. Kurtz knows Willard was sent to kill him

but does not have him killed. Instead, Willard is locked up. As
he is immobilized by a cord around his neck, Kurtz unexpectedly
drops into Willard's lap Chef's severed head. For days Kurtz
allows Willard to be with him without guards. Kurtz tells
Willard of the Vietnamese cutting off arms of childr n vaccinated
by U.S. personnel and says he wept and then realized that people
with such will power freed of judgment are unbeatable. Kurtz
asks Willard to tell Kurtz's son what Kurtz tried to be, and
Kurtz acquiesces in his own murder, which is cross-cut with the
ritual slaughter of an ox by the people under Kurtz's rule.
Kurtz's final spoken words, from Conrad's HEART OF DARKNESS, are
"the horror, the horror." After Kurtz's death, Willard finds in
Kurtz's papers the message (a version of what is in HEART OF
DARKNESS): "drop the bomb; exterminate them all."

    After Willard kills Kurtz, his followers are in awe and
allow Willard and Lance to leave (Lance seems reluctant to go).
Presumably Willard could have become the new Kurtz. By the time
they leave, Willard and Lance look more and more savage and dark
and bloody and painted: they look much like Kurtz's followers.

    During the end credits of some prints, we see bombing and
destruction, presumably of Kurtz's domain. In that version of
the story, evidently Willard called in the airstrike.

    Throughout the film, the U.S. conduct of the war is seen as
insane, excessive, and futile. A superior and brilliant officer
(Kurtz) gives up not only his country and career but also a
family, including a son he loved. Everywhere he goes, Capt.
Willard sees signs of drugged stupor, alienation, confusion, lack

of purpose. But Willard finally destroys Kurtz and returns to the U.S. military to be promoted, he says earlier in a voice over, to Major.

His is a hollow victory.

The film is sometimes difficult to follow: the soundtrack is often low and the images very dark, especially in Kurtz's territory. In the film Americans are everywhere, loud, large, yet ineffective, as in the haunting image of the helicopter burning in the tree by the river, and in the huge tail remains of an airplane whose nose was in the edge of river, and in the colored smoke, flares, and loud music by the bridge near Cambodia. The soundtrack is often loud and confusing. Sometimes, as at the bridge near Cambodia, it's a babble of voices, sounds, and music.

The film was largely misunderstood and underestimated when it first came out. Although Kilgore's attack on the village is exhilarating to most viewers, the film shows the nightmare of American involvement in Vietnam and the degradation of warfare. Audiences tend to enjoy the action and humor in the first half of the film then feel let down in the long second half by the serious and depressing actions and none-too-obvious themes. One theme: an insane war breeds insane behavior. Another theme: those with will power freed of judgment (the VC) will win. A third theme: the difference between unsanctioned insanity (Kurtz) and sanctioned insanity (Kilgore and, more so, Willard) is small (remember Willard's behavior in the hotel room at the beginning of the film). A fourth theme: many men and enormous firepower are not enough vs. a devoted enemy that takes the long view.

Casting of Brando as Kurtz is apt: Brando, the godfather and an outspoken opponent of the Vietnam war in private life. Above all a brilliant and accomplished if sometimes difficult, rebellious individual. Certainly the best choice for the role. Martin Sheen, however, though good, is less convincing. He does not have enough presence to be convincing that Kurtz would respect him so much. Better to have had Brando play both roles. We learn anyway that Willard is afraid of becoming another Kurtz, fears he will give in to his dark side, too.

The Jonestown massacre, Nov. 1978, can help us understand how masses will follow a strong leader and destroy people on a massive scale.

USA
1916

Viewing Notes Prepared by Adam Reilly

INTOLERANCE

CREDITS: Director: D.W. Griffith; produced by the Wark Producing Corporation; scenario by Griffith; music score by Griffith and Joseph Carl Breil: photography: G.W. "Billy Bitzer, assisted by Karl Brown: film editors: James and Rose Smith; sets: Frank Wortman; property master: Ralph DeLacey; assistant directors: Arthur Berthelon, Allan Dwan, Erich von Stroheim, W. Christy Cabenne, Tod Browning, Jack Conway, George Nicholls Lloyd Ingraham. Preview: Loring Opera House, Riverside, Calif, Aug 6, 1916; premiere: Liberty Theatre, New York, Sept. 5, 1916; b&w with color tints, silent, originally 14 reels in length, with current prints running approx 135 min at 24 fps.

CAST: "Of All Ages" Lillian Gish (woman who rocks the cradle).
"The Modern Story" Mae Marsh (The Dear One), Fred Turner (her father), Robert Harron (the boy), Sam de Grasse (Arthur Jenkins), Vera Lewis (Mary Jenkins), Mary Alden, Pearl Elmore, Lucille Brown, Luray Huntley, Mrs. Arthur Mackley (the uplifters), Miriam Cooper (the friendless one), Walter Long (musketeer of the slums), Tully Marshall (his friend), Tom Wilson (friendly policeman), Ralph Lewis (governor), Lloyd Ingraham, (judge) Barney Bernard (boy's attorney), Rev. A.W. McClure (Farther Farley), Max Davidson (kind neighbor), Monte Blue (striker), Marguerite Marsh (guest at the ball), Jennie Lee (woman at dance), Tod Browning (owner of racing car), Edward Dillon (chief detective), Clyde Hopkins (Jenkin's secretary), William Brown (warden), Alberta Lee (kind neighbor's wife).

"The Judean Story" Howard Gaye (Christ), Lillian Langdon (Mary), Olga Grey (Magdelene), Gunther von Ritzau, Erich von Stroheim (pharisees), Bessie Love (bride of Cana), George Walsh (bridegroom).

"The French Hugonot Story" Margery Wilson (Brown Eyes), Eugene Pallette (prosper Latour), Spottiswoode Aitken (Brown Eyes' father), Ruth Handforth (her mother), A.D. Sears (mercenary), Frank Bennet (Charles IX), Maxfield Stanley (Duc d'Anjou), Josephine Crowell (Catherine de Medicis), Georgia Pearce/Constance Talmadge (Marguerite de Valois), N.E. Lawrence (Henry of Navarre), Joseph Henabery (Admiral Coligny), Morris Levy (Duc de Guise), Howard Haye (Cardinal Lorraine), Louis Romaine (priest).

"The Babylonian Story" Constance Talmadge (Mountain Girl), Elmer Clifton (the Rhapsode), Alfred Paget (Belshazzar), Seena Owen (Princess Beloved), Carl Stockdale (King Nabonidus), Tully Marshall (high priest of Bel), George Siegmann (Cyrus), Elmo Lincoln (mighty man of valor), George Fawcett (Babylonian judge), Kate Bruce (a mother), Loyola O'Connor (a slave), James Curley (charioteer), Howard Scott (Babylonian dandy), Alma Rubens, Ruth Darling, Margaret Mooney (Girls of the marriage market), Mildred Harris, Pauline Starke (favorites of the harem), Winifred Westover (favorite of Egibi), Grace Wilson (first dancer of Tammuz), Lotta Clifton (second dancer), Ah Singh (first priest of Nergel), Ranji Singh (second priest), Ed Burns, James Burns (charioteers of priest of Bel), Martin Landry (auctioneer), Wallace Reid (boy killed in fighting), Charles Eagle Eye (barbarian chieftan), William Dark Cloud (Ethopian chieftan), Charles Van Cortlandt (lieutenant of Cyrus), Jack Cosgrove (chief eunuch).

SYNOPSIS: Four separate stories about "intolerance" through the ages are inter-woven, and connected with the motif of Lillian Gish rocking the cradle. In the Babylonian Story the priests of Bel, opposing the king's introduction of another religion, conspire to turn the city over to the Persians. The Judean Story centers on the crucifixion of Christ. The French Story, Catherine de Medicis get Charles IX to persecute the Hugonots and massacre them. And in a Modern Story a young man is mistakenly accused of a murder and sentenced to die. All four stories climax together. (Two of the sections were later released as separate features: The Fall of Babylon and The Mother and the Law.)

COMMENT: Iris Barry in D.W. Griffith: American Film Master: "Before The Birth of a Nation was released Griffith had almost completed a new picture, The Mother and the Law, a modern story which bleakly revealed the wrongs inflicted by a pious factory owner on his employees and the injustices of which the law may sometimes be capable. Suddenly the new picture seemed to him an insufficiently violent attack on prejudice and cruelty, so that he decided to weave in with his modern story three parallel stories of injustice and prejudice in other ages and so make of the film an epic sermon. The slums of today, 16th century France, ancient Babylon and Calvary itself should speak of the evil which the self-righteous have perpetrated through the centuries. He flung up sets of a size hitherto unimagined, hired players by the hundreds, shot miles of film. Into this gigantic undertaking poured his profits from The Birth of A Nation. His employees were aghast when he ordered them to construct walls so broad that any army could march round the tops of them, palace halls so vast that the crowds in them were reduced to antlike proportions. Hollywood rang with rumors. The film was two years in the making, yet out of all this footage, extravagance and passion emerged a film of unmistakable greatness and origin-ality called Intolerance.

"The film Intolerance is of extreme importance in the history of the cinema. It is the end and justification of that whole school of American cinematography based on the terse cutting and disjunctive assembly of lengths of film, which began with The Great Train Robbery and culminated in The Birth of a Nation and in this. All the old and many new technical devices are employed in it—brief, enormous close-ups not only of faces but of hands and of objects; the 'eye-opener' focus to introduce vast panaramas; the use of only part of the screen's area for certain shots; camera angles and tracking shots such as are commonly supposed to have been introduced by German producers years later; and rapid cross-cutting the like of which was not seen again until Potemkin.

"The sociological implications of the modern episode seem, perhaps, more pointed now than they did in 1916. They undoubtedly account for the fact that Lenin early in 1919 arranged to have Intolerance tour throughout the USSR, where it ran almost continuously for ten years. The film was not merely seen there; it was also used as study material for the post-revolutionary school of cinematography, and exercised a profound influence on the work of men like Eisenstein and Pudovkin. It is true that Griffith is largely instinctive in his methods where the Russian directors are deliberate and organized; but it was nevertheless in large measure from his example that they derived their characteristic staccato shots, their measured and accelerated rhythms and their skill in joining pictorial images together with a view to the emotional overtones of each, so that two images in conjunction convey more than the sum of their visible content

"The scale and sumptuousness of <u>Judith</u> <u>of</u> <u>Bethulia</u> and of <u>Intolerance</u> profoundly affected filmmaking everywhere. At home, they undoubtedly influenced Cecil B. DeMille, whose name later became synonymous with glittering spectacles. In France, the effect of Griffith's work at this period can be traced in the later productions of Abel Gance, and in Germany in those of Fritz Lang. He had conferred both magnitude and complexity as well as expressiveness on the motion pictures and, in Europe and America alike, all the most ambitious films of the 1920's reflected his influence and followed his example."

USA
1918

Viewing Notes Prepared by Adam Reilly
HEARTS OF THE WORLD

CREDITS: Directed by: D.W. Griffith; scenario: M. Gaston de Tolignac,
        translated into English by Capt. Victor Marier (both pseu-
donyms for D.W. Griffith); photography: G.W. Bitzer; technical super-
vision: Erich von Stroheim; additional European photography: D.P.
Cooper; film editors: James and Rose Smith; original musical score
arranged by: Carli Elinor and D.W. Griffith; Miss Gish's dresses by:
Nathan of London; production: Paramount-Artcraft/D.W. Griffith, Inc.;
Los Angeles premiere: Clune's Auditorium, March 12, 1918; New York
premiere: 44th Street Theater, April 4, 1918; b&w, silent, 95 minutes.

CAST: Lillian Gish (The Girl, Marie Stephenson), Robert Harron (The
      Boy, Douglas Gordon Hamilton), Adolphe Lestina (grandfather),
Josephine Crowell (mother), Jack Cosgrave (father of the boy), Kate
Bruce (mother of the boy), Ben Alexander (littlest brother), M. Emmons,
F. Marion (the boy's other brothers), Dorothy Gish (The Little Dis-
turber), Robert Anderson (Monsieur Cuckoo), George Fawcett (village
carpenter), George Siegmann (Von Strohm), Fay Holderness (innkeeper),
L. Lowy, (deaf and blind musician), Eugene Pouyet (a Poilu), Anna
Mae Walthall (French peasant girl), Mlle. Yvette Duvoisin of the Comedie
Francaise, Paris (a refugee), Herbert Sutch (a French major), Alphonse
Dufort (a Poilu), Jean Dumercier (a Poilu), Gaston Riviere, Jules
Lemontier (stretcher bearers), Georges Loyer (a Poilu), George Nicholls
(a German sergeant), Mrs. Mary Gish (a refugee mother), Mrs. Harron
(woman with daughter), Mary Harron (wounded girl), Jessie Harron
(refugee), Johnny Harron (boy with barrel), Mary Hay (dancer), Noel
Coward (boy with wheelbarrow), Erich von Stroheim (a German soldier).

SYNOPSIS: The film begins in 1912 with the inhabitants of an unnamed
         French village whose lives will be devastated by the war.
Griffith establishes a rural romance, not betweeen French lovers but
transplated Americans. The romance between the boy and the girl
(Lillian Gish and Bobby Harron) is complicated by a tomboyish street
imp (Dorothy Gish), and then the Germans attack the village. Viewers
are made to witness the appalling devastation while following the
progress of the boy, now a soldier, and the girl, expectantly awaiting
his return. In the baldly patriotic ending, the girl is reunited
to the boy overseen by a smiling portrait of Woodrow Wilson.

COMMENT: Eillen Bowser in D.W. Griffith: "On March 17, 1917,
        Griffith sailed for London to attend the opening of Intoleranc
and to discuss a British offer to make a propaganda film for the war
effort. On the same date he announced his Triangle severance and the
singing of a contract with Artcraft, Adolph Zukor's company that produced for Famous Players-Lasky (or Paramount, as it was to become
known).
        "Zukor, whose firm had already swallowed most of Triangle's
directors and stars, put up some of the money for Hearts of the World
in exchange for eventual distribution rights as well as a guarantee of
future Griffith films. Thus began a long relationship between Griffith
and Zukor.

"Hearts of the World has long been neglected as a major Griffith
film. A shortage of good prints has probably contributed more to
its disappearance than its immediate propagandistic purpose and a
nearly complete version now made should help to restore admiration for
it. Griffith had several motives in making it. He was enormously
impressed by the welcome he received in England and he needed money
badly to recover from the debts of the Wark Corporation. But when he
had toured the battlefields, slogged through muddy trenches and observed
the suffering of soldiers and civilians alike, he was genuinely determined to recreate the scene for the benefit of Americans.
"The original purpose of the film was to convince Americans to
enter the war, but before Griffith could begin work, America had
entered....The propaganda aim became our transformation into an angry,
fighting people. It was a short war for America, and Hearts of the
World had not been released long before the Armistice was in sight.
The picture made a lot of money quickly--before being drastically cut
and altered to fit the peace.
"'Viewed as drama,' Griffith said, 'the war is disappointing.'
Wisely he chose to portray the awesome holocaust in terms of a few
individuals in a small village that changes hands as the fortunes of
war sweep over it. The organization of his film was discursive in the
manner of the rambling nineteenth-century novels on which he grew up.
..Griffith discarded forever the brilliant pyrotechnics of Intolerance,
settling down to an assured style in which technical means do not
often call attention to themselves....Griffith used long explanatory
titles to avoid interrupting the flow of action with dialogue titles,
the more popular method with other filmmakers. As time went on he
was much criticized for his titles even by critics who admired his
films. Titling was a problem never completely solved in the silent
period, and certainly not by Griffith.
"As for Hearts of the World's effectiveness as propaganda,
the young Kenneth MacGowan, writing in The New Republic of July 1918,
while deploring the lack of restraint in bloody scenes of violence,
said: 'Here we have an art of pure emotion which can go beneath
thought, beneath belief, beneath ideals, down to the brute fact of
emotional psychology, and make a man or a woman who has hated war, all
war, even this war, feel the surge of group emotion, group loyalty
and group hate.'"
Sam Frank in Magill's Survey of the Cinema: "For all the charisma
of the Gish-Harron pairing in Hearts of the World, it is Dorothy Gish
as the perky, puckish Little Disturber who steals the film, making
viewers wish there was more of her. Griffith was never at ease with
comedy, but Dorothy Gish brought a manic sort of whimsy to her role
that leavened the surrounding somber melodrama, taking the edge off
it. When the film was first released, Gish's Little Disturber was
singled out for special praise by the critics and remains the film's
running highlight...."

USA
1919

Viewing Notes Prepared by Adam Reilly

BROKEN BLOSSOMS

CREDITS: Director: D.W. Griffith; production: D.W. Griffith, released through United Artists; screenplay: Griffith, based
on "The Chink and the Child" in Limehouse Nights by Thomas Burke;
photography: G.W. "Billy" Bitzer; special effects: Hendrick Sartov;
film editing: James Smith; technical advisor: Moon Kwan; original
music: Louis F. Gottschalk and Griffith; b&w with color tints, 80
minutes.

CAST: Lillian Gish (Lucy Burrows), Richard Barthelmess (Cheng Huan,
The Yellow Man), Donald Crisp (Battling Burrows), Arthur Howard
(his manager), Edward Peil (Evil Eye), Andre Beranger (The Spying One),
Norman "Kid McCoy" Selby (prize fighter).

SYNOPSIS: The story is set in Limehouse, the infamous river area of
London once inhabited by Orientals, prostitutes, and derelict
seamen. To this area comes a young Chinese boy imbued with the hope of
teaching people of the West the teaching of Buddha. He is quickly
disillusioned, working in a small Oriental shop, and daily noticing,
from afar, young Lucy, put-upon daughter of a drinking pugilist who
treats her shamefully. One day, Lucy, beaten more harshly than usual,
faints in the Oriental shop and the boy takes her to his own room and
tenderly cares for her. The pugilist eventually finds out where she
is and, with racist anger, goes and fetches her home and furiously
beats her to death. The boy then avenges her death and puts himself
out of his own misery.

COMMENT: Film Notes, Museum of Modern Art, New York: "Griffith
started production on Broken Blossoms in November, 1918,
as one of his series of program pictures for Paramount-Artcraft, but
as its importance grew in his mind, he withdrew it from this series
and reserved it to open the D.W. Griffith Repertory Season that occ-
upied the George M. Cohan Theatre in New York during the spring and
summer of 1919. Later he bought out the interest in the film held
by Adolph Zukor of Paramount, in order to make it his first contri-
bution to the United Artists program, the company which he had formed
together with Charles Chaplin, Douglas Fairbanks, and Mary Pickford,
in the hope of becoming truly independent.
"Like most of Griffith's films and many others of the period
Broken Blossoms made use of tinted stock in a variety of colors . . .
here Griffith reached his highest achievement in the use of color for
mood and atmosphere, using a variety of hues in an unrealistic way
that heightened the emotional values of this story.
"Griffith's last 'big' picture had been the war-propaganda
film, Hearts of the World (1918). This was to be very different.
From the large canvas he turned to an intimate photoplay based on one
of the stories in Thomas Burke's Limehouse Nights. Like most of
Griffith's films and all of his best ones it carried a message: the
earlier picture had roused America's fighting spirit, but this fairy
tale of non-resistance spoke of international tolerance. The part

266

of the London waif might have been made to measure for Lillian Gish, and the choice of Richard Barthelmess as the Chinese boy was fortunate. Work went unusually smoothly, and after the customary period of rehearsal, the film was completed in eighteen days at the extremely modest cost of $88,000.

"When Broken Blossoms appeared, everyone was overwhelmed, and not only by the discretion and force with which a difficult subject had been handled. Reviewers found it 'surprising in its simplicity,' hastening to explain that the photography was misty on purpose, not by accident. The acting seemed a nine-day wonder--no one talked of anything but Lillian's smile, Lillian turning like a tortured animal in a trap, Barthelmess' convincing restraint. Few pictures have enjoyed greater or more lasting succes d'estime. (It also made a substantial profit.)

"By 1919 the motion picture was learning fast how to deal as freely with ideas and feelings as with deeds, and here Broken Blossoms, despite its rather theatrical form, played an important part by scaling down dramatic action and intensifying intimate emotion. Definitely a studio picture, it emphasized a new style of lighting and photography, which, though it has been abused, was valuable. In its contrasting periods of calm and violence it borrowed something from Intolerance, just as the grim finale recalls the death of Mae Marsh in The Birth of a Nation; but there is a sureness and perhaps a sophistication here which had not formerly been evident. Out of Broken Blossoms much was to come--it cannot have been without its influence in Germany; we know that it profoundly influenced Louis Delluc and his disciples in France; and, but for it, we might never have had Charles Chaplin's A Woman of Paris."

FILM STUDIES

ABOUT THE CONTRIBUTORS

JACK BARBERA is a Professor of English at the University of Mississippi where, in addition to literature courses, he teaches an undergraduate "Introduction to Film" and a graduate course, "The Study of Film." He is co-author of Stevie: A Biography of Stevie Smith (OUP, 1987), and has published essays on the work of John Berryman, David Mamet and others. His article on the film, "Tomorrow," appeared in Southern Quarterly and was reprinted in The South and Film (UP of Mississippi, 1981).

LEO BRAUDY is Leo S. Bing Professor of Literature at the University of Southern California and Professor of English. He has also taught at Johns Hopkins University, Columbia University, and Yale University. His major works in film studies include Great Film Directors: A Critical Anthology, edited with Morris Dickstein; The World in a Frame: What We See in Films; Jean Renoir: The World of His Films; and Traffaut's "Shoot the Piano Player": A Collection of Critical Essays. Other major books include The Frenzy of Renown: Fame and its History. He has received numerous honors and awards for his books and research, and he has served on the editorial boards of numerous scholarly journals in the areas of literature and film. Since 1984 he has served on the Executive Committee of the Modern Language Association Film Division.

ROBERT CARRINGER is Professor of English and Film at the University of Illinois at Urbana-Champaign. He has written principally on American films, including Ernst Lubitsch (with Barry Sabath), The Jazz Singer, several articles on Orson Welles in PMLA and Critical Inquiry, and The Making of Citizen Kane. In addition to the Magnificent Ambersons, he has also edited the Citizen Kane videodisc for the Criterion Collection, and both of these have won national awards for design and creativity. He is presently at work on a comprehensive reconstruction of Welles's original Magnificent Ambersons film under a grant from the National Endowment for the Humanities.

DIANE CARSON teaches film theory and production at St. Louis Community College at Meramec, specializing in women in film. She has held a Fulbright Fellowship, participated in a Ford Foundation interdisciplinary curriculum project, published in Women's Studies Review and Quarterly Review of Film Studies, edited Wide Angle, and served as media coordinator and production assistant for the Smithsonian. She is working on an analysis of woman's voice in film.

KEITH COHEN is associate professor of comparative literature, University of Wisconsin-Madison. Author of Film and Fiction (Yale U.P., 1979), a novel, Natural Settings (Full Court, 1981), and critical articles on Ashbery, Cortázar, Psycho, H. Mathews among others, he is currently working on voice in films of the 1960s.

LINDA DITTMAR is an Associate Professor of English at the University of Massachusetts -- Boston, where she teaches Literature and film, American Cinema, Woman's Image, and Women Directors. The form and ideology of narrative are her special concern, notably in female, minority, and avant-garde texts. She has written on film, literature, and pedagogy (Boundary 2, Mosaic, Iris, Wide Angle, etc.), and is currently working on women's voices in film.

LESLIE FISHBEIN, Associate Professor of American Studies at Rutgers University, is the author of Rebels in Bohemia: The Radicals of THE MASSES, 1911-1917 (1982) and articles in Women's Studies, American Studies, Film & History, Labor History, and American Quarterly. Her film courses include American Film and American Myth and Documentary Expression in America.

LOUIS GIANNETTI is Professor of English and film at Case Western Reserve University. His books include Understanding Movies (Prentice-Hall, 4th ed., 1987); Flashback (with Scott Eyman, Prentice-Hall, 1986); Masters of the American Cinema (Prentice-Hall, 1981); and Godard and Others: Essays in Film Form (Farleigh Dickinson U.P. and Tantivy Press, 1975). Among the courses he has taught: Intro to Film, American Cinema Since 1940, International Cinema Since 1940, History of Cinema to 1940, Teaching Film (graduate seminar), Italian Cinema, the American Studio System, American Film Comedy, Images of Women in the American Cinema, and others.

BARRY KEITH GRANT is Associate Professor of film and popular culture at Brock University, St. Catharines, Ontario, Canada. He has edited several books of film criticism and is the author of numerous essays on film and popular music in such journals as Jump Cut, Journal of Popular Film and Television, Persistence of Vision, Literature/Film Quarterly, and Cinaction. He is currently working on a book on the films of Frederick Wiseman.

MIRIAM HANSEN teaches film and literature at Rutgers University. She has published a book on Ezra Pound and numerous articles on film, in particular on early as well as recent German cinema, on Griffith and Valentino, and on the Frankfurt School (Benjamin, Adorno, Kluge). Her book on spectatorship in American silent film, Babel and Babylon, is forthcoming from Harvard University Press. Her recent article titled "Pleasure, Ambivalence, Identification: Valentino and Female Spectatorship" was published in Cinema Journal 25 (Summer 1986).

ANNETTE INSDORF is known primarily as a film professor, critic, lecturer, translator and television personality. She is Director of Undergraduate Film Studies at Columbia University, where she holds the title of Professor as well as Chairman of the Doctoral Program in Film and Theater. She has been teaching film history and criticism at Yale University since 1975. Dr. Insdorf is the author of Indelible Shadows: Film and the Holocaust, published by Random House in 1983 to critical acclaim. Her previous book is Francois Truffaut, a study of the French director's work, published by William Morrow in 1979. She is a frequent contributor to The New York Times Arts and Leisure Section, and her articles have appeared in The Los Angeles Times, The San Francisco Chronicle, Premiere, Film Comment, Elle, Cineaste, The Boston Globe, American Film and Rolling Stone.

NEIL D. ISAACS is a Professor of English at the University of Maryland, College Park and a clinical social worker. His books range from Structural Principles in Old English Poetry to Jock Culture, U.S.A., from All the Moves: A History of College Basketball to Fiction into Film: A Walk in the Spring Rain. His study of Grace Paley's work is scheduled for 1989 publication. His short stories have appeared in Arete, his commentaries in scores of places in a variety of media. His last film course was "Myth and Legend of Baseball in Fiction and Film" and his next will be "Cinetherapy: A Look at the Psychiatric Film."

E. ANN KAPLAN directs the Humanities Institute at the State University of New York at Stony Brook, where she is also a Professor in English. She has published widely in film, feminist theory, and television studies. Her books include Women and Film: Both Sides of the Camera (Methuen, 1983), and Rocking Around the Clock: Music Television, Postmodernism and Consumer Culture (Routledge, 1987). She is finishing a book on Motherhood and Representation (Routledge, forthcoming), and plans to write a book about eary women film directors.

BRUCE KAWIN is a Professor of English and Film Studies at the University of Colorado at Boulder. He recently completed two screenplays (Grifters and The Gold Tiberius), a book of poems (Geometry of Dawn), and an introductory film textbook (How Movies Work). He has also written three books on Faulkner and three books on narrative theory (Telling It Again and Again, Mindscreen, and The Mind of the Novel).

LARRY LANDRUM teaches popular culture, film and American literature in the Department of English at Michigan State University. He is Bibliographer for The Journal of Popular Film and Television and has published numerous articles in popular culture and film. His most recent book is American Popular Culture (1982). He is currently working on a collection of critical essays on popular genres and a manuscript on the discourses of colonialization in South African popular fiction.

CECIL MACKEY, Professor of Economics and Former President, Michigan State University, teaches economics, business law, and film. Previously, he served as President of Texas Tech and at the University of South Florida. His government service included Assistant Counsel, U.S. Senate Antitrust Subcommittee; Director, Policy Development, Federal Aviation Agency; Assistant Secretary, U.S. Department of Transportation.

CHARLES MALAND is Chairperson of the Cinema Studies Program and an Associate Professor of English at the University of Tennessee. His scholarly work on film and American culture includes a number of articles and three books: American Visions: The Films of Chaplin, Ford, Capra, and Welles, 1936-1941 (1977), Frank Capra (1980), and Chaplin and American Culture: The Evolution of a Star Image (forthcoming, Princeton University Press). His film courses include Introduction to Film Studies, Film and American Culture, Film and Litearture, and Special Topics in Film.

FRED H. MARCUS is Emeritus Professor of English at California State University at Los Angeles. His publications include Film and Literature: Contrasts in Media, Short Story/Short Film, Film and Fiction: Fifteen Essays, and Perception and Pleasure. He served as a film consultant on eight short films, including The Legend of John Henry, which was nominated for an Academy Award. He has served as a visiting professor at University of California, Los Angeles, New York University, University of Southern California, and the Hawaiian Curriculum Center. He has taught a wide variety of courses on film and developed over 25 film guides.

GERALD MAST was a Professor of English and Humanities at the University of Chicago and Chairman of the Department of English. He is the author of numerous standard textbooks and studies on film: A Short History of the Movies (Fourth edition, 1986); The Comic Mind: Comedy and the Movies; Film Theory and Criticism: Introductory Readings, edited with Marshall Cohen (Third edition, 1985); Film/Cinema/Movie: A Theory of Experience; The Movies in Our Midst: Readings in the Cultural History of Film in America; Howard Hawks, Storyteller; Can't Help Singin': The American Musical on Stage and Screen. He has published numerous articles and essays on film; served as a member of the editorial boards for the Quarterly Review of Film Studies, Cinema Journal, and Literature/Film Quarterly; and developed the Film Studies Curriculum and Film Archive Study Center at the University of Chicago. He died during the summer of 1988.

JOSEPH W. MILLER has been a Lecturer in Film in the English Department at the University of Maryland from 1973 to the present. He teaches six courses in film: An American Epic: The Films of John Ford; The Heroic Myth in Contemporary Cinema; An American Comedy of Manners: The Films of Ernst Lubitsch, Howard Hawks, and Woody Allen; Film Genre as Cultural Myth; Melodrama and the Existential Crisis: The Films of Alfred Hitchcock; Film Analysis: The Rhetoric of Fictional Worlds.

JACK NACHBAR is Professor of Popular Culture and Director of the Film Studies Program at Bowling Green State University. His numerous publications on film include Focus on the Western and Western Films: An Annotated Critical Biography, and he has served as co-editor of the Journal of Popular Film and Television since its inception as the Journal of Popular Film in 1972. He has also edited and compiled important books in the area of popular culture: The Popular Culture Reader, edited with Christopher D. Geist (1983); and Currents of Warm Life: Popular Culture in American Higher Education, compiled and edited with Mark Gordon (1980).

WILLIAM H. PHILLIPS has earned degrees from Purdue, Rutgers, and Indiana. His publications include St. John Hankin: Edwardian Mephistopheles, Analyzing Films, and (in press) Writing Scripts. He has taught at five universities. Currently, he is a Professor of English at California State University, Stanislaus, where he teaches courses in writing, literature, and film analysis.

NANCY H. POGEL is a professor of American Thought and Language and teaches in the Film Thematic Program at Michigan State University. She received her A.B. in English and journalism from Grinnell College, her M.A. in American studies from the University of Wyoming, and her Ph.D. in English from the University of Wisconsin-Madison. She has delivered papers on film comedy, women in film, and American literary humor at PCA, MLA, MMLA, and CEA meetings. Her articles and reviews appear in Literature/Film Quarterly, MidAmerica, American Literature, American Humor, vol. 2 of the Dictionary of Literary Biography, American Women by Women, Midwest Miscellany, Dictionary of American Biography, Twentieth-Century Romance and Gothic Writers, and Heritage of the Midwest. With Paul Somers, Jr., she is coauthor of a chapter on "Literary Humor" in Genres of American Humor and a chapter on "Editorial Cartooning" in vol. 2 of The Handbook of American Popular Culture. She is the author of Woody Allen in Twayne's Filmmakers Series (1987).

ADAM REILLY left a monastic order of the Catholic Church to earn his M.A. in Cinema Studies from New York University. Prior to his death in 1987, he was Cinema Director of the Denver Center for the Performing Arts; earlier, he was Director of the AFI Theater at the Kennedy Center in Washington, and head of publicity for Time-Life Films and for Contemporary Films. He is author of Harold Lloyd: King of Daredevil Comedy.

NAN ROSENTHAL is Curator of Twentieth Century Art at the National Gallery of Art in Washington, D.C. For many years she was a Professor of Art at the University of California, Canta Cruz.

DAVID H. SHEPARD directs the Film & Television Study Center and is Adjunct Associate Professor of Cinema-Television at the University of Southern California. He also owns Film Preservation Associates, a specialized laboratory, and was formerly Special Projects Officer for the Directors Guild of America, Vice President of Blackhawk Films, and Associate Archivist from the AFI Collection at the Library of Congress. His films have won several Emmys and an Oscar.

ROBERT SKLAR is Professor of Cinema Studies at New York University. He is the author of Movie-Made America: A Cultural History of American Movies (1975) and Prime-Time America: Life on and Behind the Television Screen (1980), as well as many essays and articles on film, television and other cultural subjects.

TOM SOBCHACK is Professor of English and Film at the University of Utah. Publications include numerous articles as well as An Introduction to Film and the forthcoming Critical Approaches to Film: an Introduction to Film Criticism. He is currently working on a book on British silent film.

VIVIAN SOBCHACK, Associate Professor of Theater Arts, teaches Film Studies at the University of California, Santa Cruz. Past President for the Society for Cinema Studies, she has published widely on cinema in numerous periodicals and anthologies. Her current books are An Introduction to Film, 2nd Ed and Screening Space: The American Science Fiction Film.

WILLIAM A. VINCENT is Professor of Humanities at Michigan State University where he has taught since 1965. He teaches courses in history and the visual arts and has taught courses on Fellini, Hitchcock, the Hollywood Musical, Contemporary World Cinema, and Introduction to Film. He devised Michigan State's highly successful Film In Britain summer program.

GREGORY A. WALLER is an Associate Professor in the Department of English at the University of Kentucky, where he teaches courses in film and popular culture. His publications include <u>The Living and the Undead: From Stoker's "Dracula" to Romero's "Dawn of the Dead"</u> and <u>American Horrors: Essays on the Modern American Horror Film</u>. His most recent articles include "Re-placing <u>The Day After</u>" in <u>Cinema Journal</u> 26 (Spring 1987) and "Flow, Genre, and the Television Text" in <u>Journal of Popular Film and Television</u> 16 (Spring 1988).

ANDREA S. WALSH is Assistant Professor of Sociology and Adjunct Assistant Professor of Screen Studies at Clark University, Worcester, MA. She teaches courses on the sociology of mass communications and film. She has written <u>Women's Film and Female Experience 1940-1950</u>, as well as other articles on popular film, advice literature and television. Currently she is writing a history of popular images of aging in American film from the silent era to the present.

ABOUT THE EDITORS

ERIK S. LUNDE is currently Professor of American Thought and Language at Michigan State University, where he received his initial appointment in 1970. A Harvard graduate, Professor Lunde received both the M.A. and Ph.D. degrees (in 1966 and 1970) in American history from the University of Maryland. Professor Lunde has also taught at Marquette University, the University of Wisconsin-Milwaukee, Kalamazoo College and The University of Michigan. A member of the Film Studies faculty at Michigan State since 1975, Professor Lunde has offered courses in writing and film, the films of Alfred Hitchcock and the silent film. Professor Lunde is the author of Horace Greeley in Twayne's United States Authors series (number 413) and of several articles in American history and film. With Truman Morrison, he has co-hosted a local television series entitled Conversation.

DOUGLAS A. NOVERR teaches film courses at Michigan State University in the Department of American Thought and Language and in the Film Studies Thematic Program. He has published articles and delivered papers on disaster films, the sports film, and the western. The author of numerous articles in the areas of American literature, American art history, popular culture, and sports history, Professor Noverr has co-authored three books: The Games They Played: Sports in American History, 1865-1980 (with Lawrence E. Ziewacz), The Relationship of Painting and Literature: A Guide to Information Sources (with Eugene L. Huddleston), and Sport History - Selected Reading Lists and Course Outlines (with Lawrence E. Ziewacz).